The Fibre Formula

RHIANNON LAMBERT

The Fibre Formula

Feed your gut, support immunity
& live well for longer

Contents

Fibre: the missing piece — 6

What is fibre? — 8

The 30:30:30 fibre formula — 54

Recipes for a fibre-filled life — 84

Breakfasts — 86
Lunches — 110
30-minute dinners — 134
Fibre favourites — 152
Sweet and savoury snacks — 178
Desserts — 198

Index — 218
Resources and bibliography — 222
About the author — 223
Acknowledgments — 223

Fibre: the missing piece

After more than a decade in nutrition and running a clinic, I've watched our food landscape change dramatically. At the same time, the nation's health continues to decline. My research into ultra-processed foods made one thing very clear: we're missing a vital component in our modern diets, and that's fibre.

In the UK, 96 per cent of us aren't getting enough of this vital nutrient, managing only 16–18g of the recommended 30g per day. In the USA, fewer than one in ten Americans meet their own country's recommendations. Amid endless health trends, we're consistently missing one of the simplest, most powerful foundations of our health.

I call this problem the "fibre gap", and I understand why the gap exists. Fibre, gut health, and bowel habits don't feel "sexy" compared with protein and muscle gain. But the focus on protein, or any other nutrient in isolation, distracts us from the bigger picture. No single nutrient is a magic bullet to optimum health, well-being, and long-lasting youthfulness. Good health is – and always has been – about balance.

We've also become obsessed with the "quick fix", papering over issues rather than addressing root causes. We increasingly find it hard to make the time to cook from scratch. Through my work, I've tried to stem the tide on these issues, but it's obvious we need to go further. Eating more fibre is a simple, accessible way to do just that.

The Hadza peoples of Tanzania, one of the last indigenous hunter-gatherer groups, consume around 100g to 150g of fibre a day through a diet of wild plants, tubers, berries, baobab, and other foraged foods. They are eating five to ten times more fibre than the average Westerner. Without so-called diet gurus and endless diet Apps, the Hadza live in a way that supports nutritional balance and health. As a result, these peoples have highly diverse gut microbiomes and low rates of chronic disease.

This book was born out of frustration with the Western food environment – the noise, fad diets, wellness trends, and health-halo marketing that confuse more than they help. We deserve better. We deserve to understand what's happening to our health and to have realistic strategies for increasing our fibre intake. *The Fibre Formula* will arm you with the tools to achieve your 30:30:30 (30g of fibre a day, 30 different plants a week, and roughly 30 chews per bite) for better digestion and, ultimately, improved longevity.

Happily, I'm not alone in my mission. In 2025, a campaign in the UK launched with the sole purpose of increasing our consumption of beans, recognizing them as an affordable, readily available, and practical way to increase the nation's fibre intake. Through this initiative, the aim is to double our bean consumption by 2028 – it is a sign that fibre-rich foods are finally receiving the attention they deserve.

This book is your first step to joining us on the journey, effecting change that will help to protect your good health not only now, but far into the future.

Chapter One

What is

Fibre isn't just one thing: it's a whole family of complex carbohydrates – including soluble and insoluble fibre, resistant starches, beta-glucans, and pectins. Each type plays a unique role in supporting gut bacteria, stabilizing blood sugar, and keeping us fuller for longer – all crucial to long-term health.

Modern life gives us extraordinary food choice, but that abundance can be confusing. Ultra-processed foods often crowd out fibre-rich ingredients, making it easy to miss out on the very nutrients that nourish us. In fact, about 96 per cent of people fall short of the daily recommended intake of fibre.

Rather than simply suggesting a return to how our ancestors ate, this chapter focuses first on understanding what fibre is and how it works inside the body, then looks at how to make the most of the foods available today so that we can choose smarter combinations of grains, pulses and legumes, fruits, and vegetables – and close the "fibre gap".

fibre?

What is fibre?

People are often surprised to learn that fibre is, in fact, a special type of carbohydrate. It is special because it's found only in plant-based foods, by which we mean not just fruits and vegetables, but whole grains, legumes, nuts, and seeds too. Unlike other carbohydrates, though, fibre isn't digested in the small intestine. Instead, it travels largely intact into the large intestine (your colon), where it plays a vital role in keeping your gut – and the rest of your body – healthy.

There are two main types of fibre: soluble and insoluble. Soluble fibre dissolves in water to form a gel-like substance and can help lower cholesterol and steady blood-sugar levels – you can find out more about these functions on pages 39 and 41, respectively. Insoluble fibre adds bulk to your stool and helps food pass more quickly through your digestive system. This not only keeps your bowel movements healthy, it also has myriad other benefits, including supporting your immune system, improving sleep quality, and boosting mood.

Types of fibre

All fibres actually contain a mixture of both "soluble" and "insoluble" fibre. Throughout this book I'll refer not just to these simplified terms, but to the properties of fibre, such as how fermentable or viscous it is. These are the characteristics that truly shape how fibre behaves in the body.

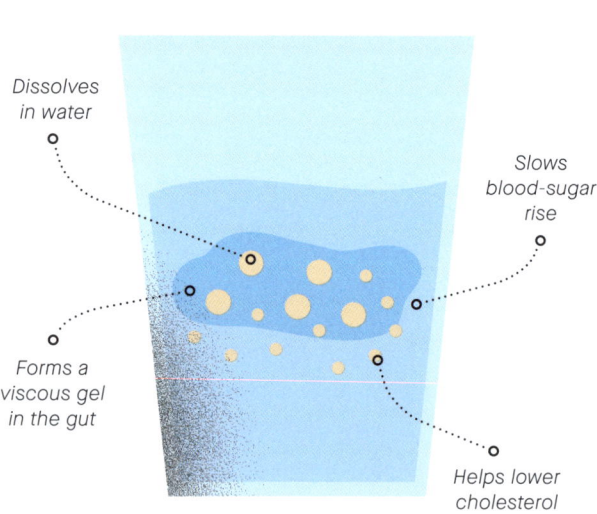

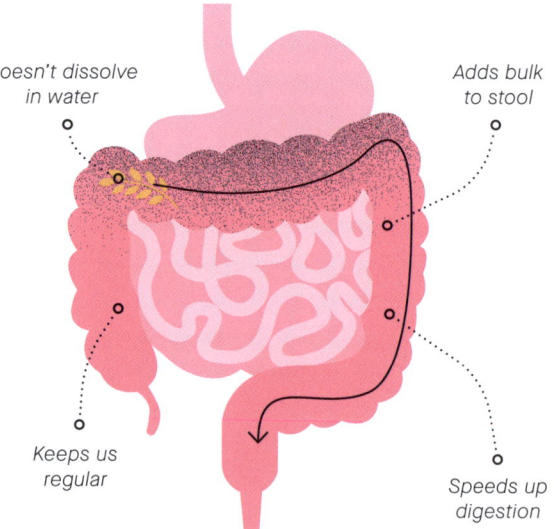

Soluble Fibre

Insoluble Fibre

What can fibre help us fight?

Studies show that diets high in fibre, especially fibre derived from whole grains, such as brown rice, wholemeal (whole-wheat) bread, oats, barley, and quinoa, are linked with a lower risk of several major diseases. These include:
- Heart disease, including angina and heart attack
- Stroke
- Type-2 diabetes
- High blood pressure
- Colorectal (bowel) cancer

SCFAs and other fibre benefits

In the past, fibre has found itself an overlooked nutrient, simply because the body can't digest it. But we now know that it is essential not only for good digestion, but also for other aspects of health. Once in the colon, fibre becomes food for our gut bacteria. Collectively, these bacteria along with other microorganisms are known as the gut microbiome. Through a process of fermentation, the gut microbes break down the fibre we eat, producing compounds called short-chain fatty acids (SCFAs). SCFAs – butyrate, acetate, and propionate among them – are incredibly important for overall health: they nourish the cells lining the colon, reduce inflammation, support our immune system, and lower the risk of diseases such as colorectal cancer. Butyrate may be linked to improved sleep quality. These fatty acids are called "short chain" because they are made up of short chains of carbon molecules (see panel, right), which helps to make them particularly water-soluble – and that means that the body is able to use them quickly and efficiently as a source of energy.

A high-fibre diet can also help with healthy weight management. That's because fibre not only slows down digestion (helping us to feel fuller for longer), but also influences the hormones that control blood sugar (reducing spikes in blood sugar after eating, staving off the urge for a sugary snack) and regulate appetite.

How can plant-based nutrition boost fibre?

As we've just learned, fibre is found only in plant foods. It stands to reason, then, that a plant-based diet, varied, interesting, and fibre-dense as it must be, will help to improve your fibre intake.

What does an SCFA look like?

Short-chain fatty acids (SCFAs) are the outcome of fibre breakdown in the gut. But, why are they called "short chain"? All fatty acids are major carbon fuel sources made of carbon, hydrogen, and oxygen. Each has a small acidic "head" and a long carbon–hydrogen "tail" that defines its structure. The number of carbon atoms in the chain determines the label short, medium, or long.

Short-chain fatty acids (SCFAs)

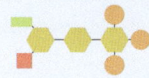

Produced when gut bacteria ferment dietary fibre, SCFAs have fewer than 6 carbon atoms – typically 2 to 6. Examples include acetate (C; 2 carbon atoms), propionate (C3), and butyrate (C4). SCFAs are one of the key benefits of eating dietary fibre. They provide energy to the cells lining the gut, help regulate metabolism, support heart health, reduce inflammation in the body, and help maintain healthy immunity. They are vital to our overall well-being.

Medium-chain fatty acids (MCFAs)

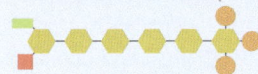

MCFAs have between 6 and 12 carbon atoms. They are found in foods such as coconut oil, palm kernel oil, and some dairy products. Unlike SCFAs, MCFAs are mostly absorbed quickly in the digestive system and used for energy. While they can be beneficial, especially for quick energy, they don't have the same wide-ranging health effects as SCFAs.

Long-chain fatty acids (LCFAs)

LCFAs have 13 or more carbon atoms. They are found in foods such as red meat, fatty fish (salmon, mackerel), nuts, seeds, avocados, and vegetable oils. They are important sources of energy, and contain essential fats like omega-3 and omega-6, but they don't reduce inflammation, nourish gut cells, and support the immune system to directly support gut health in the way of SCFAs.

Recent studies have reinforced the understanding that plant-based diets rich in dietary fibre and phytochemicals (natural plant compounds) are crucial for supporting gut health in ways more significant than simply keeping our bowel movements healthy. For a start, consuming a variety of plant foods increases the diversity and abundance of beneficial gut bacteria. These "friendly" bacteria – such as *Bifidobacterium* and *Lactobacillus* – help reduce inflammation, support immunity, and improve metabolic and cardiovascular health.

Phytochemicals (from the Greek *phyton* meaning "plant") – such as the polyphenol compounds that are especially abundant in foods like spinach, broccoli, tomatoes, and grapes, and dark berries such as blueberries – act as prebiotics that not only nourish these beneficial microbes, but also inhibit harmful ones. Some phytochemicals, such as resveratrol (found in grapes, raspberries, and peanuts), also have antioxidant and anti-inflammatory effects. These properties may provide further protection against conditions such as cardiovascular disease, neurodegenerative disorders, obesity, and cancer.

Fibre in the carbohydrate family

Carbohydrates fall into two broad categories: simple and complex. **Simple carbs** (or "simple sugars") are made up of just one or two sugar molecules and include foods such as white bread, refined sugar and fruit juice.

Variety is the spice of life

A large study published in *Nature* in 2025 found that vegans, vegetarians, and omnivores each have distinct gut microbiome "signatures". Vegans tend to have more bacteria that produce SCFAs. Importantly, omnivores who ate a wide variety of plant foods showed many of the same beneficial microbes found in vegan diets. In other words, the label you give your diet matters less than the quality and diversity of the plants you eat. Aiming for around 30 different plants each week (page 62) can help feed a broad variety of microbes, making the gut more resilient and balanced.

They release quickly into the bloodstream as a fast energy source. While this can help before exercise, or for a quick burst of energy, it may also cause blood-sugar levels to rise and fall too quickly, leaving you feeling tired or hungry. **Complex carbohydrates** are so-called because they contain chains of sugar molecules that are released more slowly in to the bloodstream. They are subdivided into starches and fibre. Our gut metabolizes starches for use in the body, while fibre travels through the gut intact to be fermented by friendly bacteria and converted to SCFAs.

Simple and complex carbs

Whole, unprocessed foods are, generally, more complex in structure, often meaning they contain more fibre.

Brown rice
A complex carbohydrate, brown rice provides fibre and sustained energy.

Potato
Potatoes can be complex or simple carbohydrates, depending on how they are prepared and cooked (page 67).

White bread
White bread is processed and therefore a low-fibre, simple carbohydrate.

Whole-grain bread
Made using, literally, whole grains, whole-grain bread is a complex carb.

White pasta
White pasta loses the whole-grain complexity during the refining process.

Resistant starch – a form of fibre

Named for its ability to "resist" digestion in the small intestine, resistant starch ferments in the large intestine, acting as a form of fibre – and so producing SCFAs. The fermented compounds help to nourish gut bacteria, reduce inflammation, and support metabolic health, including improved insulin sensitivity (page 51). There are several types of resistant starch (we label them RS1 to RS5), which are found in foods such as oats and legumes, as well as cooked and cooled potatoes, rice, and pasta. Green bananas are one of the richest natural sources of resistant starch; while uncooked oats (as in overnight oats) contain more resistant starch than cooked porridge. Including these foods in our diet can therefore enhance both fibre intake and gut health.

Fibre's time to shine

Despite all the benefits to digestion of a fibre-rich diet, most people still aren't eating enough of this superhero nutrient. Health programs all over the world agree that adults should aim for a daily fibre intake of 25–30g – but in many countries average intake is far lower (page 18). That's why experts now recommend that we make an effort to include more whole plant foods in our meals every day. A key takeaway from all these drives for more fibre in our diets is that variety matters. Different plant foods contain different types of fibre and different phytochemicals. Eating a wide range of plant-based foods ensures you're feeding diverse strains of gut bacteria, encouraging microbial diversity, which is closely linked to improved digestive and immune health, and potentially even mental health (see page 37).

Fibre travels through the gut to be fermented by friendly bacteria and converted to short-chain fatty acids.

The benefits of resistant starch

Resistant starch, which is easily incorporated into a healthy diet, acts on the body in key, positive ways.

Cool, then reheat = better for blood sugar

When starchy foods – like **pasta**, **rice**, or **potatoes** – are cooked, cooled, and even reheated, their starch structure changes, increasing resistant starch. This means that the foods release glucose more slowly into the bloodstream, helping with blood-sugar control.

Prebiotic action

Prebiotics are the whole foods that the beneficial bacteria in our gut need in order to thrive (page xx). In the large intestine, resistant starch acts as a prebiotic, boosting gut health and producing SCFAs.

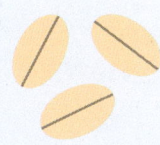

Metabolic health-booster

Research shows that resistant starch can improve insulin sensitivity and may reduce appetite, making it a helpful tool for managing weight and Type-2 diabetes (pages 40 and 50).

Naturally gluten-free

Many foods naturally high in resistant starch (such as beans, lentils, rice, and potatoes) are also naturally gluten-free, making them accessible for those with coeliac disease or gluten sensitivity.

The history of fibre intake

It's remarkable that, despite having greater access to fresh and diverse produce than ever before in the Western world, fibre intake has significantly declined. In the early 20th century, the average daily fibre intake in Western diets was estimated to be between 30g and 50g, largely owing to a diet based on unrefined grains, root vegetables, pulses, and seasonal produce.

Much of the population relied on home-cooked meals, using affordable, plant-based ingredients. Even during periods of wartime rationing, people consumed substantial amounts of whole foods, which consequentially supported higher fibre intake. Today, though, the amount of fibre in our diets has fallen dramatically. This timeline tracks global changes over the decades since the 1920s.

Fibre intake over time

1920s

UK
Post-World War I, fibre intake was high, estimated at 35–50g per day thanks to homemade, seasonal meals using locally grown whole grains, root vegetables, pulses, and fresh produce. Bread was minimally refined; processed foods were scarce. Diets were frugal but rich in plant-based staples.

USA
As in the UK, fibre intake was relatively high (30–40g per day). Rural families, especially, relied on local produce: fibre-rich staples (beans, corn, and root veg) were the heart of meals.

Mainland Europe
Fibre intake was around 30–45g per day. Fibre-rich staples such as rye, barley, beans, and root vegetables were central to daily diets, especially in rural areas.

1930s

UK
Post-war, diets remained modest, but fibre intake stayed high: oats, legumes, cabbage, and skin-on potatoes were staple. Economic hardship in the Great Depression limited access to luxuries, preserving a whole-food, fibre-rich diet for many.

USA
During the Great Depression, most families cooked at home, relying on staples like beans, corn, oats, and potatoes with skins, as well as seasonal fruits and vegetables. Fibre intake dipped only slightly below early 20th-century levels.

Mainland Europe
Meals continued to feature whole grains, legumes, root veg, and cabbage, often grown locally or in home gardens. Fibre intakes remained substantial.

1940s

UK
World War II made a significant impact. Rationing included wholemeal bread, potatoes, vegetables, and dried legumes. Government campaigns like "Dig for Victory" encouraged homegrown produce. This was a time of unexpectedly balanced and fibre-friendly nutrition.

USA
Rationing and food conservation boosted fibre-rich staples, while "Victory Gardens" supplied additional fresh produce. Despite economic and logistical challenges, many Americans maintained plant-based, fibre-containing diets.

Mainland Europe
Government and local initiatives encouraged self-sufficiency, supporting a likely fibre intake of about 25–40g daily.

Fibre-rich diets in ancient times

Interestingly, research into ancestral diets gives us insight into how far we've drifted from fibre-rich eating patterns. It's estimated that early human populations may have consumed 100–150g of fibre per day, thanks to their reliance on wild plants and unprocessed foods. Even today, the Hadza people of Tanzania, a modern-day hunter-gatherer tribe, consume significantly more fibre than people in industrialized nations. They also exhibit far more diverse and resilient gut microbiomes.

1950s

UK
Rationing ended in 1954. The British diet began to diversify, but home cooking remained the norm. Even so, fibre intake likely declined to about 30g per day.

USA
Post-war economic boom brought more processed and convenience foods. Refined white bread, canned foods, and sugary snacks began to displace fibre-rich staples. Intake likely fell to around 20–30g fibre per day, though seasonal foods, in rural areas especially, remained high.

Mainland Europe
Food industrialization accelerated. White bread and refined cereals increased. Fibre intake remained moderate thanks to local gardens and home-cooked meals, but a downward trend had begun.

1960s

UK
A cultural and dietary shift from supermarkets, frozen foods, and TV dinners; intake of legumes and whole grains fell. Diets of refined carbs rose, and fibre levels likely dropped slightly below 30g, as eating patterns leaned in to convenience.

USA
Convenience foods, sliced bread, breakfast cereals, and canned goods continued to replace whole grains and legumes]. Many adults likely consumed around 18–25g fibre daily. Even so, homegrown foods still added to fibre intakes.

Mainland Europe
Urbanization and supermarket culture brought more refined, sugary, and packet foods. Total fibre fell to around 20–30g daily in many places.

1970s

UK
Fibre intake fell to 25–30g per day, owing to industrialized foods (breakfast cereals, white bread, etc). Meat consumption rose. In working-class homes especially, home cooking and vegetables remained the norm.

USA
Average intakes are thought to have been around 15–20g per day – another dip. Health-focused families or those preserving traditional cooking habits consumed higher levels.

Mainland Europe
Industrialized food production and supermarket shopping meant refined bread, white rice, and packaged foods increasingly replaced higher fibre foods, lowering intake to about 15–25g per day. General awareness of dietary fibre was still limited.

Fibre and the environment

The Planetary Health Diet, outlined in the EAT-Lancet Report (published in October 2025), presents a model for how we can eat to protect both the health of humans and the planet. Centred around vegetables, fruits, whole grains, legumes, nuts and seeds, it encourages a shift toward plant-rich meals while limiting red and processed meats, free and added sugars, and excess salt. Small, flexible amounts of dairy, fish, poultry, and eggs can be included where needed, but the emphasis remains on plants as the foundation of every plate. This model is not only sustainable for the planet as it's projected to halve food-system emissions by 2050, but is also grounded in evidence-based research that supports our well-being. The Lancet Commission estimates that global adherence to this diet could prevent up to 15 million premature deaths each year and substantially reduce rates of chronic disease. It is no coincidence that fibre sits at the heart of this model, whereby foods highest in fibre are often the very ones that provide our body with essential nutrients for long-term health and help protect the planet through lower environmental impact.

1980s

UK
Branded convenience foods, and low-fat, high-sugar, and fast food rose. Consumption of white bread peaked. Messaging began to promote fibre for digestive health, but average intake lowered to about 22–25g daily.

USA
Fast-food culture and ready meals became established. Fibre intake remained low, around 15–18g per day, as white bread, refined cereals, and processed snacks dominated. Nutrition education was limited: few made an effort to increase fibre intake.

Mainland Europe
Fibre intake declined, often given as 15–20g per day. Rural and Mediterranean regions retained slightly higher intakes through homegrown vegetables, legumes, and whole grains.

1990s

UK
Average UK fibre intake fell below 20g per day, as processed foods became dominant. Advertising heavily influenced diet, as did "grab-and-go" and ready meals. Despite growing evidence for fibre's health benefits, trends declined into the early 2000s.

USA
Growing awareness of diet-related chronic disease gave fibre some attention, yet intake remained at 15–17g per day. Whole-grain bread, cereal, and fruit intake increased modestly, but processed foods dominated.

Mainland Europe
Early whole-grain campaigns began. Fibre intake in urban areas was still low (15–20g per day), but Mediterranean regions maintained slightly higher levels owing to cultural norms.

Modern times

The modern, Western diet contains far more refined carbohydrates, ultra-processed foods, and added sugars than ever before, while intakes of whole grains, legumes, and fibrous vegetables have sharply decreased. The current average intake of fibre in the UK, USA, and mainland European countries sits well below the WHO's recommended 30g (page 18). This shift reflects broader changes in food production, industrial milling practices, and eating habits, all of which have contributed to a significant reduction in dietary fibre and, consequently, poorer gut-health outcomes across the whole of the Western world.

The map on pages 18–19 breaks down the global averages of the modern-day world.

Why are we eating less fibre?

Despite decades of nutrition advice, many people still don't eat enough fibre. Several key factors are driving this global fibre gap.

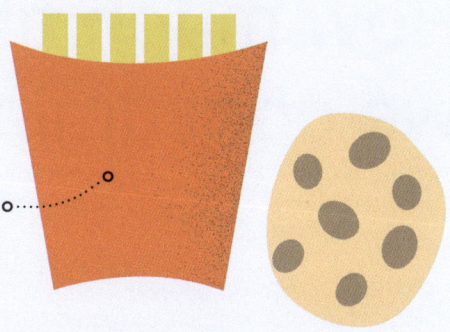

Processed and ultra-processed foods
Most modern diets are heavy in low-fibre, packaged foods.

Shifting eating patterns
We've moved away from traditional, plant-rich meals toward more meat, dairy, and refined carbohydrates.

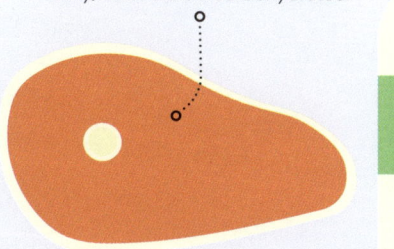

Lack of awareness
Many people don't realize how important fibre is or which foods contain it.

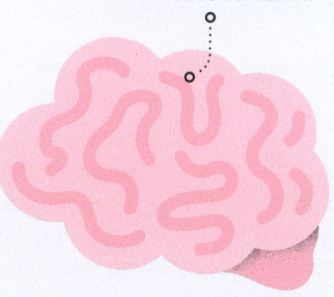

Convenience and cost
Foods like pulses, legumes, nuts, and whole grains are often seen as harder to prepare or more expensive.

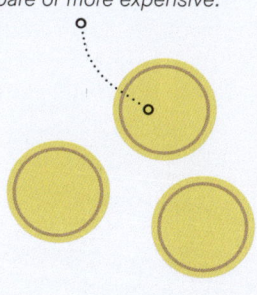

Marketing and advertising
Highly processed, low-fibre foods are aggressively marketed, especially to children.

Busy lifestyles
Time-poor consumers often choose quick, pre-packaged options that are low in fibre.

What is fibre?

How much fibre are we consuming today?

Improving fibre intake globally could prevent millions of chronic disease cases and enhance quality of life worldwide. Success stories from Denmark and other Nordic countries and Ghana, highlight the power of coordinated public health strategies, food industry reformulation, policy measures, and consumer education.

So, what's the global picture?

This map gives a sense of population fibre intake across the world. The gram figures represent the average adult daily intake in each of the featured countries, while the percentages (where data is readily available – unfortunately in some territories it is not) reveal the proportion of the adult population meeting the WHO's recommended 30g of fibre per day. Finally, I've indicated the main fibre sources in each country.

Key to symbols

 Average adult daily intake

 Percentage of the adult population meeting 30g target

 Main food sources

*No age-range is given for this data

**Based on recommendations for whole-grain consumption

***Based on recommended amounts of fruit and vegetables

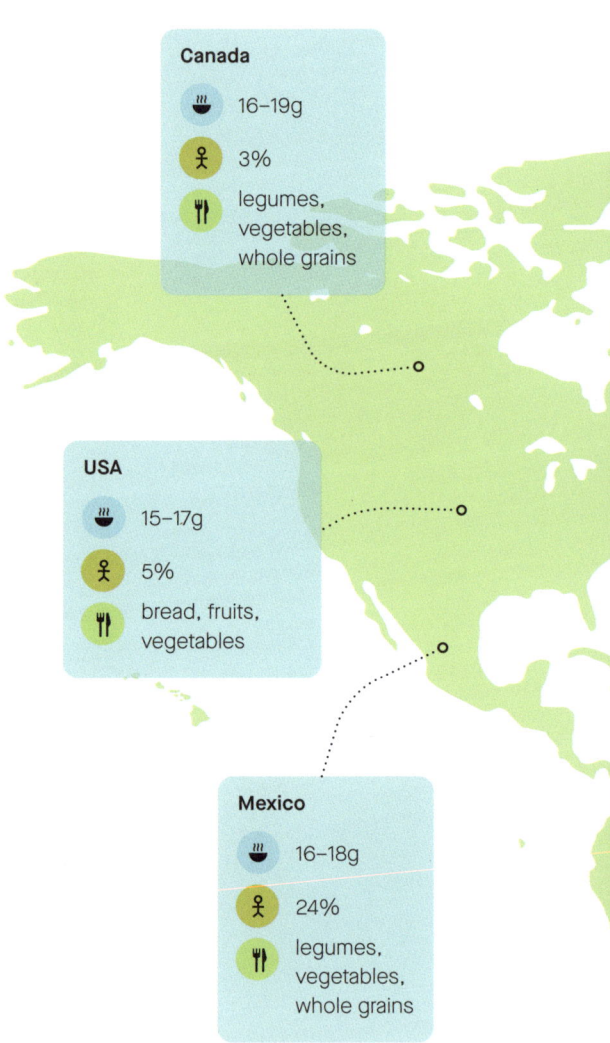

Canada
- 16–19g
- 3%
- legumes, vegetables, whole grains

USA
- 15–17g
- 5%
- bread, fruits, vegetables

Mexico
- 16–18g
- 24%
- legumes, vegetables, whole grains

Argentina
- 9g*
- 6%***
- fruits, vegetables, whole grains

18   The Fibre Formula

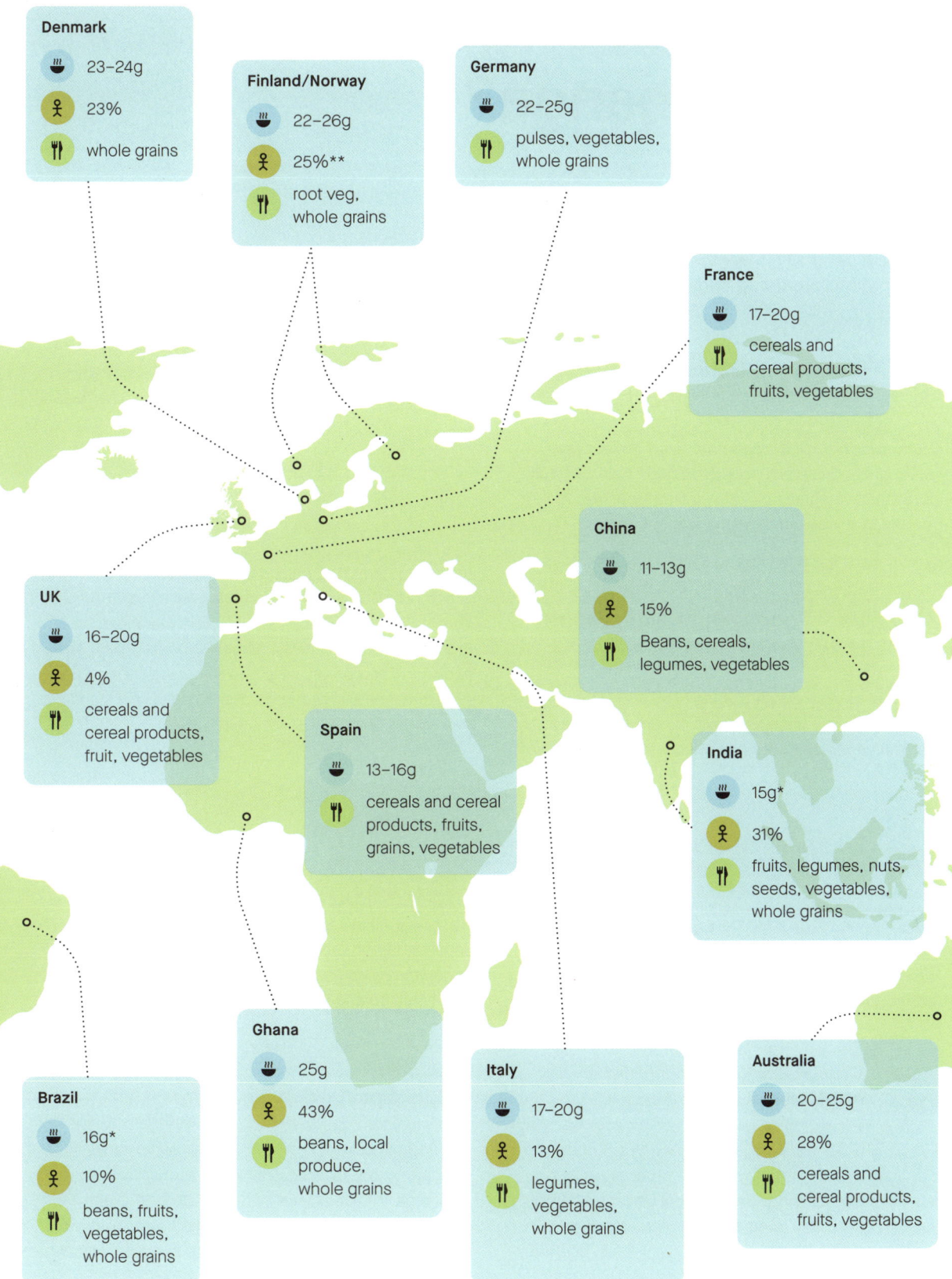

How are nations making positive change?

The good news is that while intakes all over the world are generally lower than they should be, many nations are trying to do something about it.

 Denmark – Danish Whole Grain Partnership (DWGP)

A long-running collaboration between government, NGOs, and industry, launched in 2008. It successfully increased average whole grain intake from 36g to 82g per day by 2019 – now the highest in Europe.

 UK – Food & Drink Federation (FDF) Action on Fibre

Industry-led initiative partnering brands and retailers to launch high-fibre lines. By 2023, it had delivered about 1.5 billion additional servings of fibre into UK diets.

 EU (general) – School Meal Fibre Standards & Labelling

More than 15 EU countries enforce minimum fibre standards in school meals (generally 10g of fibre per 1,000 calories). EU regulations also standardize nutrition labelling and claims (pages 70–71).

 Australia

The Health Star Rating System (since 2014) nudges manufacturers toward higher fibre products via front-of-pack labelling. The National Obesity Strategy (launched in 2022) integrates nutrition standards supporting fibre intake.

 France

The voluntary Nutri-Score label scores foods on fibre and other nutrients (page 70). The PNNS (Public Dietary Guidance) promotes pulses, legumes, whole grains, fruits, and vegetables. A proposed national strategy on food-nutrition-climate could strengthen fibre promotion.

 USA

The Dietary Guidelines for Americans (2020–2025) highlight pulses, legumes, whole grains, nuts, and vegetables. The Food & Drug Administration's (FDA) 2024 "Healthy" Label Update includes fibre thresholds. A Front-of-Package Nutrition Label Proposal (2025) aims to clarify fibre content. The Healthy, Hunger-Free Kids Act (2010) mandates fibre-rich school meals, with standards maintained beyond the Act's expiry date.

 Japan

The 2025 Dietary Reference Intakes raised fibre targets to 20–22g per day for men and at least 18g for women – although, that's still below WHO recommendations. The Japanese Food Guide Spinning Top emphasizes grains, vegetables, and beans; and also seaweed, which is a significant source of fibre.

 Spain

The 2025 Royal Decree on School Meals mandates daily fruit and vegetables (≥45% seasonal/local, ≥5% organic), weekly fish, and vegetarian/vegan options, and it bans sugary drinks. Indirectly, then, it is supporting increased fibre intake in school lunches.

Is sex a factor?

Looking more closely at UK figures specifically reveals an apparent anomaly between men and women when it comes to fibre intake. In those aged over 65, only 1% of women but 8–9% of men hit the target. Is that statistic as meaningful as it seems? Probably not, particularly when we take into account the relevance of age.

Different dietary patterns

Surveys show women are more likely to avoid bread, potatoes, or carbohydrate-rich foods (sometimes owing to diet culture or weight-control signalling), which are major fibre sources in the UK diet. This avoidance can unintentionally lower fibre intake.

Different energy requirements

Men generally eat more calories than women because of higher energy needs. As fibre is tied to food volume, a higher food intake means men are more likely to reach higher absolute fibre amounts, even if their diets aren't especially fibre rich.

Appetite and physiological changes

Appetite tends to decline with age, especially in older women, and reduced food intake means less chance of meeting fibre targets. Men, on average, may sustain higher intake levels into older age.

Portion sizes and food choice

Men often consume larger portions of starchy foods like bread, cereals, rice, and potatoes – all key fibre contributors. Women, particularly older women, may eat smaller portions or lighter meals, reducing fibre-intake opportunities.

So the gender gap isn't because men are necessarily choosing more fibre-rich foods, but rather that their overall greater calorie intake and different dietary patterns make it easier to eat more fibre. Nonetheless, the fact remains that both sexes in the UK – at over 65, but also throughout life – are consuming far below the recommended 30g of fibre per day. However, simple daily changes – switching to whole-grain bread, adding beans to meals, or snacking on fruit – can close the fibre gap and support lifelong health.

Simple daily changes – switching to whole-grain bread, adding beans to meals, or snacking on fruit – can close the fibre gap and support lifelong health.

What is fibre?

How have UPFs affected fibre intake?

Ultra-processed foods (UPFs) have become a dominant part of modern diets in many countries, often making up over half of the daily calories we consume. These foods, ranging from packaged snacks and ready meals to sugary drinks and instant noodles, are typically made from refined ingredients that have been stripped of their natural fibre. As a result, diets high in UPFs tend to be low in fibre and other essential nutrients. Even when fibre is added back in to processed products in isolated forms (such as inulin or oat fibre), it may not provide the same benefits as fibre from whole foods. Over time, a dietary pattern that loads up on UPFs can increase the risk of digestive issues, weight gain, and chronic disease.

There's no doubt that UPFs have become an issue for our diets, but it's important to approach that issue with empathy and nuance. For many people, UPFs are not simply a matter of poor choice, they are often the most accessible, affordable, and time-efficient options available. Factors like income, food education, cultural background, and limited access to fresh produce all play a significant role in shaping eating habits. The widespread marketing of UPFs, especially to children and low-income communities further complicates the picture. Addressing the fibre gap, therefore, isn't just about urging people to "eat better"; it also means tackling systemic problems, improving food education, and making healthy, fibre-rich foods more accessible and appealing for everyone, regardless of circumstance.

To close the global fibre gap, we need more than just nutritional guidelines – we need systemic change. That includes public-health policies that support better food education, transparent labelling, reformulation of processed products, and subsidies that make fibre-rich foods more affordable. School-meal programmes, community initiatives, and urban food-access projects also play a vital role. Encouraging a return to whole, minimally processed plant foods is important but we must do so with empathy, recognizing that for change to be lasting, it must be made possible and practical for all.

Levels of fibre in processed foods

The Nova framework, developed in Brazil in 2009, categorizes foods into four groups, from un- (or minimally) processed to ultra-processed. Understanding fibre distribution across these groups highlights how processing can influence diet quality.

1. No or little processing
Whole or almost-whole foods, with no added ingredients. With skin, these foods provide good levels of fibre.

2. Processed cooking ingredients
Foods to cook and season our food (salt, vegetable oils, sugar, vinegar, and so on). They provide no fibre.

3. Processed foods
Group 1 foods with added Group 2; or minimally processed (canned beans, say). May contain good levels of fibre.

4. Ultra-processed foods
Additive-packed, industrial. Often low in fibre. Exceptions, such as high-fibre cereal, still have many additives.

Making choices

There are very few individuals or families in the world for whom choice – in whatever form and for whatever reason – is genuinely straightforward. When it comes to choosing between foods on a weekly shopping budget, it can be helpful to know whether high-fibre processed foods or low-fibre whole foods are the better option, enabling you to make informed decisions to buy not just the best value for money but the best "health-value" for money.

What's better? High-fibre processed or low-fibre whole foods?

You should aim to consume more *minimally processed*, *high-fibre* foods but if you're choosing between high-fibre ultra-processed foods (such as fortified bars, high-fibre cereals, and fibre-added yogurts) and low-fibre minimally processed foods (such as white rice, peeled potatoes, and white bread), the high-fibre option often wins out in terms of gut health and satiety – *but only to a point*. The tables below offer the best way to think about the options.

Can I trust the label?

A popular low-calorie snack bar often praised for its fibre content is a clear example of a well-marketed UPF. While it contains 5g of fibre per bar, it also comes with a long list of ingredients: wheat flour, oligofructose, vegetable fats (palm, shea), sugar, fructose, fat-reduced cocoa powder (8%), humectant (glycerol), water, wheat fibre, egg white powder, raising agents (diphosphates, sodium bicarbonate), salt, flavourings, thickeners (locust bean gum, xanthan gum), emulsifiers (soy lecithin), whole milk powder, and antioxidant (tocopherol-rich extract). It's a perfect example of how fibre can be engineered into a product that is otherwise far removed from a whole food.

High-fibre ultra-processed foods

High-fibre UPFs (such as fortified bars, high-fibre cereals, and fibre-added yogurts) contain fibre, but also many additives.

Pros	Cons
• Convenient • Can boost fibre intake quickly (especially if fortified) • May help close the fibre gap for people who eat very few plant foods	• Often contain added sugar, salt, emulsifiers, and preservatives • May lack *diverse* types of fibre (such as resistant starch, inulin, pectins) • May promote overconsumption owing to being engineered for taste

** High-fibre UPFs can supplement an otherwise whole-food-rich diet, but not replace it.**

Low-fibre minimally processed foods

Low-fibre, less-processed foods (such as white rice, peeled potatoes, and white bread) are more "natural".

Pros	Cons
• Typically free from additives and closer to how foods occur in nature • Easy to digest and tolerated by people with sensitive guts or during illness	• Don't provide good amounts of fuel for a proliferation of healthy gut microbes • Can cause blood-sugar spikes and won't keep you full as long • Miss the opportunity to improve diversity in the microbiome

** Low-fibre minimally processed foods are fine in moderation, alongside higher-fibre whole foods.**

Why does my gut need fibre?

When we talk about "gut health", we often mean the trillions of microbes, bacteria, fungi, and viruses that live in our large intestine. Clinically, though, the term actually refers to the well-being of the entire gastrointestinal tract, from mouth to rectum. The gut does more than digest food. It plays a vital role in immune defence, energy production, hormone balance, mood regulation, and nutrient synthesis. Fibre is central to all of this, as it feeds our gut microbes and supports the production of the short-chain fatty acids (SCFAs) that keep the gut lining strong. Feeding the gut fibre is key to feeling and functioning well.

Gut health is increasingly recognized as a core indicator of overall health, yet studies suggest it has deteriorated across much of the industrialized world. Compared with previous generations, today we tend to have less diverse gut microbiomes, a trend linked to processed diets, high use of antibiotics, reduced exposure to environmental microbes – and, significantly, low fibre intake. The typical Western-style diet, high in refined carbohydrates, fats, sweeteners, and additives, can deplete beneficial bacteria and reduce production of the SCFAs that help regulate inflammation and immunity.

Evidence now links microbial shifts to rising rates of non-communicable diseases such as obesity, Type-2 diabetes, heart disease, inflammatory bowel disease (IBD), and depression and anxiety. One global study found that countries with the highest intake of minimally processed plant foods had more resilient and diverse microbiomes and notably lower rates of chronic disease.

More microbes, more balance

A diet rich in plant-based whole foods high in fibre, polyphenols, and prebiotics supports the growth of beneficial microbes. These microbes ferment fibre to produce metabolites like SCFAs, which nourish colon cells, strengthen the gut barrier, and regulate the immune and hormonal pathways that influence appetite, mood, sleep, and energy levels. In contrast, ultra-processed foods, hydrogenated fats, emulsifiers, artificial sweeteners, and additives can disrupt microbial balance and weaken gut function.

Top 5 gut benefits of a high-fibre diet

Gut microbiome modulation

Fibre is fermented by gut bacteria to produce short-chain fatty acids (SCFAs). These help maintain the strength of the gut lining, reduce inflammation, regulate lipid and glucose metabolism, and may protect against colorectal cancer and metabolic disorders.

Cholesterol reduction and heart health

Soluble fibre binds bile acids in the intestine, which are then excreted. The liver uses cholesterol to make more bile, lowering circulating LDL ("bad") cholesterol levels. This contributes to a reduced risk of cardiovascular disease.

Blood-glucose regulation

Soluble fibre forms a gel in the gut that slows the absorption of glucose, reducing postprandial blood-sugar spikes. This can lower the risk of Type-2 diabetes.

Anti-inflammatory effects

High-fibre diets are linked to lower systemic inflammation, as measured by markers such as C-reactive protein. Chronic inflammation underpins many diseases, including heart disease, diabetes, and some cancers.

Weight management

Fibre increases satiety because it slows gastric emptying and adds bulk to meals. This can lower overall calorie intake, helping prevent obesity, a risk factor for multiple diseases.

A feedback loop

Eating the right amounts of fibre is only one part of the puzzle. We also need to ensure that the gut is at optimal health to make *the best use of* the fibre our diet provides. It's a kind of fibre–gut feedback loop. Give the gut what it needs but also make sure that the gut can make the best of what it has. So, how do we do this?

Regular exercise and adequate hydration further support healthy digestion and gut integrity, but minimizing stress levels is one of the most important ways to ensure the gut is in good working order.

The Gut–Brain axis

Stress doesn't just affect your mind. Acute stress (sudden stress in response to a specific trigger) takes only minutes to disrupt microbial diversity and weaken the tight junctions in the intestinal lining. This increases gut permeability (so-called "leaky gut"), in which, harmful bacteria and toxins, say, can cross the intestinal barrier into the bloodstream, causing inflammation in the body. Chronic (long-lasting) stress drives sustained changes in the microbiome, hampers barrier function, and shifts immune responses. This can contribute to gut–brain disorders and conditions such as irritable bowel syndrome (IBS; page 34) and post-traumatic stress symptoms, and can worsen IBD symptoms.

Emerging evidence highlights SCFAs as key messengers in the gut–brain axis, signalling to affect mood, cognition, and neurological function. Their production depends heavily on SCFA-producing microbes that thrive on fibre-rich diets, emphasizing (once again) that promoting microbial diversity through varied plant intake is fundamental to supporting both gut and brain health. Research reveals fascinating mechanisms: stress hormones, like cortisol, reduce SCFA production, impair gut and blood-brain barriers, and alter the gut's microbial composition. There are even sex-specific responses: women may experience more pronounced microbiome shifts under acute stress than men. And, new evidence links the gut microbiome to brain function via neural circuits that connect the gut to the amygdala (which helps regulate emotions, stress, and memory) and hippocampus (crucial for learning and forming memories).

Gut–Brain communication

The microbes in your gut produce chemicals, such as SCFAs and neurotransmitters, which influence your immune and endocrine (hormonal) systems. Likewise, your thoughts and emotions can affect digestion and gut function.

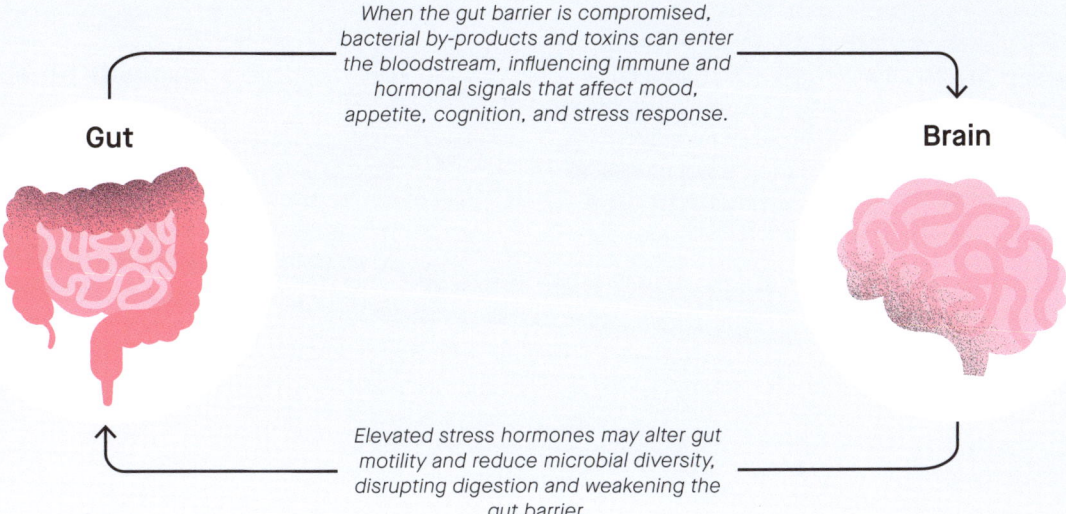

When the gut barrier is compromised, bacterial by-products and toxins can enter the bloodstream, influencing immune and hormonal signals that affect mood, appetite, cognition, and stress response.

Elevated stress hormones may alter gut motility and reduce microbial diversity, disrupting digestion and weakening the gut barrier.

What does my stool tell me about my fibre intake?

Having regular, healthy bowel movements is a key – although often overlooked – marker of digestive health. A healthy stool is typically soft but well-formed, passed without straining, and occurs regularly. While frequency varies from person to person, anything between three times a day to three times a week can be considered normal, as long as it's consistent.

Fibre plays a central role in maintaining this balance: *soluble fibre* helps soften stools by holding on to water, while *insoluble fibre* adds bulk and supports regular movement through the gut (page 38). For some, simply "eating more fibre" doesn't seem to help with gut or bowel problems, and may even make things feel worse. This tells us that both types of fibre are essential for healthy bowel habits.

Not all fibre is equal. A diet overloaded with insoluble fibre, like raw wheat bran, can sometimes irritate the gut lining or worsen bloating, especially in those with a sensitive digestive system. Individuals with conditions such as irritable bowel syndrome (IBS) or coeliac disease may find that certain fibres trigger discomfort, while their body is better able to tolerate others. In short, how your body responds to fibre depends on a range of factors. Hydration is also important: fibre needs water to work properly (page 73). Things don't stop there – there are other influences like stress (page 27), gut motility, and hormonal fluctuations, which can all impact how your gut functions and how it processes fibre. Your toileting habits and your stools' appearance are good indicators as to what is going on inside you when it comes to your gut.

Getting the right fibre for your gut

Now that we know that not all fibre works the same way and some types may suit you better than others, what sources are available and which work best when? Among the most researched interventions are psyllium husk, wheat bran, and kiwi fruit, each with its own benefits and quirks.

Psyllium husk (soluble fibre)

 Constipation-predominant IBS (IBS-C)

 Gently eases stool passage through the gut; well-tolerated for many gut types

 Risk of choking and blockages if too much is consumed

Wheat bran (insoluble fibre)

 Sluggish bowels (speeds up transit time)

 Often too coarse for those with a sensitive gut or IBS (can lead to bloating/discomfort)

Kiwi fruit (soluble + insoluble fibre)

 Sluggish bowels (speeds up transit time; also contains digestive enzyme actinidin)

 Provides a whole-food approach with added benefit of other natural enzymes

Psyllium husk for healthy stools

A type of soluble fibre derived from the husks of the *Plantago ovata* seed, psyllium husk, when mixed with water, forms a gel-like substance that helps soften stools and increase regularity. What makes psyllium unique is its versatility: it's one of the few fibres effective for both constipation and diarrhoea. It also has prebiotic properties, helping to feed beneficial gut bacteria and support overall microbiome health. The research around psyllium is strong, particularly for relieving symptoms of constipation-predominant IBS (IBS-C) and improving overall stool consistency. However, it's crucial to take psyllium with plenty of water: without enough fluid, it can lead to blockages rather than relief. It's also wise to introduce it gradually to avoid bloating, and to space it out by a couple of hours from any medications, as it can interfere with their absorption.

What does a healthy stool look like?

To help us better understand what's happening in our gut, the Bristol Stool Chart (see panel, right) offers a visual guide. It's important to remember that a *normal* stool appearance for you may not be normal for someone else. That said, stool types 3 and 4 are considered the ideal: they're soft, formed, and easy to pass without straining. Types 1 and 2 often suggest constipation: typically linked to not getting enough fibre, fluids, or exercise. These stools are hard, lumpy, and uncomfortable to pass. Types 5 to 7 can indicate that you have eaten too much fibre too quickly, a sensitivity to certain fibre types, or an imbalance in gut health. At this end of the scale, stools become loose, mushy, or diarrhoea-like.

Fibre and hydration work together to keep digestion running smoothly. Without enough fluid, fibre can lead to hard, dry stools; sudden increases in fibre, especially without adequate water, may cause bloating. Rather than aiming for perfection every day, it's more useful to watch overall patterns: occasional variations in stool consistency are normal, but persistent trends toward either extreme may indicate that your fibre intake, fluid levels, or gut health need attention. If you have ongoing concerns about your bowel habits, a GP or registered dietitian can provide personalized guidance.

Bristol Stool Scale

The Bristol Stool Scale is a visual guide for identifying the health of your poo. Gradually increasing fibre, alongside drinking plenty of water, can help bring stool consistency toward the ideal type 3–4 range.

Type 1
Small, hard, separate lumps; difficult, often painful to pass.

Type 2
Lumpy, sausage-shaped; firm, dry; uncomfortable to pass.

Type 3
Sausage-shaped with surface cracks; firm but passes easily.

Type 4
Smooth, soft, sausage- or snake-like; easy to pass.

Type 5
Soft blobs with clear-cut edges; passes easily but can lack shape.

Type 6
Fluffy pieces with ragged edges; mushy consistency.

Type 7
Watery, entirely liquid stool – diarrhoea.

What's the difference between prebiotics and probiotics?

Prebiotics are specific types of fibre found in certain plant-based foods. They "feed" the good bacteria in your gut, helping it – and myriad other physiological processes – function optimally. Probiotics are live bacteria that are found in fermented foods. While these are not found in fibre foods themselves, they are important to support your microbiome for optimal gut health so that your body can make the most of the fibre – and other nutrients – you eat.

Why do I need prebiotics?

Unlike most nutrients, prebiotic fibres are resistant to digestion. They pass through the stomach and small intestine without being broken down, and eventually reach the colon intact. Here, they become food for millions of beneficial bacteria.

As these beneficial bacteria "feed" on the prebiotics (through a process of fermentation), they produce helpful compounds like short-chain fatty acids (SCFAs), which, as we saw on page 11, have anti-inflammatory and gut-healing effects that are good for your entire health and well-being.

Not all the fibre you eat is prebiotic – only certain types of fibre feed good bacteria and help them grow. Among those types are foods containing compounds such as inulin, pectin, and fructooligosaccharides. You can find these in fruits such as apples, dates, prunes and bananas; vegetables such as asparagus, leeks, onions, chicory, and garlic; and whole foods and pulses, such as wheat bran, nuts, and beans. Resistant starch (page 15) is another source. Eating a variety of prebiotic foods helps maintain a diverse and healthy gut microbiome, which in turn supports digestion, immunity, and even mental well-being.

What are probiotics?

Unlike prebiotics, which feed your existing gut bacteria, probiotics add new strains of beneficial bacteria directly into your digestive system. These microbes help balance the gut microbiome and support a healthy immune response. In the UK, USA, and the EU, the word "probiotic" is classified as an unauthorized health claim and can't be used on food labels or packaging to imply a health benefit. Instead, you might see phrases such as "contains live cultures" or "fermented with live bacteria". During your food shop, check the labels of fermented foods (below and opposite) for specific strains, like *Lactobacillus acidophilus* or *Bifidobacterium lactis*, which are good, active probiotic sources.

Probiotics – the four Ks

One way to remember some of the most popular groups of probiotic foods is to think of the four Ks. Adding some or all of these to your diet, along with other probiotic-rich foods such as yogurt, miso, tempeh, and certain aged cheeses, will support your gut microbiome.

1. Kefir
A tangy, fermented milk drink

2. Kombucha
A slightly fizzy fermented tea

3. Kimchi
Spicy fermented Korean vegetables

4. Sauerkraut
Fermented cabbage

What are fermented foods?

Fermented foods like the four Ks (opposite, below) are among the best sources of probiotics. We now know far more about them than ever before. During fermentation, natural bacteria and yeasts break down the sugars and fibres within plant-based foods, softening their cell walls and making certain nutrients more bioavailable. This process also produces beneficial compounds known as postbiotics, sometimes called "zombie bacteria", which remain active even after the microbes have become inactive. These by-products may continue to support immune and gut health, much like how a vaccine made from inactivated microbes can still train the immune system to respond to it. In other words, even though the bacteria are no longer alive, their components can still have powerful, health-promoting effects.

A 2025 study of more than 6,000 adults found that increasing fermented-food intake by just three portions per day for three weeks led to notable improvements in well-being (one portion is about 1 tablespoon of miso or half a cup of kimchi). Around half of participants reported a significant improvement in mood (47%), energy levels (56%), and hunger control (52%), and four in ten reported signs of reduced bloating (42%). The effects were especially pronounced among participants who were living with obesity. The findings suggest that even short-term increases in fermented-food intake can lead to meaningful benefits for gut comfort and day-to-day well-being. What does this tell us? The gut responds quickly to positive dietary changes!

Eat a diet rich in prebiotic fibres and probiotic foods to support a thriving, balanced gut microbiome.

What are healthy-gut supplements and are they worth taking?

Probiotics are widely available in many forms. Synbiotics are supplements or foods that combine both prebiotics and probiotics. These aim to improve the survival of probiotics in the gut by feeding them the prebiotic fibres they need to thrive. However, healthy individuals really don't need to supplement, as food sources are enough. Getting your probiotics from food is usually more reliable, more affordable, and safer (supplements are expensive and often unregulated). Many probiotic-rich foods, like the four Ks (see box, opposite) can be made easily and cheaply at home.

Prebiotics
Prebiotics come from certain types of fibre-containing foods and "feed" the beneficial bacteria already in the gut.

+

Probiotics
Probiotics exist in certain foods (usually aged or fermented foods) and add beneficial bacteria to your gut.

=

Synbiotics
Synbiotics are the combination of prebiotics and probiotics in synthetic (manufactured) supplement form.

Do I have to choose between fibre and protein?

The short answer to this question is no – there is absolutely no scientific or metabolic need to choose between fibre and protein. In fact, it's important that we reframe our thinking, unpicking decades of high-protein, low-fibre narrative to bring fibre back into our diets in a healthy, sustainable way – while still getting enough protein for optimum health, too.

Is protein essential?

In the body, protein supports growth, cell repair, hormone balance, enzyme production, and immunity. Country-by-country recommendations suggest that adults need around 0.75g protein per kilogram of body weight daily – that amounts to about 53g of protein each day for a 60kg woman and 55g each day for a 75kg man.

You need only look at the list of foods in the box (right) to see that, whatever your dietary preference, it's relatively easy to hit around 50g of protein a day. That means that most of us consume more protein than the body needs to function well. Indeed, in my work at the Rhitrition clinic, I have yet to see a true case of protein deficiency (whereas I frequently see fibre deficiency). In the context of Western diets, it's worth questioning, therefore, how useful extra protein really is and why we talk so much about protein when looking at nutrition.

In modern times, protein has become entwined with strength, youth, beauty ideals, and wellness marketing. Yes, protein matters and needs increase with age (women benefit from maintaining intake through menopause and beyond; page 48). But any cultural fixation on "high-protein everything" runs the risk of leaving fibre – the nutrient that protects against heart disease, diabetes, bowel disorders, and even supports healthy weight management – forgotten. In fact, the better way to think of things is to look at how fibre and protein work together for optimum health, and even to focus on foods that can provide both, so that the body is getting everything it needs, in balance.

The main actions of protein on the body

While there is much focus on protein as a means to build muscle in a health-and-fitness sense, its actions on the body are far more physiologically varied and significant than any focus on aesthetic ideal might suggest.

Growth and maintenance Protein provides the body with structural "building blocks" to grow new tissue and maintain healthy muscles, bones, and organs throughout life.

Enzyme production Enzymes, which are mostly proteins, catalyze countless biochemical reactions inside and outside cells, facilitating processes like digestion and energy production.

What does 50g protein look like?

No single food source should provide all your daily protein, but it's useful to see side by side how easy it can be to reach 50g protein each day.

Chicken breast
170g (6oz)

Raw, shelled peanuts
200g (7oz)

Tofu or edamame
400–450g (14–16oz)

White fish (cod) or oily fish (salmon)
150g or 170g (5½oz or 6oz)

Beans or pulses
600–700g (1lb 5oz–1lb 8oz)

Hormone production Many hormones, such as insulin and growth hormone, are proteins or polypeptides that act as chemical messengers for the brain to regulate various bodily functions.

Structure provision Proteins like collagen, elastin, and keratin contribute to the structural integrity of tissues such as skin, hair, nails, bones, and cartilage.

Immune support Protein is essential for producing antibodies, which fight infections and bolster the immune system.

Fluid balance Proteins like albumin help maintain the body's fluid balance, preventing swelling (oedema).

Nutrient transportation and storage Some proteins move substances like oxygen (haemoglobin), glucose, cholesterol, vitamins, and minerals throughout the bloodstream and within cells. Others provide storage – for example, the protein ferritin stores iron.

Challenging the narrative

While most of us already meet our daily protein needs for all these physiological benefits, many still fall short on fibre. In order to challenge the narrative that we need to increase protein to optimize strength, weight maintenance, and timeless ageing, it's worth taking each of these in turn to consider where fibre fits in to those ideals, too. The specific circumstances of each of these outcomes highlight protein–fibre interactions, but taking steps to get the right balance of fibre and protein in our diet, no matter the goal, is an approach that can benefit everyone, not just when the aim is an aesthetic one.

The better way... is to look at how fibre and protein work together for optimum health, and even to focus on foods that can provide both.

The consumerism effect

The protein health obsession isn't new. In the 1960s and 70s bodybuilding appeared on the scene, messaging that we need to be eating enough protein to fulfil shape, size, and muscle goals! In the 80s, popular bodybuilder figures like Arnold Schwarzenegger appeared in marketing that endorsed protein powders. Today, a protein shake is accepted as a normal supplement – among the public as well as for athletes. This popularity has proved huge commercially: between 2007 and 2012, UK sales of protein products skyrocketed from £73m to over £170m. Between 2010 and 2015, product launches exhibiting "high-protein" labels rose nearly 500%! Today, social-media platforms drive the high-protein trend to phenomenal levels – with record surges for products like protein bars. These days we even see high-protein cereals and high-protein chocolate bars. All of which have been driven by consumer demand.

1960s–70s: Protein powders gain traction in bodybuilding.

2007–2012: Mass-market growth; sales in the UK double.

2013–15 onward: Social media fuels lifestyle marketing; consumers embrace protein.

2020s: Protein becomes cultural currency; "high protein" labels dominate food aisles.

Building strength
Building strength depends not just on protein intake but also resistance exercise and, importantly, overall diet quality. Plant proteins like beans, lentils, and soy can make good inroads for – and even meet – your daily protein needs (remember: 53g of protein each day for women and 55g each day for men) while boosting fibre.

Achieving a healthy weight
For those tackling overweight or obesity, protein can certainly support satiety. However, its reputation as a metabolism-boosting nutrient is overstated and inaccurate – high-protein diets (below, right) are a red herring. Sustainable weight loss still depends on energy balance. In this case, it's better to look to fibre. Fibre plays an even greater role in appetite regulation, slowing digestion, and nurturing the gut microbiome all of which support healthy body weight. Importantly, for anyone looking to achieve a healthy weight, carbohydrate foods are not the enemy. Whole-grain bread, brown rice, oats, and legumes are not only good carbohydrate sources but also contain both protein and fibre, delivering balanced energy that helps manage hunger and stabilize blood sugar.

Easing menopause
During menopause, protein becomes increasingly important in the female diet to help counteract age-related muscle loss (known medically as sarcopenia). Protein supports the maintenance of lean body mass, which can decline as a result of hormonal changes. Higher protein intake may also help manage postmenopausal body weight by enhancing satiety and supporting metabolism. Additionally, protein contributes to bone health, which is especially important as oestrogen levels fall and the risk of osteoporosis (a condition adversely affecting bone density) rises.

But what does this mean in practice? For postmenopausal women, while recommended daily levels (around 0.75g per kilogram of body weight pre-menopause) can maintain lean mass, optimal protein intake of around 1–1.6g per kilogram of body weight per day is associated with better muscle function, increased strength, and improved physical capacity and resilience. Consistent protein consumption across meals (for example, eating about 20–25g of protein per main meal) supports metabolic balance and helps manage body composition during hormonal transitions.

In the SPOON trial (2025), 84 postmenopausal women were, for 18 months, randomly assigned to one of two groups: one received a whey protein supplement providing 40g of protein per day, while the other received a placebo. Researchers measured circulating branched-chain amino acids (BCAAs) and markers of insulin sensitivity. Although the protein group had significantly higher BCAA levels, they showed no improvement in insulin sensitivity or menopausal symptoms compared with the placebo group. This suggests that simply increasing protein intake isn't enough to improve metabolic health after menopause: it's the overall quality, balance, and context of the diet that matter most, including fibre-rich, plant-based foods that support gut health and metabolism.

Choosing protein-fibre power foods
We need protein but we already get enough of it. Fibre is the nutrient missing from our plates. Rather than asking "Do I need more protein?", a more useful question is: "Am I getting enough fibre, and where can I swap animal proteins for plant proteins to boost both?" That's because when you choose beans, lentils, whole grains, nuts, seeds, and soy, you naturally cover your protein needs while also increasing fibre intake. And that's where the real health gains lie, from supporting your microbiome to reduce your risk of chronic disease.

In short, then, by leaning in to plant proteins and whole carbohydrate sources, you get the best of both worlds: all the protein you need, plus the fibre and nutrients that protect your heart, gut, and long-term health. As with so much about diet and well-being: balance always wins over excess.

High-protein diets

Popular among athletes and dieters, high-protein diets often focus on meat, eggs, and dairy, leaving little room for fibre-rich plant foods and meaning that fibre intake in these adult groups can fall well below recommended levels. This can result in hard, dry stools (Bristol Types 1–2; page 27) leading to constipation, and reduced microbial diversity, especially in low-carb or bodybuilding-style meal plans.

Protein + Fibre power foods

Here are a top 10 of protein + fibre foods. If you can increase these in your diet, you are giving your body good amounts of protein without sacrificing fibre.

Almonds
(30g/1oz)
Protein **6g**
Fibre **4g**

Lentils
(150g/5½oz)
Protein **12g**
Fibre **10g**

Butter (lima) beans, cooked
(150g/5½oz)
Protein **10g**
Fibre **9g**

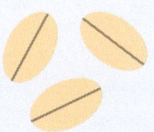
Oats, dry
(40g/1¾oz)
Protein **5g**
Fibre **4g**

Chia seeds
(25g/1oz)
Protein **4g**
Fibre **9g**

Quinoa
(185g/6½oz)
Protein **8g**
Fibre **5g**

Chickpeas, cooked
(150g/5½oz)
Protein **11g**
Fibre **9g**

Tofu, firm
(150g/5½oz)
Protein **15g**
Fibre **2g**

Edamame, shelled
(100g/3½oz)
Protein **11g**
Fibre **5g**

Tempeh
(100g/3½oz)
Protein **11g**
Fibre **9g**

Can I eat fibre if I have IBS?

Irritable bowel syndrome (IBS) is a common condition that affects how the gut works. Symptoms vary but often include bloating, abdominal pain, wind, constipation, diarrhoea, or a mixture of all. Because fibre directly affects how food moves through the gut, it can play a role in either easing or worsening symptoms.

IBS is a chronic functional gut disorder affecting approximately 10–15% of the population in the UK, around 12% in the USA, and 8–12% across mainland Europe. Although its symptoms are physical and can be debilitating, the precise cause remains uncertain. IBS may have a hereditary component, and can occur when food moves either too quickly or too slowly through the gut, or when there is heightened sensitivity in the intestinal lining. Stress is also known to exacerbate symptoms, supporting evidence that IBS may stem partly from disrupted communication between the brain and gut, the so-called Gut–Brain axis (page 25).

What we do know is that IBS does not present in the same way for everyone, and fibre can have different effects depending on dominant symptoms. Eating too little fibre can make constipation and discomfort worse. On the other hand, eating too much fibre, or the wrong type, can trigger bloating, excess gas, and loose stools. This is why fibre can feel confusing if you have IBS – what may trigger symptoms in one person, may not trigger symptoms in another.

In IBS with constipation and bloating, increasing soluble fibres such as psyllium, chia seeds, flaxseeds, and oats may help soften stools, support regularity, and reduce discomfort. In contrast, for those with IBS with diarrhoea, too much fibre or certain types (for example, wheat bran or high-FODMAP sources; opposite) can worsen loose stools and urgency. This highlights why there is no single "IBS-friendly" fibre. What to eat and what to avoid depend on both the type of fibre and the individual's symptom patterns. A dietitian can help navigate that path specifically for you.

What are FODMAPs?

As we already know, fibre is not a single nutrient and the effect it has on the body depends on how it behaves in the gut. Gut bacteria can quickly break down readily fermentable fibres such as inulin and fructooligosaccharides (FOS), often added to snack bars, yogurts, and cereals. This rapid fermentation produces gas, which can worsen bloating and pain in sensitive people. Some fibres, like psyllium husk (page 27), dissolve in water to form a gel and are only moderately fermented. They can soften hard stools, ease constipation, and improve overall IBS symptoms with less bloating. Insoluble fibres (for example, wheat bran) add bulk and speed up transit. Some people with IBS tolerate them well, but others find that they irritate the gut if introduced too quickly.

Some fibres also fall under the category of FODMAPs – short-chain carbohydrates that are easily fermented in the gut and can trigger symptoms like bloating, pain, and diarrhoea in some people with IBS. Many high-FODMAP foods are also naturally high in fibre. For example, beans, lentils, onions, and certain fruits provide excellent fibre, but for those with IBS can be harder to tolerate. This is where the overlap between FODMAPs and fibre can become confusing – foods that are normally encouraged for gut health may worsen symptoms in sensitive individuals.

> There is no single "IBS-friendly" fibre. What to eat and what to avoid depend on both the type of fibre and the individual's symptom patterns.

Adopting a low-FODMAP diet

The low-FODMAP diet is one strategy sometimes used to manage IBS. It involves temporarily reducing high-FODMAP foods before reintroducing them step by step to identify personal triggers. Importantly, this is not a diet to follow long term nor to attempt without support. Cutting out many high-FODMAP foods on your own can unnecessarily reduce fibre intake and restrict the diet more than is helpful. For this reason, the low-FODMAP diet should be carried out only with support from a registered dietitian who can ensure your fibre intake remains balanced, help you reduce and then reintroduce foods carefully and sustainably, and avoid unnecessary long-term dietary restriction. Not everyone with IBS needs a low-FODMAP diet, but when used correctly, it can be a useful tool for finding out which fibre-rich foods you tolerate best so that you have the best chance of being able to eat a well-rounded, balanced diet that minimizes your IBS symptoms.

Top 5 tips for an IBS-friendly, fibre-rich diet

1. Increase your fibre intake gradually
Sudden jumps in fibre often worsen bloating.

2. Hydrate well
Fibre needs water to work effectively.

3. Choose soluble, moderately fermentable fibres
Oats, chia seeds, linseeds, and psyllium are often well tolerated.

4. Be cautious with "added fibre" foods
Products that contain added fibre such as inulin or FOS may cause extra gas and bloating.

5. Remember: it's personal
What flares symptoms in one person may be fine for another – be prepared for trial and error.

FODMAP foods

These are examples of low, medium, and high FODMAP foods. Talk to a dietitian before going on any kind of restrictive diet.

Low	Medium	High
• Blueberries	• Aubergine (eggplant)	• Apples
• Carrots	• Avocado	• Asparagus
• Cucumber	• Brazil nuts	• Blackberries
• Grapes	• Broccoli	• Cauliflower
• Green beans	• Brussels sprouts	• Dates
• Kale	• Butternut squash	• Garlic
• Kiwi	• Cannellini (navy) beans	• Honey
• Oranges	• Courgettes (zucchini)	• Leeks (bulb and white part)
• Parsnip	• Celery	• Legumes
• Pineapple	• Nectarines	• Mangoes
• Potatoes	• Pineapple	• Mushrooms
• Quinoa	• Ricotta	• Onions
• Rocket (arugula)	• Raspberries	• Pears
• Strawberries	• Sweetcorn	• Pulses
• Tomatoes	• Sweet potatoes	• Watermelon

Can fibre help reduce rates of bowel cancer?

One thing I've seen time and again is how low fibre intake seems quietly to contribute to serious health issues, particularly colorectal (bowel) cancer. This type of cancer has been rising alarmingly over recent years, especially among younger adults in many Western countries. Despite the advances we've made in screening and treatment, bowel cancer remains one of the most common and serious cancers of all.

In the UK, colorectal cancer is the third most diagnosed cancer and the second leading cause of cancer death. Screening programmes have helped stabilize rates among older adults, but there seems to be a trend toward more cases among younger people. Hugely concerning, it is clearly linked to lifestyle factors like low-fibre intake, poor diet, and less physical activity. In the USA and in Germany, similar trends are emerging. Even in Italy, where the traditional Mediterranean diet is rich in fibre, modern shifts toward ultra-processed foods are changing the picture. On the other side of the coin, colorectal cancer rates are notably lower in certain parts of Africa and South Asia – regions where traditional, high-fibre diets have long prevailed.

The common thread is the same: diets low in fibre, high in processed foods, and increasingly sedentary lifestyles lead to higher cancer rates for certain kinds of cancer. While multiple factors influence cancer incidence, consistent evidence suggests that fibre-rich diets could be a powerful component of prevention strategies. In Western countries, we all need to prioritize fibre as a vital, nourishing part of our everyday lives.

Throughout my work, I've met many people who felt overwhelmed by the confusing health messages out there. It's easy to feel like prevention is complicated or out of reach, but it's really about the small, consistent steps we take every day. Adding fibre is one of those simple, loving acts we can do for ourselves. Together, by understanding and embracing this, we can help turn these troubling trends around, one meal at a time.

Fibre and different types of cancer

Higher fibre intake is strongly linked to lower colorectal cancer risk and may benefit the prevention of other cancers.

Cancer type	Evidence strength	How might fibre be helping?
Colorectal (bowel)	Strong	By improving digestion and gut health to reduce risk.
Breast	Moderate	By helping to reduce oestrogen levels to reduce risk.
Stomach	Moderate	By lowering glycaemic load to reduce risk.
Endometrial	Moderate	By helping to regulate hormones to reduce risk.
Pancreatic	Limited	By potentially offering a protective role to reduce risk.
Lung	Limited	Through links with overall healthier diet patterns.

Can fibre improve my mood?

We've long known that what we eat shapes how we feel physically, but scientists are now uncovering just how much it might influence how we think and feel too. On page 25 we learned about the Gut–Brain axis, a busy two-way system that plays a crucial role in our overall well-being.

Fibre is one of the main dietary contributors in the conversation between our gut and our brain. Short-chain fatty acids (SCFAs; page 11) don't just keep the gut lining healthy, they may also help regulate inflammation and support the production of serotonin. Often called the "feel-good" hormone, serotonin helps regulate mood, sleep, and even appetite. Remarkably, even though serotonin's effects are experienced in the brain, about 90% of it is produced in the gut! By fuelling the bacteria that influence serotonin production, and therefore the gut–brain connection, fibre could be one way our diet supports our mental well-being.

Fibre may also reduce inflammation through a healthier gut environment by balancing its pH and keeping the gut barrier strong. This can mean fewer inflammatory compounds are able to circulate through the body: inflammation has been tied to both low mood and poor sleep quality. Studies show that people eating the lowest amount of fibre tend to sleep worst and report more symptoms of depression and anxiety; while those eating more fibre, report the opposite.

Cognitive health, fibre, and ageing

Preliminary research into the connections between fibre and brain health in older adults is especially intriguing. A recent analysis of US data found that people over age 60 who consumed more fibre performed better on certain tests of thinking speed and mental processing, with benefits levelling off at around 34g of fibre per day. Although not every area of memory improved, the study has highlighted that meeting fibre recommendations could be one simple step to help protect the brain as we age. Another compelling study in adults aged over 60 found that a simple prebiotic supplement, designed to feed gut bacteria (page 29), not only reshaped the gut microbiome but also led to measurable improvements in cognitive performance. Together, these findings suggest that supporting the gut with fibre and prebiotics could become an accessible way to help maintain brain health as we get older – although we need much more research before we can say for sure.

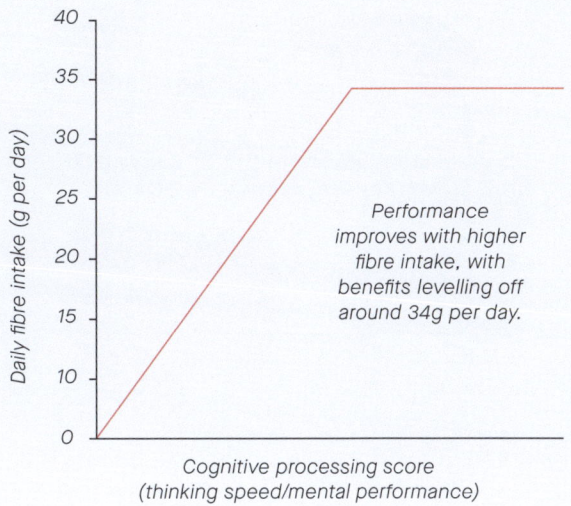

Performance improves with higher fibre intake, with benefits levelling off around 34g per day.

How does fibre impact my heart health?

The search for everyday dietary habits that can protect cardiovascular health has never been more crucial. Fibre continues to stand out as one of the simplest yet most effective tools we have to help keep our heart and circulation in top condition.

What's the scale of the problem?

Heart and circulatory diseases are the leading cause of death worldwide, responsible for almost one in three deaths, amounting to around 20 million deaths each year. In the UK alone it's estimated that one in 12 people are living with a heart or circulatory condition. In Germany, statistics from 2019 show that around 1.1 million inpatient hospitalizations and 174,000 rehabilitations were related to atherosclerotic cardiovascular disease diagnoses. The picture is no less startling on the other side of the Atlantic: in the USA approximately 695,xxx people die from heart disease each year (about one in every five deaths). Additionally, about 805,000 Americans have a heart attack annually. Of these heart attacks, 605,000 are first-time occurrences, while 200,000 are in individuals who have previously experienced a heart attack.

Fibre's effects on circulating cholesterol

Soluble fibre binds to bile acids in the small intestine, preventing them from being reabsorbed into the bloodstream. As a result, the liver draws on circulating cholesterol to produce more bile acids, which helps lower levels of LDL ("bad") cholesterol in the blood. In diets low in soluble fibre, more bile acids are reabsorbed and cholesterol is recycled rather than excreted. Regular intake of soluble fibres such as beta-glucan (oats, barley) and psyllium husk may significantly reduce LDL cholesterol concentrations and support heart health.

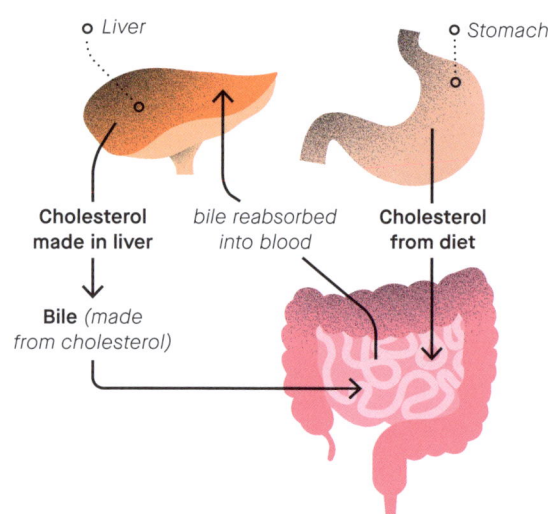

Most bile is reabsorbed, so cholesterol is reused and remains in circulation.

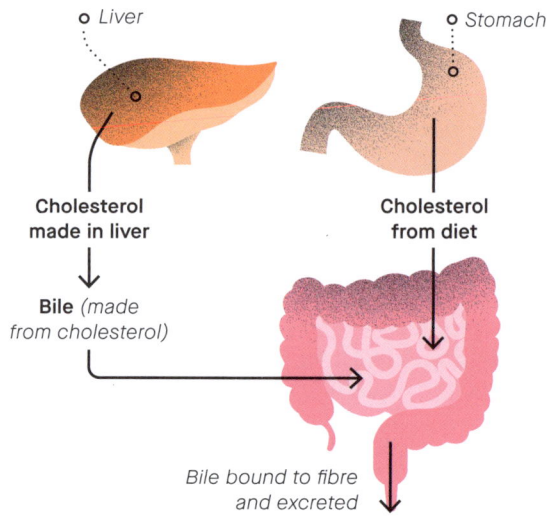

Bile acids bind to soluble fibre and are excreted, reducing circulating LDL cholesterol.

Decades of research have consistently linked higher fibre intake with a lower risk of cardiovascular disease, coronary heart disease, stroke, and Type-2 diabetes. Large-scale analyses show that those who consume the most fibre have up to a 30% lower risk of developing heart disease compared to those who eat the least. Furthermore, just 5g extra fibre each day can reduce blood pressure, cholesterol, and markers of inflammation – all of which impact heart health.

Why is fibre so good for the heart?
Fibre's heart benefits are thought to stem from several different mechanisms.

Lowering cholesterol
Cholesterol is a fatty, wax-like substance that the body needs in small amounts for making hormones, building cells, making bile acids (which help us digest fats from food), and other functions. However, too much of the wrong kind, known as low-density lipoprotein (LDL) cholesterol, can lead to a deposit build-up in the artery walls. Over time, these deposits, called plaques, can narrow or block arteries, raising the risk of heart attacks and strokes. Soluble fibres, though, found in foods like oats, barley, beans, and some fruits, form a gel in the gut that binds to bile acids. Normally, once they've done their job, bile acids are reabsorbed and recycled in the body, but when fibre locks on to them, they're carried out and excreted instead. This sets off a chain reaction: the liver pulls cholesterol out of the bloodstream to make new bile acids. Some of that is LDL cholesterol, therefore lowering blood levels and reducing the risk of plaque build-up (see diagram, opposite).

Maintaining healthy weight
Fibre slows digestion and helps you feel fuller for longer, which reduces the likelihood of overeating. Maintaining a healthy weight in turn lowers blood pressure and improves blood-sugar control – two key risk factors for heart disease.

Making short-chain fatty acids
Prebiotic fibres (page 28) trigger an effect that produces short-chain fatty acids (SCFAs) in the gut. These enter the bloodstream and have wide-reaching effects, from helping lower inflammation to helping moderate blood-sugar and cholesterol levels (page 11).

Contributing to the bigger picture
High-fibre diets rarely exist in isolation – by definition they are rich in fruits, vegetables, legumes, whole grains, nuts, and seeds. These foods provide not just fibre, but a wide array of vitamins, minerals, antioxidants, and plant compounds that also protect the heart. In other words, fibre may partly serve as a marker of an overall diet that supports cardiovascular health.

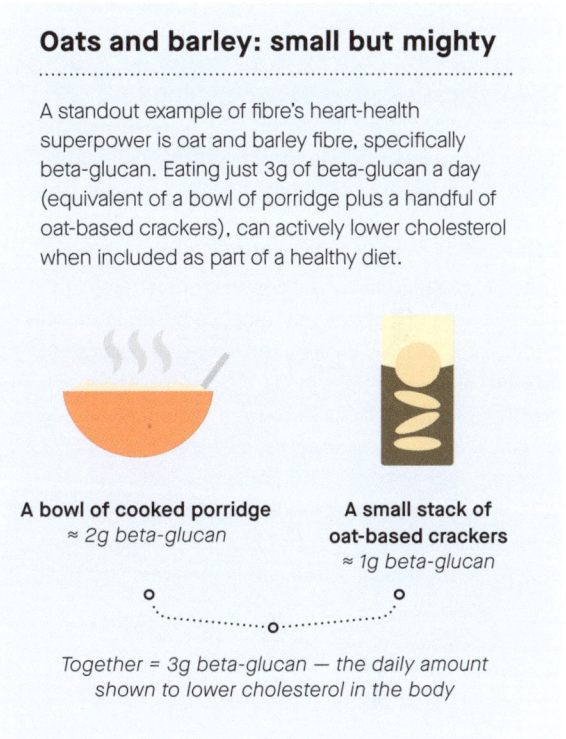

Oats and barley: small but mighty

A standout example of fibre's heart-health superpower is oat and barley fibre, specifically beta-glucan. Eating just 3g of beta-glucan a day (equivalent of a bowl of porridge plus a handful of oat-based crackers), can actively lower cholesterol when included as part of a healthy diet.

A bowl of cooked porridge
≈ 2g beta-glucan

A small stack of oat-based crackers
≈ 1g beta-glucan

Together = 3g beta-glucan — the daily amount shown to lower cholesterol in the body

Just 5g extra fibre each day can reduce blood pressure, cholesterol, and markers of inflammation – all of which impact heart health.

Can fibre help me manage my weight?

Weight management is so much more complex than counting calories. Whether you want to lose or gain weight, fibre plays an important role. That's because many fibre-rich foods are not only good for digestion and gut health, but also provide energy and essential nutrients, optimizing health whatever your weight-management goals.

What is a "healthy" weight?

There is no straightforward answer to this question – "healthy" weight needs to look at your genetics (some people are naturally smaller and lighter or taller and heavier) and your overall health to determine what is healthy *for you*. If, though, you are underweight due to stress, illness, or low appetite, and if as a result you are fatigued, nutrient deficient, immuno-compromised, or suffering hormonal imbalance or other signs of ill health, a gradual increase in weight (about 0.5–1kg per week) may help, especially paired with light activity to build muscle mass. If you are overweight or obese, a careful, sustained weight-loss programme that optimizes nutrient intake and is paired with exercise, can help you lose weight safely and sustainably. (Note that, if you're struggling with gaining or losing weight, seek support from a healthcare professional or registered dietitian.)

Why fibre works for weight gain

Carbohydrates are the body's main source of energy, and, as we know, fibre is a type of carbohydrate found in plant foods. The misconception that "carbohydrates cause unhealthy weight gain" has led many people to cut them out unnecessarily. In reality, whole-grain and fibre-rich carbohydrate foods provide both energy (needed for weight gain) and fibre (needed for gut health and nutrient absorption). This makes them ideal for underweight individuals trying to eat more without sacrificing the nutritional quality of their diet by relying on ultra-processed options.

Weight-gain superfoods

Practical foods to include in a fibre-rich, but balanced healthy weight-gain diet, include:

Carbohydrate sources
Whole-grain starchy carbs such as brown rice, oats, and potatoes.

High-quality protein foods
Protein-rich foods including beans, lentils, dairy, eggs, fish, and meat.

Energy-dense plant foods
Energy-dense fibre sources like nuts, seeds, and avocados.

Dairy foods
Smoothies, yogurts, and milk-based puddings made with whole ingredients.

Why fibre works for weight loss

In the UK alone there are an average of 136,000 monthly searches for "how can I lose weight fast". In 2021, a study found that 45% of people globally are actively trying to lose weight at any one time. The figure increased to 60% of people in Chile, and more than 50% in Spain, Peru, Saudi Arabia, Singapore, and the USA. Clearly weight is a growing concern all over the world: research published by *The Lancet* suggests that more than one billion people worldwide are living with obesity. This comprises roughly 880 million adults and 159 million children.

Fibre-rich whole foods are fundamental to sustainable weight loss: research published in 2025 provides compelling evidence that they can represent a practical and effective strategy within a minimally processed dietary pattern. In a well-controlled UK-based trial, adults with overweight or obesity followed two distinct eight-week diets: one based on minimally processed foods and the other on ultra-processed foods (UPFs). Both diets were nutritionally matched, and aligned with national dietary guidelines. However, participants lost significantly more weight on the minimally processed diet – it is likely that fibre played a contributing role in this outcome. Minimally processed meals tend to be naturally higher in dietary fibre, which supports appetite regulation through greater satiety, slower digestion, and reduced energy intake over time. These findings highlight the importance of food *form and structure*, not just nutrient content, and suggest that fibre-rich, whole foods may support weight-loss efforts more effectively than their ultra-processed counterparts.

Carbohydrate choice matters

It's not the carbohydrates themselves that drive weight changes – it's the quality of those carbohydrates. Fibre-rich foods like whole grains, fruit, beans, and vegetables provide energy for weight gain while also supporting digestion, stable blood sugar, and long-term health. In contrast, refined and ultra-processed carbohydrates (such as white bread, biscuits, and sugary cereals) give quick calories but little else. By choosing whole, fibre-containing carbohydrates, you can optimize both your calorie intake and the nutritional value of your diet. Put simply, carbohydrates – including fibre-rich carbohydrates – complement each other when it comes to healthy weight gain or healthy weight loss.

Feeling full

One of fibre's most valuable traits is its ability to increase satiety (feeling full) by adding bulk, slowing digestion, and giving sustained energy release. Hand in hand with protein (which triggers fullness hormones; page 30), fibre is a weight-stabilizing hero. Plant-based proteins, such as beans, lentils, and quinoa, naturally combine both fibre and protein, delivering the double benefit in one package (animal proteins contain little to no fibre).

Regulating blood sugar

Fibre can level out blood-sugar spikes and crashes, which are often responsible for mid-morning and afternoon cravings and slumps. By slowing digestion, a high-fibre diet releases glucose into the bloodstream gradually and steadily, so we are more likely to resist the urge to snack, particularly on sugary foods. (On the other hand, ultra-processed foods hijack our brain's dopamine system to give a rapid hit of pleasure, followed by a crash that drives us to go back for more.)

Healthy bacteria (again)

As we know, prebiotic dietary fibre feeds beneficial bacteria, and in turn produces short-chain fatty acids (SCFAs). While the relationship between SCFAs and body weight is still being clarified, some evidence suggests that specific changes in gut bacteria and their fermentation activity may support a healthier weight. Studies in obese patients have found microbiome imbalance with an overgrowth of harmful bacteria.

How might resistant starch help with weight loss?

Resistant starch (page 15) bypasses digestion, and may offer two potential benefits for weight management. First, because the small intestine does not absorb some of the starch, the energy (number of calories) in the food is slightly lowered compared with the same food without resistant starch. Second, once resistant starch reaches the colon, gut bacteria ferment it to produce SCFAs. These may increase feelings of fullness, improve the body's response to insulin, and support overall metabolic health. However, much of the research on resistant starch and weight control is rodent-based. Although there appear to be consistent benefits for satiety, fat metabolism, and body composition in rodents, evidence in humans is mixed. A few small trials suggest possible reductions in appetite or body weight; many others show little or no effect. It's a case of watch this space.

How do weight-loss drugs change my nutritional needs?

Over the past few years, weight-loss injections have made headlines around the world. Once prescribed almost exclusively for people with Type-2 diabetes, drugs such as Ozempic®, Wegovy®, and Mounjaro® are now being used far more widely for weight management.

Demand has surged, with prescriptions rising sharply in the UK and USA, fuelled in part by social media and celebrity endorsements. For many, these medicines seem to offer a quick solution to weight loss and undoubtedly save lives, but they also raise important questions about long-term nutrition and health.

What is GLP-1 and how does it work?

At the heart of these treatments is glucagon-like peptide-1 (GLP-1), a hormone naturally released from the gut after eating. GLP-1 helps regulate appetite by slowing gastric emptying, moderating post-meal blood glucose, and signalling to the brain that we have consumed enough food. Medications such as semaglutide (sold as Ozempic or Wegovy) and tirzepatide (sold as Mounjaro, which also mimics another gut hormone, called GIP) act on the same GLP-1 receptors in the gut, pancreas, and brain, but remain active much longer than the body's own GLP-1.

How do weight-loss injections work?

Weight-loss injections provide extra GLP-1 – a hormone that the body naturally releases after we eat and which regulates appetite. GLP-1 medications have longer-lasting effects in the body, thus reducing cravings for food over a longer period of time and suppressing our need to eat.

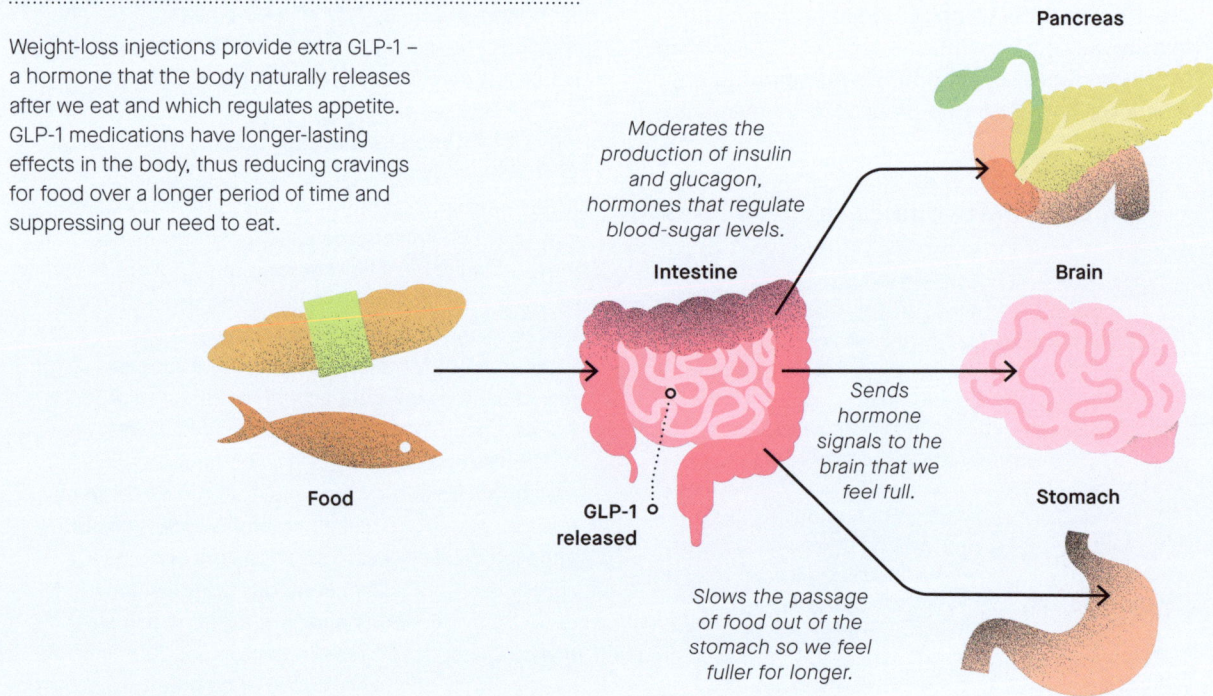

Suppressing appetite

While originally developed to improve blood-sugar control in Type-2 diabetes, these medications' strong appetite-suppressing effects also drive significant weight loss. People often describe a sudden quietening of "food noise" (the constant urge to eat), alongside satisfaction with much smaller meals. But this reduced appetite brings challenges as well as benefits. Because the medications reduce appetite and slow digestion, one of the nutrients most at risk of being reduced in the diet is fibre, along with protein and essential vitamins and minerals. Fibre is especially vulnerable when portion sizes shrink or when meals become more protein-centred, yet we know it is crucial for digestion, appetite regulation, and long-term metabolic health.

Slowing the gut

GLP-1 medicines slow the rate at which food leaves the stomach. This effect can help with blood-sugar control and satiety, but it increases the risk of digestive side-effects, such as nausea, bloating, or constipation. Fibre becomes particularly important here. As we know, insoluble fibre adds bulk to stool and keeps bowel movements regular (page 26), while soluble fibre, such as beta-glucan (found in oats and barley) and pectin (in apples, pears, and berries) helps normalize digestion and stabilize blood glucose. People who cut back on meal size but fail to include these fibres may notice sluggish digestion or irregular stools.

Getting the fibre fix

For those using GLP-1 medications, it is clear that there is increased risk of key nutrient deficiencies – this applies to micronutrients such as iron and calcium, but also to fibre. The lack of nutritional diversity and fibre also leads to poor gut health. The focus for anyone taking GLP-1s should be on nutrient density and variety in smaller portions. Prioritizing fibre-rich foods within smaller, regular meals helps support gut health, maintain satiety, and ensure that reduced calorie intake does not come at the expense of long-term well-being. In the context of the use of these medications, fibre is not just a background nutrient, it is central to good digestive function and to good health beyond weight loss. Fibre-rich plant foods provide both nourishment and digestive support without large food volumes.

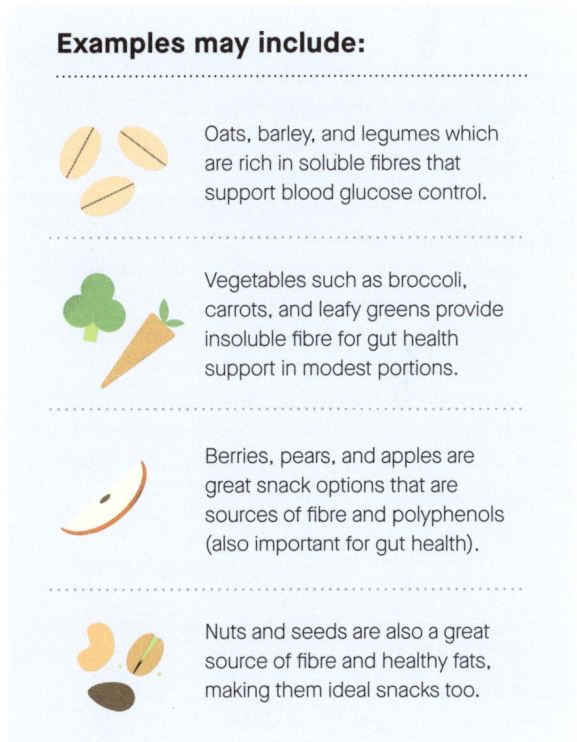

Examples may include:

- Oats, barley, and legumes which are rich in soluble fibres that support blood glucose control.
- Vegetables such as broccoli, carrots, and leafy greens provide insoluble fibre for gut health support in modest portions.
- Berries, pears, and apples are great snack options that are sources of fibre and polyphenols (also important for gut health).
- Nuts and seeds are also a great source of fibre and healthy fats, making them ideal snacks too.

Fibre is especially vulnerable when portion sizes shrink or when meals become more protein-centred.

How does fibre affect my performance in sport?

During exercise, blood is directed away from the gastrointestinal (GI) tract and toward the working muscles. This is a normal physiological response that ensures oxygen and nutrients are delivered where they're needed most – primarily to the limbs and peripheral tissues. However, this shift in blood flow means there's less oxygen – along with fewer other resources – available for digestion. So, if you eat a fibre-rich meal too close to a sports session, your gut will struggle to manage the digestive load. As a consequence, you may experience symptoms such as bloating, abdominal discomfort, cramping, urgency, or even diarrhoea (particularly common in endurance athletes where GI distress is already prevalent).

You might, given all that, think that fibre shouldn't therefore feature at all in an athlete's diet, but that would be a huge misconception. Fibre is essential for athletes just as it is for everyone else because it supports regular bowel function, helps stabilize blood-glucose levels, and contributes to long-term cardiovascular and metabolic health. Nonetheless, to optimize your sporting performance and your fibre intake, there is one important thing you need to take into account: exactly when you eat your fibre.

Not "if" or "how", but "when"

As a general rule, athletes should eat high-fibre meals at least 3–4 hours before prolonged or intense activity. This allows enough time for digestion and minimizes the risk of gut discomfort during exercise.

In the 60–90 minutes before endurance training or racing, the focus should shift to "simple sugars". These are carbohydrates that contain very little fibre and are quickly absorbed into the body to provide a rapid release of energy. They include foods such as white bread, sweets, sports drinks, and low-fibre cereal bars.

You may be surprised to hear me encouraging simple sugars. But this is where the nuance comes in. These foods are ultra-processed, low in fibre, and offer very few nutrients overall – but in the context of endurance sports nutrition (such as running training and racing), they have a place. When used appropriately, they can provide fast, accessible energy without placing unnecessary strain on the digestive system.

For those regularly experiencing gut issues during endurance fitness sessions, adjusting fibre intake around exercise can be a simple and effective change. Over time, it's also possible to train the gut to tolerate slightly higher amounts of fibre or carbohydrate closer to exercise, but do this gradually – and ideally with the support of a sports nutritionist who can guide you through the transition safely and effectively.

Should I eat fibre to fuel a race?

For endurance or racing athletes, fibre plays an important but often misunderstood role. While fibre is essential for long-term health, including digestive function and metabolic regulation, it's one nutrient you may want to avoid too close to a competition. Fibre's ability to slow down digestion is one of its many benefits to the general population, but this effect can become problematic when the goal is quick energy release for exercise.

> Athletes should eat high-fibre meals at least 3–4 hours before prolonged or intense activity.

Timing your sports nutrition

If you're an athlete, eat fibre strategically – away from training windows and around rest days to ensure optimum nutritional benefit without compromising performance. Immediately before a race or workout, foods made up of simple sugars will give you the energy you need with minimal bloating or discomfort.

Eat a balanced meal that includes slower-releasing carbohydrates (page 12) for sustained energy and moderate amounts of fibre. If you're prone to gastrointestinal discomfort during exercise, choose lower-fibre options (page 23), reserving higher-fibre foods for after training or on rest days.

Aim to begin exercise well-hydrated. Fluid needs depend on body size, sweat rate, and training conditions.

2–3 hours before exercise

Sports drinks provide quick-release carbohydrates and hydration to support energy needed for exercise.

Choose low-fibre, quick-release carbohydrate foods (page 23). These foods and drinks are easy to digest and low in fibre, reducing some risk of bloating or discomfort during training.

60–90 minutes before exercise

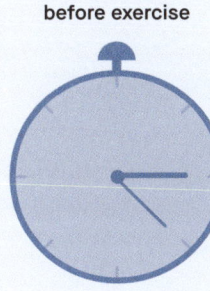

Can fibre help relieve symptoms of menopause?

All women born with ovaries will experience menopause. Despite that certainty, the term itself was coined only in 1821 – by French physician Charles de Gardanne. Then, it wasn't until the mid-20th century that scientists began to study hormonal changes more closely – with the discovery of oestrogen and the introduction of hormone replacement therapy (HRT), especially.

Large-scale research, like the Women's Health Initiative (WHI) launched in the 1990s, revealed potential risks associated with HRT, which led to a decline in prescriptions and stalled progress in menopause research for over a decade. Only in the past 10–15 years has menopause gained more serious attention. Although there is no evidence-based "menopause diet", emerging research suggests that what we eat may influence how we experience this natural transition.

Phytoestrogens and the Mediterranean diet

Diets rich in whole plant foods have consistently been linked with reduced menopause symptoms. A key area of interest is the role of phytoestrogens. These are naturally occurring plant compounds that can mimic the effect of estrogen in the body. In particular, adherence to the Mediterranean diet – which includes abundant pulses, legumes, whole grains, extra virgin olive oil, fruit and vegetables – has been associated with better health outcomes after menopause, such as improved bone density, lower cholesterol, and reduced inflammation. A 2022 study found that women with obesity who followed a Mediterranean diet experienced fewer and less severe menopausal symptoms overall. Specifically, higher legume intake was associated with reduced physical symptoms, and extra virgin olive oil appeared to ease psychological symptoms.

Populations with higher intakes of these foods often report fewer vasomotor symptoms (those linked to the relaxation and contraction of the blood vessels, like hot flushes and night sweats). Notably, consuming two servings of soy per day may offer symptom relief. This is especially true for women who produce equol, a compound derived from the metabolism of soy isoflavones by specific intestinal bacteria. Only about 30–50% of all adults have the right gut microbes to produce equol, which may enhance the beneficial effects of soy on menopausal symptoms.

A recent cross-sectional study in Australia involving over 200 peri- and postmenopausal women found that adherence to a Mediterranean-style diet was associated with improved physical functioning, general health, and joint/muscle comfort, although it was not directly linked to symptom severity. Similarly, a systematic review of interventional studies concluded that the Mediterranean diet can help reduce blood pressure, body weight, and cholesterol levels among postmenopausal women.

While findings overall are mixed, and cultural, genetic, and lifestyle differences may also play a role, they do appear to support the growing consensus that a plant-forward, wholefood-rich dietary approach, particularly one based on Mediterranean principles, may offer significant benefits during menopause, especially when rich in fibre and phytoestrogens. Diet is not a cure-all, but making fibre- and plant-focused changes can support overall health during menopause.

Soybeans for menopause

A 2025 analysis of a low-fat vegan diet with added daily soybeans showed significant reductions in the frequency and severity of hot flushes, alongside improved plant-based dietary index scores. Soybeans provide a unique mix of high-quality plant protein, soluble fibre, and isoflavones (which act as mild phytoestrogens in the body). Isoflavones can help support bone and heart health; while soy fibre can contribute to better digestion and cholesterol management, while its protein supports muscle mass as oestrogen levels decline (page 32).

Fibre, gut health, and hormonal balance

Good gut health is essential not only for our overall well-being, but also for supporting hormonal (particularly oestrogen) balance. In one large study of 17,000 menopausal women, those with higher intakes of fibre from fruits and vegetables, along with soy, experienced a 19% reduction in hot flushes compared to the control group. Similarly, findings from the UK Women's Cohort Study, which involved over 900 women, indicated that a gut-friendly diet rich in prebiotic fibre may help delay the onset of natural menopause.

While more robust research is needed in this area, current evidence supports the benefits of a predominantly plant-based, fibre-rich diet as a sensible and safe nutritional strategy during the menopause transition. If you're experiencing troublesome symptoms, it's always advisable to speak with a healthcare professional for a personalized plan.

Those with higher intakes of fibre from fruits and vegetables, along with soy, experienced a 19% reduction in hot flushes.

Top 10 fibre-rich phytoestrogen foods

Many fibre-rich foods are also top-class sources of phytoestrogen. Among them are:

1. Soybeans (and its products, including tempeh, tofu, miso, and edamame)

2. Flaxseeds

3. Sesame seeds

4. Lentils

5. Chickpeas

6. Chia seeds

7. Rye

8. Barley

9. Oats

10. Nuts (especially cashews, pistachios, and almonds)

Can fibre make me look and feel younger?

From collagen powders claiming to smooth wrinkles, to omega-3s touted for skin elasticity, and vitamins A and C praised for repair and radiance, the search for the nutritional fountain of youth grows ever wider. Ageing well is big business. But, beyond the hype, what does science actually tell us about the relationship between diet and ageing? Two main markers – skin health and bone health – are good ways to see whether eating more fibre can help us look and feel younger.

Examining the science

The skin's microbiome (the "skin flora"), consists of about 1,000 diverse microorganisms that primarily inhabit the outer layers of the epidermis and the upper portions of hair follicles. This complex community is critical in maintaining skin health by providing a barrier against harmful pathogens and by modulating the immune system. A balanced microbiome helps protect the skin and supports its structural and functional integrity.

While some research has explored the link between individual micronutrient deficiencies and skin function, there is limited clinical evidence to support any notion that specific foods or dietary patterns lead to optimal skin health. However, populations with higher intakes of plant-based foods have been found to experience less photoageing (skin damage caused by persistent sun exposure) compared with those consuming a typical Western diet rich in red and processed meats, full-fat dairy, refined carbohydrates, and sugary drinks.

The Gut–Skin axis

On pages 24–25 we introduced the idea of the Gut–Brain axis – well, there is a Gut–Skin axis, too. Emerging research suggests that Western-style diets may disrupt the gut microbiome, which can lead to systemic inflammation in the body. This includes compromising skin quality – manifested as reduced elasticity and firmness, and uneven pigmentation. In contrast, plant-based diets, rich in fibre, polyphenols, and antioxidants, have been shown to support a diverse gut microbiome and may positively affect skin appearance and function.

Fibre and the skin

One observational study found that for every 5g increase in daily fibre intake, patients undergoing immunotherapy for melanoma (cancer of the skin) experienced a 30% lower risk of disease progression or death. This could suggest that fibre may enhance treatment outcomes through immune modulation and by reinforcing the links between the gut–skin axis and immunity. Supporting this notion, animal research has shown that the process of gut microbes fermenting dietary fibre to produce short-chain fatty acids (SCFAs; page 11) enhances skin-barrier function (such as improving the activity of keratinocytes, cells in the skin's dermis, which form part of the immune system), and reduces allergic skin inflammation. It stands to reason, then, that there is potential for fibre to play a protective role in maintaining skin integrity.

Additionally, data from the Nurses' Health Study (conducted in the USA looking at data over a 22-year period from 1984 to 2016 and published in 2025), linked higher midlife intake of fibre and high-quality carbohydrates with up to a 37% increased likelihood of healthy ageing – further suggesting that fibre intake may influence skin-cell ageing and resilience over time.

While direct research on fibre specifically impacting skin-age markers remains limited, mounting evidence supports its role in improving skin-related health through immune support, enhanced skin-barrier integrity, and systemic ageing pathways. These findings point toward fibre as a subtle but powerful ally in maintaining skin vitality as we age.

Fibre and the bones

As we get older our bones become more brittle, our joints more stiff, and the ligaments that hold everything together more loose. But there is plenty we can do to preserve the integrity of our bones and joints into old age. In fact, some studies suggest that dietary fibre may play a protective role in joint health. As we already know short-chain fatty acids (SCFAs), which are the direct result of the fermentation of fibre in the gut (page 11), have anti-inflammatory properties that can help reduce systemic inflammation – a key factor in age-related joint degeneration. One large cohort study found that individuals with higher fibre intake had a significantly lower risk of developing symptomatic knee osteoarthritis. Finally, as we know, fibre plays a significant role in weight management (page 40). Reducing the strain on weight-bearing joints may help regulate immune responses implicated in autoimmune conditions such as rheumatoid arthritis.

Data from the Nurses' Health Study... linked higher midlife intake of fibre and high-quality carbohydrates with up to a 37% increased likelihood of healthy ageing.

Keeping your chromosomes young

An exciting recent research analysis of more than 5,600 adults in the USA showed that, for every 10g increase in fibre per 1,000 calories, telomeres (the protein caps at the ends of chromosomes) were on average 83 base pairs longer. As each year of chronological age equates to about 15½ fewer base pairs, this means that biological ageing slowed by around five years. The study controlled for variables including smoking, body mass index, alcohol use, and physical activity, suggesting a meaningful link between more fibre and preserved cellular youth.

1. Young and healthy
Telomeres are long and protective, safeguarding chromosomes from damage and keeping cells youthful.

2. Early adulthood
Each cell division shortens the telomeres slightly, a natural part of ageing. But antioxidants and a high-fibre diet help slow the process.

3. Midlife
Shorter telomeres make DNA more vulnerable, increasing oxidative stress and reducing the cell's ability to repair itself.

4. Older age
Critically short telomeres trigger cell ageing and dysfunction, contributing to inflammation, slower regeneration, and age-related disease.

Can fibre manage my diabetes?

An estimated 537 million adults worldwide are currently living with diabetes. Around 90–95% of these cases are of Type-2 diabetes, which is often linked to diet and lifestyle. In other words, a significant number of diabetes' patients have a disease that is manageable with the right nutritional and lifestyle advice.

In the UK, 3.9 million people have been formally diagnosed with diabetes. However, estimates that include undiagnosed cases push that figure upward to more than 4.8 million. If current trends continue, every year will see another half a million people on the diabetes spectrum. If Type-2 diabetes accounts for around 90% of the UK's cases (reflecting the global picture), Type 1 makes up about 8%, and rarer forms the remaining 2%. In the USA, 29.7 million people have been diagnosed with diabetes (all types) – again with the breakdown reflecting the global picture that around 90% are Type 2. Understanding the role of diet, and particularly the role of dietary fibre, is crucial in both the prevention and management of this condition.

Types of diabetes

Type-1 diabetes is an autoimmune condition, where the body's immune system mistakenly attacks insulin-producing cells in the pancreas. This means it cannot be prevented or managed through lifestyle changes alone. Type-2 diabetes, on the other hand, is a chronic condition where the body *becomes resistant* to insulin or the pancreas doesn't produce enough of it. As a result, glucose from the carbohydrates we eat cannot be moved out of the bloodstream and into the body's cells for energy effectively. The pancreas tries to compensate for this by producing more insulin. Over time the response becomes less successful and blood-glucose levels remain too high.

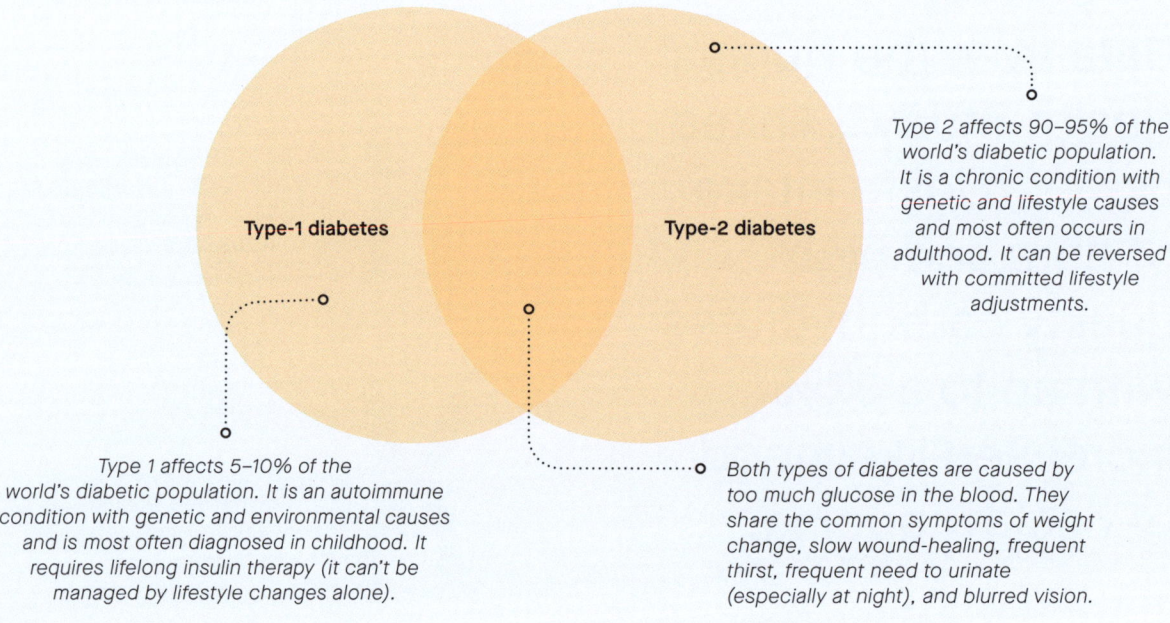

Type 1 affects 5–10% of the world's diabetic population. It is an autoimmune condition with genetic and environmental causes and is most often diagnosed in childhood. It requires lifelong insulin therapy (it can't be managed by lifestyle changes alone).

Type 2 affects 90–95% of the world's diabetic population. It is a chronic condition with genetic and lifestyle causes and most often occurs in adulthood. It can be reversed with committed lifestyle adjustments.

Both types of diabetes are caused by too much glucose in the blood. They share the common symptoms of weight change, slow wound-healing, frequent thirst, frequent need to urinate (especially at night), and blurred vision.

Fibre for blood-sugar stability

Historically, those with Type-2 diabetes have been advised to adopt a low-carbohydrate diet. However, newer evidence suggests that, in fact, higher carbohydrate diets are more effective, because the stress of restrictive eating and frequent weight cycling leads to poorer metabolic outcomes, including impaired glucose uptake, increased liver fat, and reduced insulin secretion. Rather than eliminating carbohydrates, then, a balanced diet that includes high-fibre, nutrient-dense carbohydrates (page 40) may lead to improved outcomes. These foods are rich in phytonutrients and have a lower glycaemic index, meaning they produce a slower, more stable rise in blood glucose. Furthermore, fibre slows gastric emptying and glucose absorption, reducing post-meal blood-sugar spikes. Finally, high-fibre diets are associated with improved insulin sensitivity, lower fasting glucose levels, and reduced risk of even developing Type-2 diabetes. Overall, for individuals living with diabetes, increasing daily fibre intake to between 25g and 35g may support better blood-sugar control and long-term metabolic health.

Diabetes and the gut

Research underscores the pivotal role of the gut microbiome in regulating metabolic health and blood-glucose control. As we know, a fibre-rich diet increases levels of short-chain fatty acids (SCFAs). These strengthen the intestinal lining, reduce inflammation, and improve insulin sensitivity, changes associated with enhanced glucose metabolism and reduced insulin resistance. By nurturing a more diverse and stable gut microbiota, dietary fibre may act as a natural modulator of metabolic function.

Recent science

A 2023 randomized, placebo-controlled trial found that a prebiotic, fibre-enriched nutritional formula significantly improved both HbA1c (a key marker of blood-sugar control) and quality of life in individuals with Type-2 diabetes, also promoting growth of beneficial SCFA-producing gut bacteria. In a 24-week pilot trial, consuming 20g of a diverse prebiotic fibre supplement each day, led to a modest but statistically significant reduction in HbA1c among pre-diabetic adults with baseline HbA1c under 6%. Large cohort data from the Melbourne Collaborative Cohort Study (2023) revealed a 25% lower incidence of Type-2 diabetes among participants with higher cereal fibre intake (although this effect appeared to be partly mediated by body mass index). Furthermore, a 2024 meta-analysis highlighted that fibre intake measurably improved glycaemic control in individuals with Type-2 diabetes. These findings suggest that integrating high-fibre foods and prebiotic supplements can support blood-sugar regulation, enhance insulin sensitivity, and protect against diabetes.

So, while diabetes remains a growing global challenge, the evidence is clear: increasing fibre intake is one of the most effective, accessible, and empowering dietary strategies we have to support blood-sugar control and enhance quality of life for those with diabetes.

> For individuals living with diabetes, increasing daily fibre intake to between 25g and 35g may support better blood-sugar control and long-term metabolic health.

Eat the whole fruit

Eating whole fruit not only increases dietary fibre, but also mitigates the resulting increase in blood sugar. This is because the intact plant cell structure and fibre matrix in whole fruit help regulate digestion and absorption, leading to a steadier rise in blood glucose.

Eating 6 medium oranges = 12–15g of dietary fibre

150ml fresh orange juice from 6 medium oranges = 1g of dietary fibre

Can fibre help flush out plastics and heavy metals?

Environmental toxins, such as plastics and heavy metals, pose a growing concern for health. They are substances (natural and synthetic) in our air, water, soil, and food. Plastics can take anywhere from 20 to over 500 years to degrade, but even then they don't disappear – they break down into microplastics, which enter the food chain and so our body. While not a concern for most of us, research suggests that heavy metals (lead, mercury, and so on) may disrupt the balance of the gut microbiome. Amazingly, though, fibre is emerging as a way the body could tackle both.

The plastics problem

The rate at which plastic decomposes depends on the type, environmental conditions, and how it is discarded.

Microplastics are found in food packaging, clothing fibres, personal care products, and household items, meaning they can easily end up in the air we breathe and the food and drink we consume. Unsurprisingly, microplastics have now been detected in everything from bottled water and table salt to household dust.

Estimates suggest that the average adult may ingest between 39,000 and 52,000 microplastic particles each year. These figures seem alarming enough, but gaps in current testing methods suggest that our actual exposure is (worryingly) likely to be far greater.

Where do dietary plastics come from?

Everyday sources of dietary plastics include food packaging, cling film (plastic wrap), tea bags, plastic-lined coffee cups, and reheating leftovers in plastic containers. But before panic sets in, this doesn't mean you need to throw out all the plastic boxes you own. It's more about being aware of where exposures come from and making small, achievable swaps where possible, like reducing single-use plastics or choosing glass or stainless steel for hot-food storage.

Heating food in plastic containers can cause harmful chemicals such as bisphenol A (BPA) and phthalates to leach into the food, especially when the plastic is not labelled as microwave-safe. These chemicals are known endocrine disruptors, meaning they can interfere with hormone function and have been linked to reproductive and metabolic health issues. Repeated heating may increase the risk of exposure over time, especially when using old plastic containers, where tiny flakes of the container walls can find their way in to the food inside.

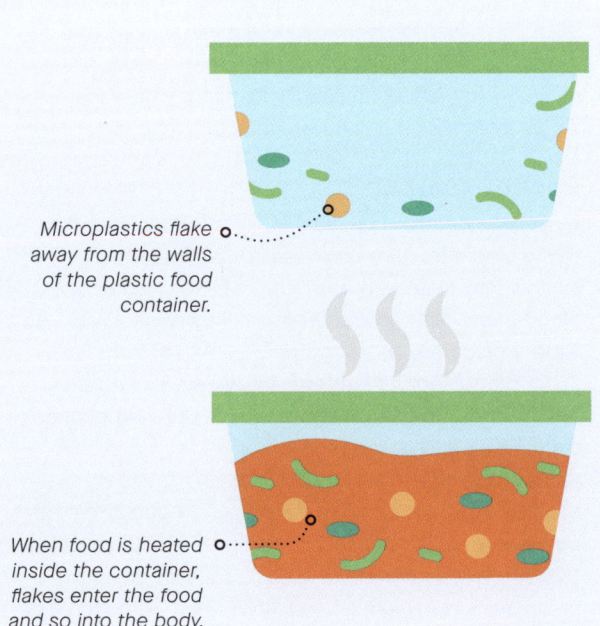

Microplastics flake away from the walls of the plastic food container.

When food is heated inside the container, flakes enter the food and so into the body.

What happens to microplastics in the gut?
Recent studies show that, once ingested, microplastics don't just remain in the gut: they can cross biological barriers in the body. They have been detected in the bloodstream, lung tissue, placenta (of pregnant women), breast milk, and even brain.

Alarmingly, one 2024 study estimated that in individuals with prolonged high exposure, brain tissue could contain up to 0.5% plastic by weight. While this area of research is still evolving, it raises important questions about how microplastics interact with the body and what steps we can take to reduce their accumulation.

What's the fibre solution for plastics?
Incredibly, emerging research suggests that our dietary fibre intake may offer a surprising line of defence against these marauding microplastics. A review conducted in 2024 explored how different types of dietary fibre, particularly soluble fibres, such as beta-glucan and pectin (page 43), may help limit microplastic accumulation in the body.

One proposed mechanism for this, demonstrated by animal and cell models, is that dietary fibre may reduce the transportation of plastic particles across the gut barrier and into blood and lymph circulation. The theory is that soluble fibre forms a thick, gel-like matrix in the gut creating a viscous environment that helps trap unwanted substances, such as bile acids and toxins – but also potentially microplastics. The trapped particles then move through the digestive system so that we excrete them via the stool. In other words, they are prevented from crossing into the bloodstream or lymphatic system. Some early human research along these lines is beginning to show promise – with studies suggesting that high-fibre diets may lower levels of plastic-associated chemicals in blood and urine. While these studies are still limited in scale and are in their infancy – we still need much more research to be sure – the potential is significant.

The problem with heavy metals
Heavy metals such as mercury, cadmium, arsenic, and lead occur naturally in the environment but have become more widespread through industrial pollution, and contaminated water and soil. These metals can accumulate in plants, fish, and animal products – and that means that our diet is often our main source of exposure to them. As alarming as this might sound, in most developed countries overall exposure is generally low, and well below safety thresholds. However, in some parts of the world where soil or water contamination is higher, levels can be slightly more concerning.

What happens to heavy metals in the gut?
Once inside the body, heavy metals are not easily broken down or excreted. Over time, they can build up in the body's tissue and may begin to have adverse effects on our organs, such as the liver, kidneys, and brain. More recently, research has shown that they may also disrupt the gut microbiota (the community of microbes that support digestion), immunity, and metabolic health. High exposure to certain metals has been linked with changes in the diversity and function of gut bacteria, increased inflammation, and damage to the intestinal barrier that acts to regulate what passes from the gut into the bloodstream and helps protect the body from toxins and pathogens.

What's the fibre solution for heavy metals?
Recent studies have suggested that people who consume more dietary fibre tend to have lower blood concentrations of heavy metals. Certain fibres – especially soluble types such as pectin, beta-glucan, and resistant starch – can bind to heavy metals in the gut, reducing how much heavy metal is absorbed into the bloodstream and promoting its removal through the stool. Fibre may also help by supporting a more resilient gut microbiota, counteracting some of the damage heavy metals cause to intestinal cells and beneficial bacteria. However, as with plastics, this research is very much still in its infancy and we need to know a lot more before we can confirm how different fibre types influence heavy-metal absorption in humans. Nonetheless, it raises an exciting possibility that a diet rich in varied fibre sources could help the body defend itself not just against toxins from food, but from the environment too.

Chapter Two

The 30:30:30

The 30:30:30 Fibre Formula is a simple yet transformative framework that brings together three evidence-based habits to nourish the body and support a healthy gut: 30 different plants a week, 30 chews per mouthful, and 30g of fibre a day.

Research shows that eating around 30 different plant foods each week – from fruits, vegetables, and grains to nuts, seeds, and herbs – supports a more diverse gut microbiome. This diversity is linked to better digestion, stronger immunity, and even long-term protection against chronic disease. Variety, not perfection, is what matters most. Then, taking the time to chew each mouthful – around 30 times – aids digestion, enhances satiety, and reduces bloating. Finally, the goal of 30g of fibre remains the benchmark for optimal gut and digestive health.

This chapter provides the practical advice you need – whatever your lifestyle or health goals – to put the 30:30:30 Fibre Formula into practice.

fibre formula

The 30:30:30 fxormula

The 30:30:30 formula is a simple yet powerful way to structure eating habits for long-term health. The aim is for 30g of fibre per day, 30 different plant foods each week, and 30 chews per mouthful.

Each "30" is backed by research, and together they offer a practical framework for supporting gut health, weight management, and overall well-being.

Taken together, the 30:30:30 formula empowers individuals with a framework that is evidence-based, practical, and flexible. It is not a diet of restriction, but a lifestyle approach that celebrates variety, balance, and awareness of key nutritional and dietary needs.

30 grams of fibre per day

Despite being one of the strongest dietary predictors of good health, fibre remains the most under-consumed nutrient globally, with average intakes in the UK, USA, and elsewhere falling far short of recommendations (page 18–19). A large 2019 meta-analysis in *The Lancet* found that consuming 25–30g of fibre daily was associated with reductions in cardiovascular disease, Type-2 diabetes, colorectal cancer, and overall mortality. Importantly, different types of fibre play distinct roles: soluble fibres (like oats, beans, and psyllium) improve blood-glucose control and cholesterol, while insoluble fibres (whole grains, vegetables, nuts) promote regular bowel movements and support gut motility. Emerging studies also highlight the importance of fermentable fibres (inulin, resistant starch), which feed beneficial gut microbes, producing short-chain fatty acids, such as butyrate. These, in turn, strengthen the gut barrier and reduce inflammation (page 13).

30 plant foods per week

The idea of eating 30 different plants weekly comes from the American Gut Project, one of the largest microbiome studies to date. This research has shown that dietary diversity (rather than just the total amount of fibre we consume) is strongly linked to a healthier gut microbiome. As we've seen, plants in this context include fruits, vegetables, herbs, spices, legumes, nuts, seeds, and whole grains, each offering a unique make-up of fibre and phytochemicals in their different forms. Recent reviews have shown that people who consume a more diverse range of plants have greater microbial diversity, which in turn supports immune function, metabolic health, and even mental well-being through the Gut–Brain axis (page 27). Practically, this could mean adding another type of fruit to your snack list, adding chickpeas to a salad, or sprinkling seeds over breakfast porridge, which are all small changes that contribute to that weekly plant tally.

The 30:30:30 formula empowers individuals with a framework that is evidence-based, practical, and flexible.

30 chews per bite

Mindful eating is increasingly recognized as a tool for improving digestion and regulating appetite. Studies suggest that chewing each bite around 30 times slows eating speed, enhances satiety signals, and reduces overall food intake without feelings of deprivation. It also encourages us to engage all five senses (taste, smell, sight, touch, and even hearing) to fully appreciate our food. Mechanistically, thorough chewing helps break food down into smaller particles, making nutrients more accessible for digestion, while also allowing gut hormones, such as GLP-1 (page 42) and others, to signal fullness more effectively. Beyond physiology, chewing slowly creates space to connect with the eating experience improving satisfaction, reducing mindless snacking, and helping re-establish healthier relationships with food.

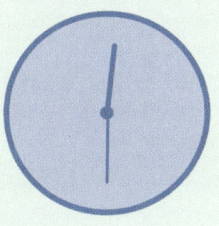

Bonus 30: 30-minute meals

The idea that meals should take no more than 30 minutes to prepare gives a bonus boost to the other 30s.

Studies consistently highlight time as one of the biggest barriers to healthy eating. By focusing on quick, wholefood meals, such as stir-fries, grain bowls, or hearty salads, it becomes easier to integrate fibre-rich, plant-diverse foods into daily life without the overwhelming task of lengthy cooking. When you're planning your meals for the week, try to choose those that are quick and easy.

The recipes in this book primarily concentrate on nutritional content over cooking time (although, of course, the faster you chop, the quicker the recipes will be, and there are plenty of options that anyway fall within 30 minutes). However, to get you started with looking for clever hacks and time-savers, while still boosting fibre, I have also included a recipe section dedicated to "Bonus 30" meals (pages 134–53). As you get used to incorporating more fibre into your diet, and it becomes habit, you can start to find other exciting ways to keep the cooking time down while pushing the fibre content up!

Favourite speedy recipes
- Green butter bean mac and fibre cheese (page 137)
- Harissa-spiced hispi wedges with date and almond tabbouleh and mint yogurt (page 141)
- Persian herb and grain stewed lentils and caramelized onions (page 153)

How much fibre is in my food?

The rise of ultra-processed and convenience foods has led to a decline in home cooking, particularly in Western countries like the UK and the USA. As a result, in some places average fibre intake has dropped to around 18–19g per day, well below the recommended 30g for optimal health.

As we've learned, fibre is typically found in the more wholesome parts of our diets – fruits, vegetables, grains, pulses, legumes, and whole grains – but it can also be surprisingly present in foods like dark chocolate, popcorn, and coconut chips.

This book features 60 delicious recipes, each containing at least 8g of fibre per serving, making it easier for you to reach your 30g-a-day target – all while celebrating variety, flavour, and nourishment by enjoying 30 different plant foods per week. However, knowing where to find other fibre-rich foods will help you to integrate more fibre into your everyday life in ways beyond the recipes themselves. Once finding the fibre superheroes becomes a habit – once you're simply pulling them instinctively from the shelves during your weekly shop – hitting your 30g target is going to be easier than ever. Over the following pages we'll look at some general know-how on recommended intakes by age, how to pick the best loaf of bread, and how to be gentle on your gut as you increase your fibre intake. We'll also provide the key to your fibre fix: the tables showing which foods are most fibre-rich.

Daily fibre recommendations by age

The daily fibre needs for males and females at around age 18 is about 30g and 25g respectively (page 76). But changing fibre needs doesn't stop there. This table shows the recommended daily fibre intake for adults from the age of 19 onward.

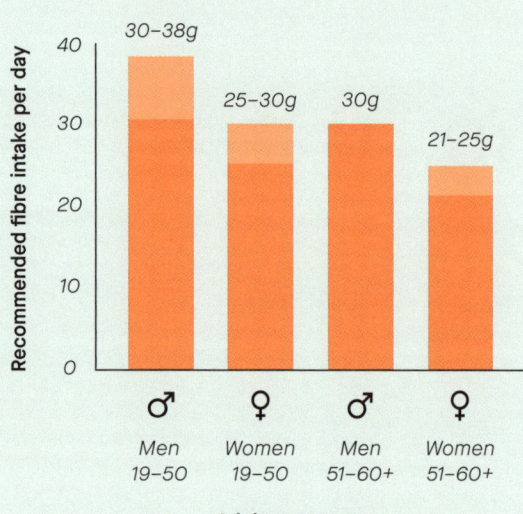

Note that while we can talk in averages, men and women have different needs throughout their lives, and individual needs will vary from person to person. In older age, fibre needs tail off as our metabolism slows down.

> **Once finding the fibre superheroes becomes a habit… hitting your 30g target is going to be easier than ever.**

Adjusting to more fibre

Increasing the variety of plant-based foods in your diet naturally boosts your fibre intake. While this is beneficial for long-term gut health, a sudden increase can lead to temporary digestive symptoms such as gas, bloating, diarrhoea, or constipation. To help your body adjust more comfortably, bear in mind the following tips.

Sit tall and chew thoroughly Good eating posture supports the natural flow of digestion. Chewing well ensures food reaches your stomach in a form that's easier to process.

Keep your body active Gentle movement, such as stretching or yoga, can stimulate digestion and help reduce bloating or discomfort.

Take it slowly Introduce new plant foods one at a time. Give your digestive system time to adapt before adding another.

Stay well hydrated Drinking fluids is essential for helping fibre move smoothly through the digestive tract, and for supporting digestion (page 75).

The best loaf

Breads made with whole grains, seeds, or oats offer significant fibre advantages over loaves of white bread. They can aid digestion and support heart health, while promoting better blood-sugar balance. Options like wholemeal, rye, multigrain, and porridge breads deliver added nutrients and longer-lasting energy, too.

White Containing minimal fibre (around 2.7g per 100g), white bread falls short of being a fibre source.

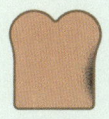

Wholemeal and high-fibre white Providing around 6–7g fibre per 100g, wholemeal (whole wheat) and high-fibre white are a fibre source in public-health guidelines.

Multigrain or seeded These loaves often offer the highest fibre levels (up to about 10g), depending on the added seeds and grains. **Chia seeds** are standout – they are one of the highest fibre sources known, offering around 34g per 100g. **Other nuts and seeds**, such as almonds, pumpkin, and sunflower (all great bread toppings) provide moderate fibre and essential nutrients, even if servings are small.

Rye Containing about 6g fibre per 100g, often has a lower glycaemic response (the rate at which it releases sugar into the bloodstream) than other breads, making it a good option.

Sourdough Made with whole-wheat flour, sourdough offers similar fibre to wholemeal (about 6g per 100g), while white sourdough provides only about 3g. Both forms offer fermentation-related gut benefits (page 29).

Porridge bread Made with oats or a mixture of oats and wholemeal (whole-wheat) flour, porridge bread offers around 5–6g fibre per 100g. The oats' soluble fibre (beta-glucan; see page 39) can help support heart health and steady blood-sugar levels. They give a moist texture and a slightly nutty flavour.

The fibre tables

The following tables are organized from most fibre-rich to least – according to food group and then each food itself. Everything is measured to 100g so that you can instantly compare which foods can boost the fibre-content in your diet and which might be best left on the shelf.

Fibre in vegetables

(per 100g; about 1 cup cooked veggies or 1½ cups raw)

Vegetable	Fibre per 100g
Kale	4.7
Brussels sprouts	4.5
Green cabbage	4.1
Aubergine (eggplant)	3.3
Potato (with skin)	3.3
Broccoli	3.1
Carrots	2.9
Beetroot (Beet)	2.9
Green beans	2.7
Spinach (raw)	2.2
Cabbage (raw)	1.9
Cauliflower	1.8
Celery (raw)	1.1

Fibre in fruit

(per 100g; about ¾–1 cup fruit)

Fruit	Fibre per 100g
Avocados	6.7
Raspberries	6.5
Blackberries	5.3
Pomegranate	4.0
Kiwi	3.0
Pear (with skin)	3.1
Apple (with skin)	2.6
Bananas	2.6
Blueberries	2.4
Peach	2.0
Apricots	2.0

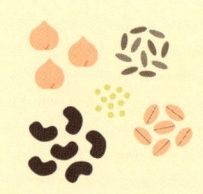

Fibre in whole grains and legumes

(per 100g; about ½ cup cooked grains)

Whole Grains

Grain	Fibre per 100g
Barley (hulled)	17.0
Rolled oats (dry)	10.4
Farro	7.0
Bulgur (cooked)	4.5
Quinoa (cooked)	2.8

Legumes

Legume	Fibre per 100g
Black beans (cooked)	8.7
Split peas (cooked)	8.3
Lentils (cooked)	7.9
Chickpeas (cooked)	6.2

Fibre in nuts and seeds
(per 100g; about ½–¾ cup nuts and seeds)

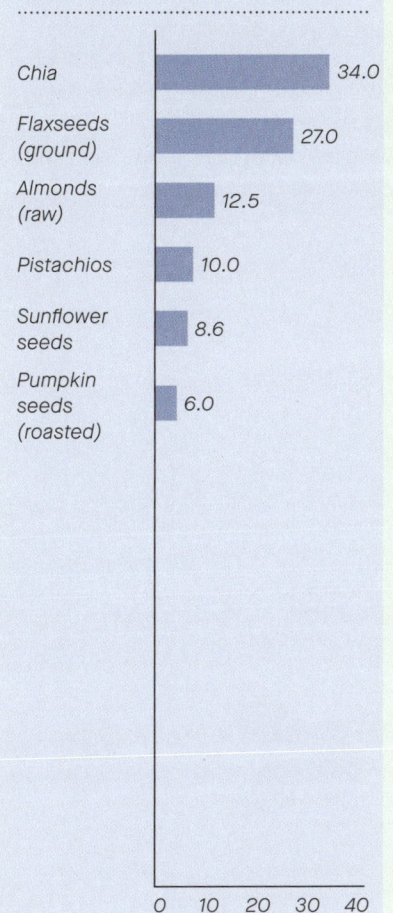

Food	Fibre per 100g
Chia	34.0
Flaxseeds (ground)	27.0
Almonds (raw)	12.5
Pistachios	10.0
Sunflower seeds	8.6
Pumpkin seeds (roasted)	6.0

Fibre in bread
(per 100g; about 3 slices)

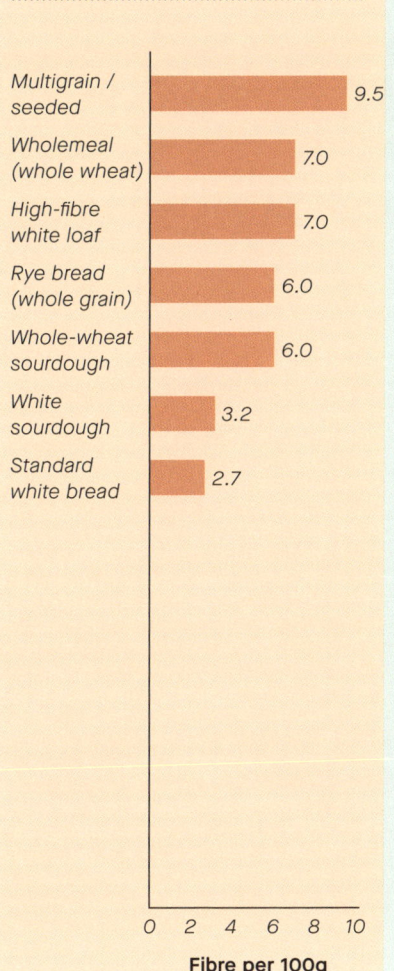

Food	Fibre per 100g
Multigrain / seeded	9.5
Wholemeal (whole wheat)	7.0
High-fibre white loaf	7.0
Rye bread (whole grain)	6.0
Whole-wheat sourdough	6.0
White sourdough	3.2
Standard white bread	2.7

Fibre surprises
(per 100g)

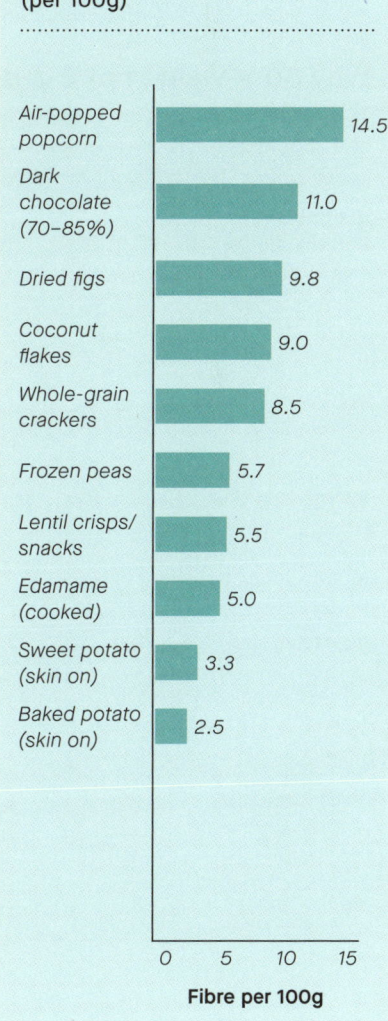

Food	Fibre per 100g
Air-popped popcorn	14.5
Dark chocolate (70–85%)	11.0
Dried figs	9.8
Coconut flakes	9.0
Whole-grain crackers	8.5
Frozen peas	5.7
Lentil crisps/snacks	5.5
Edamame (cooked)	5.0
Sweet potato (skin on)	3.3
Baked potato (skin on)	2.5

The 30:30:30 fibre formula

How do I hit 30 plants a week?

I often share the 30:30:30 approach in clinical practice and professional work as a simple yet effective way to make a concerted effort to enhance gut health and improve fibre intake. At first people wonder how on earth they may reach the target of 30 different plants in just one week, but – with a few tips, techniques, and know-how – it's easier than you may think.

Over the following pages, I've highlighted the practical techniques you can use to hit your 30-a-week target not just easily and with bags of flavour, but with positivity – and hopefully even joy! First, though, the answer to a question that my clients so frequently ask me...

Why 30-a-week, not 5-a-day?

Five-a-day campaigns focus solely on our intake of fruit and vegetables. The 30-a-week system focuses on "plant points" that highlight the importance of the range of plant-based foods you're eating, rather than just the number. In this context, a "plant" refers to any food grown from the ground, not just fruits and vegetables. In other words, it includes whole grains, legumes (like beans and pulses), nuts, seeds, herbs, and spices too.

Why is this important? Your gut microbiome is home to trillions of bacteria that thrive on different plant compounds. By consuming a wide variety of plant-based foods, you help cultivate a rich and diverse microbial ecosystem – your "gut garden".

Research from the American Gut Project shows that people who eat 30 or more different types of plant foods per week have a significantly more diverse gut microbiome than those who eat 10 or fewer.

Scoring plant points

One of the best ways to ensure you're getting a broad range of plant-based foods is to count plant points. Every distinct type of plant you consume earns a point (this isn't related to the amount you eat, but rather the variety of the foods you're eating), making it easier and more engaging to track variety in your diet.

A useful tool for this is the "Super Six" – six core plant food groups that all contribute to your plant-point total (see panel, below).

What are the "Super Six" core plant foods?

Incorporating a mixture of these food groups in your diet throughout the week helps you reach the 30-plant-point goal to support a healthier, more resilient gut.

Vegetables

Fruit

Whole grains

Legumes

Nuts & seeds

Herbs & spices

60 "Super Six" starter wheel

To get you started, this wheel of 60 plants provides double inspiration for how to rack up the 30 plants on your plate. The list is by no means exhaustive (the world of edible plants is vast), but it's a good starting point for readily available fibre nutrition.

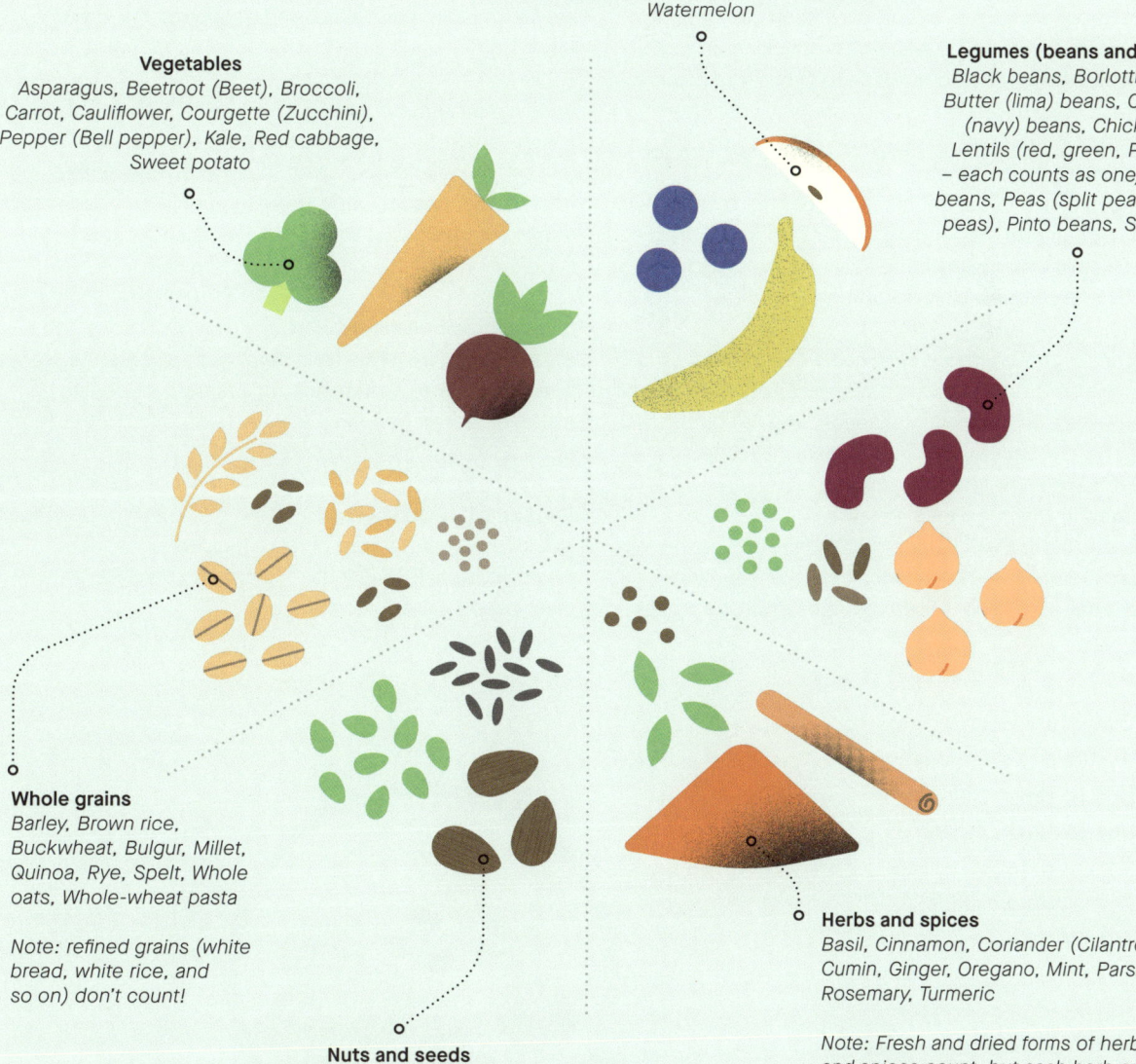

Fruits
Apples, Bananas, Berries (such as blueberries or raspberries, each scoring 1 point), Grapes, Kiwi, Mango, Oranges, Pears, Pomegranate, Watermelon

Vegetables
Asparagus, Beetroot (Beet), Broccoli, Carrot, Cauliflower, Courgette (Zucchini), Pepper (Bell pepper), Kale, Red cabbage, Sweet potato

Legumes (beans and pulses)
Black beans, Borlotti beans, Butter (lima) beans, Cannellini (navy) beans, Chickpeas, Lentils (red, green, Puy, etc. – each counts as one), Kidney beans, Peas (split peas, garden peas), Pinto beans, Soybeans

Whole grains
Barley, Brown rice, Buckwheat, Bulgur, Millet, Quinoa, Rye, Spelt, Whole oats, Whole-wheat pasta

Note: refined grains (white bread, white rice, and so on) don't count!

Nuts and seeds
Almonds, Brazil nuts, Chia seeds, Flaxseeds, Hazelnuts, Pistachios, Pumpkin seeds, Sesame seeds, Sunflower seeds, Walnuts

Note: Nut butters count if made from the whole nut (that is, 1 portion of whole-almond butter = 1 almond point).

Herbs and spices
Basil, Cinnamon, Coriander (Cilantro), Cumin, Ginger, Oregano, Mint, Parsley, Rosemary, Turmeric

Note: Fresh and dried forms of herbs and spices count, but each herb or spice counts only for ¼ point – so you need to clock up 4 different herbs or spices in your food to make 1 point (page 83).

The 30:30:30 fibre formula

Making room for more plants: simple, supportive tips

Adding more plant-based foods to your meals doesn't have to be complicated. With a few gentle changes and a bit of curiosity, you'll soon find yourself naturally enjoying a more colourful, fibre-rich plate. Start slow, be kind to your body, and remember: every plant counts.

Fill your plate with colour and variety
Aim to fill half your plate with vegetables whenever you can. Choose a mixture of colours – each colour brings different flavours and nutrients. Try snacking on a rainbow of raw vegetables – add hummus, guacamole, or fresh salsa to put even more variety in your week.

Re-think the role of meat
You don't have to cut out meat entirely, but think of it as a side or garnish, rather than the main focus of the meal. This simple shift makes more room on the plate for plant foods and so those all-important plant points.

Choose high-fibre foods with heart-healthy fats
Healthy fats from plants are a wonderful addition to your diet. Olives, avocados, nuts, seeds, and nut butters offer flavour, satiety, and nourishment all in one.

Try a meat-free meal each week
Pick one night a week to go vegetarian – build your meals around fibre-rich beans, lentils, whole grains, and greens. You might even discover a new favourite!

Start your day with whole grains
Breakfast is a great opportunity to include more plant-based variety. Try oatmeal, buckwheat, barley, or quinoa topped with fruit, nuts, or seeds for a delicious, filling start to the day.

Go for your greens
Leafy greens like kale, spinach, rocket (arugula), or Swiss chard are full of fibre and nutrients. Eat them raw, or when you cook them, steam, stir-fry, grill (broil), or braise to retain their flavour and goodness. Try mixing a few different kinds into your meals throughout the week.

Build a meal around a salad
A large bowl of leafy greens can be the foundation of a satisfying and nourishing meal. Add vegetables, fresh herbs, beans, lentils, tofu, tempeh, or mycoprotein to make it hearty and filling. See the salad recipes in the Lunches chapter, on pages 110–133, to help.

Enjoy whole fruit for dessert
Swap out sugary treats for nature's own sweets. A juicy peach, a slice of watermelon, or a handful of berries can make the perfect end to a meal – fresh, light, sweet (in a good way), and satisfying.

Start small, build slowly
Making changes to your diet is a journey, not a race. Begin with small, manageable steps. Try the "1-2-3" plant-based plate (below).

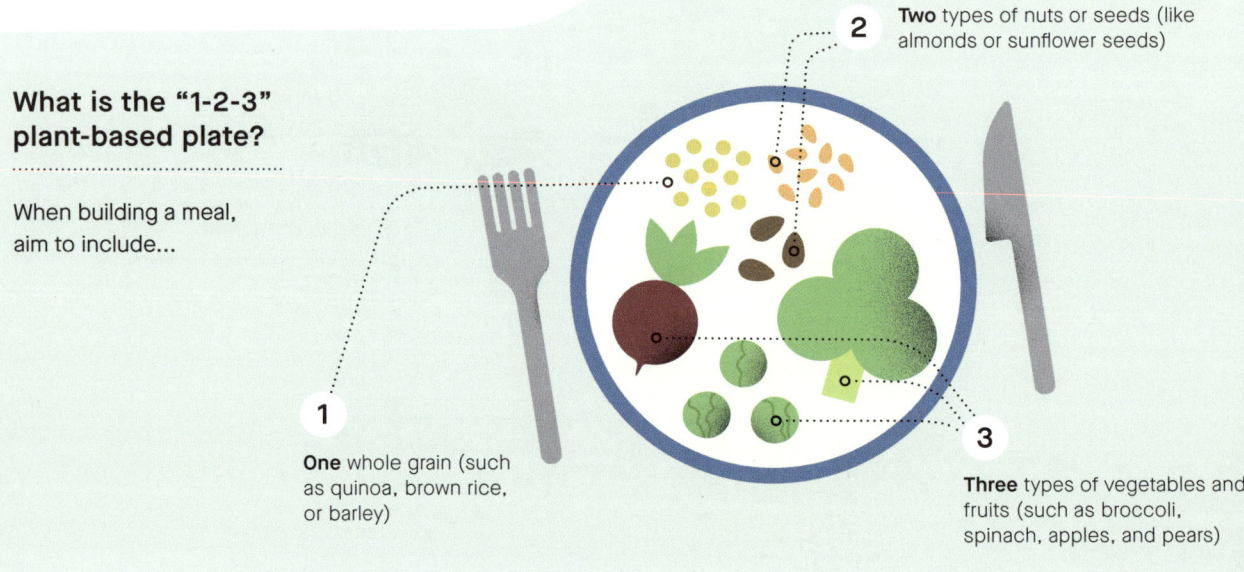

What is the "1-2-3" plant-based plate?

When building a meal, aim to include...

1 **One** whole grain (such as quinoa, brown rice, or barley)

2 **Two** types of nuts or seeds (like almonds or sunflower seeds)

3 **Three** types of vegetables and fruits (such as broccoli, spinach, apples, and pears)

Should I use fibre supplements as a boost?

Ideally, we should get our daily fibre from whole plant foods because these foods offer not only fibre, but also essential nutrients and plant compounds that supplements simply can't provide. That said, fibre supplements can play a role for some people, particularly those with restricted diets, chronic constipation, or certain health conditions. They may also offer short-term support during times of digestive imbalance. Remember, though, they should never replace a diverse, fibre-rich diet – and they can come with side effects. Supplements can cause bloating, gas, or discomfort if introduced at high dosages too quickly, or taken without enough fluids, and they may not be suitable for everyone.

The following table highlights some of the most readily available supplements and their action on the body. Always consult your doctor or a registered dietitian before starting a fibre supplement, especially if you have digestive issues, take regular medications, or are pregnant. All supplements should be introduced gradually with plenty of water and under professional supervision. And remember – they are not a substitute for real food!

Fibre type	Study highlights (2020–2025)	Main benefits	Common drawbacks
Psyllium + pectin	>10g/day improved stool output and frequency (RCT meta-analysis)	Constipation relief, cholesterol lowering	Gas; bloating if introduced too quickly
FOS (Inulin-type)	Improved frequency, softened stools; few side effects for most	Prebiotic, gentle laxative effect	Bloating, not ideal for IBS-sensitive guts
Acacia fibre	Helped with IBS symptoms and microbial diversity in two trials	Prebiotic effect, better tolerated than inulin	Less impact on metabolic markers
Inulin + FOS	Boosted memory and cognitive function in older adults	Brain health (potential gut–brain axis effect)	No effect on muscle strength
Oat beta-glucan	Lowered synthetic chemical levels (PFAS) in blood after 4 weeks of use in healthy adults	Detox support, cholesterol, and blood-glucose control	Early-stage research; long-term effects unknown

What healthy swaps can I make?

The simplest way to approach increasing your fibre intake is to make small food swaps – substituting foods you consume every day for more fibre-rich alternatives.

If you're an omnivore, a good first step is to turn your meat-based dishes into half beans or pulses and half meat (such as on page 162). For families, there are so many amazing swaps that quickly accumulate to increase everyone's intake. The table below gives a list of everyday swaps (with added benefits) to help you work toward maxing out the fibre potential of each day.

Pasta
Swap white for whole-wheat or legume-based pasta.
- *Adds protein with very little change in taste or texture*
- *Try the recipe on page 137*

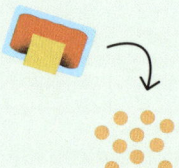

Minced (ground) meat
Swap half for lentils, grains, or beans in chilli, meatballs, etc.
- *Provides plant protein while reducing saturated fat*
- *Try the recipe on page 177*

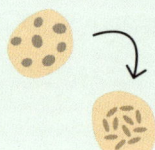

Biscuits (cookies)
Swap for oat-based biscuits or homemade fibre-rich alternatives.
- *Less sugar, and a slower release of energy*
- *Try the recipe on page 193*

Bread
Swap white for whole-grain, seeded, or rye bread.
- *Doubles the fibre content; feeds your gut microbiome*
- *Try the recipe on page 173*

Rice cakes
Go for chickpea crackers or a small handful of nuts and seeds instead.
- *Boost of healthy fats, and long-lasting energy*
- *Try the recipe on page 185*

White chocolate
Swap for dark chocolate with at least 70% cocoa solids.
- *More antioxidants; less added sugar*
- *Try the recipe on page 194*

Rice
Try brown rice, quinoa, pearl barley, spelt, or bulgur wheat.
- *B-vitamins, better blood-sugar control, deliciously nutty*
- *Try the recipe on page 169*

Crisps
Swap for air-popped popcorn or roasted chickpeas.
- *Fewer ultra-processed ingredients*
- *Try the recipe on page 181*

Flour
Use wholemeal (wholewheat) flour.
- *Nutrient-rich; slow sugar release*
- *Try the recipe on page 201*

Jam (jelly)
Swap for homemade fruit compôte.
- *More omega-3s; far less sugar*
- *Try the recipe on page 91*

Leave the skin on

One of the simplest ways to boost your daily fibre intake is to leave the skin on fruits and vegetables wherever possible. The skin of foods like potatoes (see table below for the potato lowdown), carrots, apples, pears, and cucumbers are rich in insoluble fibre, which helps to support healthy digestion and regularity. Rather than peeling, give the produce a good scrub to remove dirt and enjoy the extra nutrients and fibre on your plate. Even vegetables like courgettes (zucchini) and aubergines (eggplants) offer more fibre when eaten with their skins. This easy swap reduces waste and supports a more satisfying, gut-friendly plate with minimal effort.

What about vegan cheese?

Common commercial varieties of vegan cheese, made from refined oils and starches like coconut oil, potato starch, or tapioca (such as those from Violife or Sheese) are usually fibre-free. In contrast, vegan cheeses made from whole-plant ingredients, such as cashews, almonds, tofu, or oats, may provide a small amount of fibre – typically 0.5–2g per 30g serving. For those looking to boost fibre intake, choosing artisanal or homemade vegan cheeses – made with legumes, nuts, or seeds – can be a better option. These retain more of the fibre naturally found in whole plant foods and can contribute modestly to your daily fibre goals.

Preparation type	Skin on/off	Processing level	Fibre (per 30g)	Fibre (per 150g)
Crisps (from sliced potatoes)	Skin off (usually)	Processed	~1.2g	~6.0g
Baked potato (with skin)	Skin on	Minimally processed	~1.0g	~5.0g
Potato wedges (with skin)	Skin on	Minimally processed	~0.8g	~3.5–4.0g
Roast potatoes (with skin)	Skin on	Processed	~0.7g	~3.5g
Crisps (from potato flakes/starch)	Skin off	Ultra-processed	~0.6g	~3.0g
Roast potatoes (without skin)	Skin off	Processed	~0.4–0.5g	~2.0–2.5g
Chips/fries (oven or fried)	Skin off	Processed	~0.4–0.5g	~2.0–2.5g
Boiled potatoes (peeled)	Skin off	Minimally processed	~0.4g	~2.0g

Can I get fibre from my drinks?

From smoothies and juices to coffee, green tea, and even fruit-infused water, can the drinks we consume contribute to our fibre intake? Yes… a little. While it's essential to prioritize whole foods as the primary source of dietary fibre, some drinks can offer a small fibre boost, depending on how they're prepared.

We should all think of drinks primarily as tools for hydration, but in some cases – like a blended smoothie or even a fibre-rich hot chocolate (opposite) – they can provide a top-up. Importantly, though, proper hydration helps your body absorb fibre from all your food – there's more about this on the following pages.

Fruit smoothies

Smoothies on average provide 3–5g of fibre per 250ml (1 generous cup) serving, depending on the fruit and whether the smoothie includes whole fruit or just juice. But, eating whole fruit is generally more beneficial than drinking it as a smoothie (page 67). This is because whole fruit contains intact fibre, especially insoluble fibre, which slows digestion and promotes feelings of fullness. When fruit is blended into a smoothie, some of this fibre, particularly the physical structure that aids in slowing sugar absorption, is partially broken down. While smoothies still contain fibre, the mechanical blending can reduce the effectiveness of fibre's benefits by speeding up sugar absorption and potentially leading to quicker blood-sugar spikes. Additionally, it's easier to consume larger amounts of fruit (and therefore more sugar) in smoothie form, which may impact dental health, calorie intake, and feelings of satiety.

Plant-based "milks"

Oat, soy, and almond milks vary widely. Oat milk can have around 1–2g fibre per 250ml (1 generous cup), soy milk about 1g, almond milk usually less than 1g. The benefit of soy milk over the other types is that it contains more protein.

Coffee and tea

Neither coffee nor brewed black or green tea have any fibre at all per cup (where a cup is 250ml). Matcha tea, which is drunk with the whole leaf powder (rather than being brewed then strained) can offer about 1g of fibre per serving (or 1 teaspoon of powder gives around 2g of fibre). The fibre in fruit teas is generally negligible, if present at all.

> While it's essential to prioritize whole foods as your primary source of dietary fibre, some drinks can offer a small fibre boost, depending on how they're prepared.

Dark chocolate hot chocolate

I am a huge fan of a dark chocolate hot chocolate, so imagine how excited I was to learn that dark chocolate, rich in cocoa flavanols, has been shown to potentially support stem-cell activity related to vascular repair. Bear with me while I give you the caveats for this first: there is, though, currently no strong evidence that dark chocolate directly increases stem cells in other tissues or broadly promotes stem-cell regeneration. So, while initial findings are promising, we need more human studies to confirm these effects and their health implications. Now for the really good news: when it comes to fibre there is much more evidence. While the fibre content of hot chocolate is typically low (around 1g per 250ml), final fibre varies based on the recipe. The use of milk powder, cocoa solids, and whether or not there is added fibre in the final drink make a difference. The fibre content of a dark hot chocolate depends mainly on the cocoa content, but here's how you can make your hot chocolate work for you in this and other ways.

Cocoa powder (unsweetened, dark) contains about 6–8g of fibre per 28g (1oz) of powder.

A standard serving for hot chocolate uses about 1–2 tablespoons (5–10g) of cocoa powder, providing roughly 1–3g of fibre.

Additional ingredients like sugar or whipped cream add little or no fibre.

If prepared with milk or a plant-based milk (which generally has minimal fibre), the fibre mainly comes from the cocoa.

So, a typical 250ml (1 generous) cup of dark hot chocolate might provide around 1–3g of fibre, depending on how much cocoa you use and its fibre density. If you want a higher fibre result, using more pure, high-fibre cocoa powder or adding ingredients like ground flaxseed or oat bran, can boost the fibre content to make the hot chocolate work harder.

What can the labelling tell me?

Most people know to check food labels for fat, sugar, and salt – but fibre? Not so much. Despite its critical role in digestive, heart, and even mental health, fibre is often the forgotten nutrient. Add in the confusion of ultra-processed foods and the fact that nutrition labels differ slightly from country to country, it's no wonder so many people are unsure where to begin.

Top 5 cheat sheet

Here are a top-five tips for knowing you're on the right track with the fibre-content of the food you buy – regardless of where you are in the world!

 Products high in fibre but low in free sugars are a good bet: a cereal with 7g fibre and under 5g sugar per 100g is generally a nutritious choice.

 Foods with more than 3g fibre per serving are good; foods with more than 5g fibre per serving are excellent.

 Look for fibre-rich foods at the top of the ingredients list – that indicates that there are proportionally more of them in the product you're buying.

 Consider the labelling in light of what you actually see – the closer a food is to its natural state, likely the greater its overall nutritional value.

 Avoid "low carb" or "net carb" marketing that may subtract fibre content to appear lower-carb – it can be misleading.

Above all, it's worth remembering that it's always better to swap ultra-processed foods for whole-food versions – cooking the staples, such as rice or potatoes, yourself makes a real difference.

Traffic lights: the UK
In the UK, the front-of-pack traffic-light system flags levels of fat, saturated fat, sugars, and salt, but not fibre.

Nutri-Score: the EU
The Nutri-Score system (in countries such as France, Spain, and Germany) gives foods an A–E letter rating and a colour based on overall nutritional quality, awarding positive points for fibre, protein, and fruit or veg content.

NutrInform battery: Italy
Italy's plain-looking system presents nutrients as battery icons that show how much energy, fat, saturated fat, sugar, and salt each portion contributes to daily intakes.

The keyhole and the heart: Scandinavia
Scandinavian countries use the Keyhole symbol to mark healthier choices higher in whole grains and fibre. Finland also uses a heart symbol to identify foods that are lower in salt and saturated fat and higher in fibre, helping consumers quickly spot heart-healthy options.

Nutrition Facts Label: the USA
The US Food and Drug Administration (FDA) uses the Nutrition Facts Label – a straightforward table identifying the fat, cholesterol, and sodium, and breakdown of total carbohydrates into dietary fibre, total sugars, and added sugars. To be defined as a "healthy food" products must contain meaningful amounts of ingredients such as fruits, vegetables, or grains, and include at least one "nutrient to encourage" (fibre, potassium, calcium, iron, or vitamin D), while limiting added sugar, salt, and saturated fat.

A word on chicory root

In many cases, manufacturers increase fibre content by adding isolated ingredients such as inulin, a soluble fibre commonly extracted from chicory root. While inulin can contribute to overall fibre intake and support gut health, products that rely heavily on it may still be low in other beneficial nutrients and high in sugars, refined starches, or additives. For this reason, it is important to look beyond the front-of-pack claims and consider the overall nutritional quality of the food you buy.

The pros and cons of fibre labelling

The pros of putting fibre information on a label are:
- Labels provide quick insights into how fibre-rich a food might be.
- Labels help guide healthier choices on the go.
- Labels help identify marketing spin versus actual nutritional value.

The cons of putting fibre information on a label are:
- Labels aren't always easy to interpret.
- Fibre isn't highlighted on front-of-pack marketing in every country.
- Some foods contain added fibres that don't have the same benefits as whole-food sources.

Labelling in the UK

On most UK labels, fibre is listed in the "Carbohydrates of which sugars/fibre" section of the nutrition panel. Terms like "multigrain" or "made with whole grains" don't guarantee high fibre – check the actual grams of fibre to be sure. Also, look out for the following:

1. Fibre per serving
- Look at the portion size ("per bar", "per slice", and so on) to see actually how much fibre you'll be eating.
- With that label in mind, aim for 8g fibre per meal and 3–4g per snack.

2. The ingredients list
- Look for whole grains, seeds, nuts, legumes, fruit/vegetable powders, oats, bran, chicory root (inulin), or psyllium: good fibre sources.
- The closer a fibre-rich food is to the top, the more of it there is.

3. Misleading claims
- Some "health" foods (such as protein bars) may have very little fibre or rely on added fibres (polydextrose, inulin) for texture.

Labelling in the USA

The US Food and Drug Administration recognizes fibre as a nutrient lacking in the US diet, but there is no front-of-pack labelling to flag high-fibre foods. Fibre content can usually be found in one of these ways:

1. Fibre per serving
- Fibre is listed under "Total Carbohydrate" on the Nutrition Facts Label.
- Fibre is expressed in grams per serving.
- It is often shown as % Daily Value (%DV) – based on a 28g-per-day reference point. For example: 5g fibre = 18% DV.

2. Types of fibre
- Occasionally, you'll see soluble and insoluble fibre broken down separately, but it's not an FDA requirement.

3. The ingredients list
- Look for fibre-rich ingredients, such as: whole-grain wheat, oats, and barley; added fibres such as inulin or chicory-root fibre; and psyllium husk, flaxseed, and chia seeds.

Can I trust the marketing?

Marketing health – whether through nutrient buzzwords or statements, or diet trends (see panel, below) – is big business. As soon as "high in fibre" pops up on a sticker, the food itself must be healthy and bursting with fibre, right? What do these marketing claims actually mean?

In both Europe and the USA, the use of nutrition and health claims on food packaging is strictly regulated to ensure accuracy and to protect consumers. In the EU, claims are governed by Regulation (EC) No 1924/2006 and must be scientifically substantiated. The European Food Safety Authority (EFSA) evaluates the evidence, and the European Commission approves claims for inclusion in the EU Register. In the USA, the Food and Drug Administration (FDA) regulates claims under the Nutrition Labeling and Education Act (NLEA) of 1990. Claims are categorized as authorized, qualified, or structure/function, with varying levels of scientific scrutiny. While authorized health claims require FDA approval, structure/function claims do not but must still be truthful and not misleading.

Popular claims in the EU and USA

Nutrition claims in the EU describe the content of a nutrient in the food. In the USA these are defined by the FDA and describe levels of nutrients:

- "High in fibre" (EU) – at least 6g fibre/100g food
- "Source of fibre" (EU) – at least 3g fibre/100g food
- "Excellent source of fibre"(USA) – 20% or more of the Daily Value (DV) per serving
- "Good source of fibre" (USA) – 10–19% of the Daily Value (DV) per serving

Health claims link a nutrient to a beneficial effect on the body. They must be authorized (by the FDA in the USA), and carry a qualifying statement if evidence is limited:

- "Fibre contributes to normal bowel function"
- "Plant sterols may reduce blood cholesterol"
- "Beta-glucan from oats can help maintain normal blood-cholesterol levels"
- "Soluble fibre from oats, as part of a diet low in saturated fat and cholesterol, may reduce the risk of heart disease"

Function claims require no pre-approval but must be truthful, such as "Fibre helps support digestive health."

The diet business

So many diets are marketed promising long-lasting health and well-being. Here are four of the most popular and how they might affect your fibre intake.

Juice diets remove the fibre-rich pulp from fruits and vegetables, leaving a concentrated sugar solution with no fibre. This can lead to blood-sugar spikes and hunger crashes, and over time may contribute to sluggish digestion and a less diverse gut microbiome.

Carnivore diets eliminate all plant foods, delivering next to zero dietary fibre, and stripping the diet of critical nutrients.

Intermittent fasting isn't inherently harmful, and may be beneficial for some, but long fasting windows can reduce overall fibre consumption over the course of the day. If you don't prioritize fibre-rich foods during your eating windows, your digestion can slow down and your stools may harden and become difficult to pass.

Ketogenic diets, by design, restrict carbohydrate intake, cutting out a significant source of fibre (page 12). Many keto followers also lean on well-marketed, processed "keto snacks", which are often virtually fibre-free.

Can I have too much fibre?

In many Western countries, the real issue isn't getting *too much* fibre, it's not getting *enough*. With this in mind, it's unlikely you'll consume too much fibre unless you suddenly change your diet or rely heavily on supplements without proper hydration or adjustment time.

Extremely high fibre intakes, typically above 70g per day, may interfere with the absorption of essential minerals such as iron, zinc, and calcium. That's because some typically high-fibre grains, nuts, and seeds are also rich in compounds called phytates. These can bind minerals together and make them harder for the body to absorb and use. Individuals with sensitive digestive systems or conditions like Irritable Bowel Syndrome (IBS) may find that some types of fibre, especially insoluble or fermentable ones, worsen their symptoms. In rare cases, very high intakes may cause intestinal blockages, particularly in individuals with slowed gut motility. Certain foods high in prebiotic fibres, like Jerusalem artichokes and legumes, can be especially fermentable and may produce excess gas if not introduced gradually. For these reasons, consume a diverse mixture of plant foods, rather than relying on one kind, stay well hydrated (below), and increase fibre intake little by little.

Minimizing the side effects of increased fibre

It's really hard to eat "too much" fibre, but increasing your fibre intake too quickly can be a problem if your digestive system isn't used to processing this vital nutrient. Common symptoms include gas, bloating, and cramping. To minimize side effects of an increased fibre intake, do three simple things:

 Increase fibre gradually over several days or weeks, not all at once.

 Drink plenty of water (see panel, below).

 Listen to your body – some people with IBS or a sensitive gut may need to be more cautious.

The importance of water

Eating large amounts of fibre without drinking enough water can lead to uncomfortable digestive symptoms such as bloating, gas, cramping, and even constipation. That's because fibre is like a sponge – absorbing water so that the fibre softens and swells. That effect keeps our stools (page 27) easy to pass, preventing blockages and aiding digestion. Aim to drink 6–8 glasses of water each day and if your stools are hard to pass, address your diet and potentially increase your water intake. (If this persists, speak to a dietitian or doctor.) Note that even though tea and coffee are diuretics, they can still count toward daily fluid intake.

6–8 glasses per day

What are the trends – and the myths – about fibre?

Wellness trends gained traction in the 1970s in the USA, driven by alternative health and self-care philosophies. In the 1990s, lifestyle magazines began to promote wellness as aspirational, linking it with beauty, fitness, and luxury. Today, social media – fuelled by branded content – has brought a "wellness" explosion. Today's wellness trends reflect both its counter-cultural origins and its evolution into a multi-billion-dollar industry.

There has been a move on social media toward fibre as the next great "hack" – from bowls of pastel-hued oats to so-called detox drinks. Some practices are harmless and can support increased fibre intake, but others distort the science or rely on unsupported claims. Below and opposite are some of the most prominent fibre-related wellness trends, assessing their validity and exploring whether they genuinely benefit health, or simply capitalize on cultural wellness phenomena.

Green powders
Often seen as a shortcut to better health, green powders are concentrated blends of dried and ground vegetables, herbs, algae, and grasses. They're promoted for their high vitamin and mineral content and often boast long lists of nutrients. However, they typically contain virtually no fibre and are not a substitute for the complex texture, bulk, and nutritional matrix of fruits and vegetables in their natural state.

Worryingly, these products are not always subject to strict regulation, and the accuracy of their nutrient claims can be difficult to verify, particularly when the powders are bought online from lesser-known brands that may lack independent testing or quality control. While these powders may help fill the gap on days when fruit and vegetable intake is low, they cannot replace real food and won't improve your fibre levels.

Sea moss
This trendy seaweed is promoted as a gut and skin saviour, but the actual scientific evidence for that claim is extremely limited. While it does contain some vitamins and minerals, claims around detoxification, immunity, or fibre-related benefits are largely unproven. Like any single "superfood", sea moss is unlikely to offer much without a balanced, fibre-rich diet around it.

Gut-cleansers
Often marketed as teas, powders, or juice fasts, these products usually promise to "reset" or "clean out" your digestive system. In reality, the gut is not a pipe that needs cleaning! These cleanses rarely contain much fibre at all and can even disrupt digestion if they lack solid food or hydration. In addition to this, full juice cleanses typically exclude most other essential nutrients from the diet, including protein, healthy fats, and fibre – making them nutritionally unbalanced and unsustainable in the long term.

Chia-seed water
TikTok's "internal shower" drink has brought chia seeds newfound popularity. The claim is simple: 1–2 tablespoons of chia seeds soaked in a glass of water, then drunk, are a natural laxative to "flush out the gut" and support weight loss. It's true that chia seeds are nutritionally dense (1 tablespoon provides roughly 5g of dietary fibre, alongside small amounts of protein, omega-3 fatty acids, and micronutrients). Hydrated, they can bulk and soften stools to help relieve mild constipation in those with low fibre intake. However, the online claims are far broader than evidence supports. The idea that chia water "melts fat" or significantly suppresses hunger is misleading. The plumped seeds may give a brief sense of fullness, but the volume needed to meaningfully blunt appetite is impractical, and the calories from those additional seeds negates any supposed weight-loss benefit.

Fibre maxxing
Popular in certain online wellness spaces, this involves aggressively increasing fibre through powders, seeds, and fortified snacks. While increasing fibre intake is something we all need to do, suddenly ramping up intake can cause bloating, cramps, or constipation, especially without adequate hydration (page 73). A gradual increase in fibre intake from whole foods is far more effective (and sustainable).

Adaptogenic mushrooms
These fungi, such as lion's mane, are gaining popularity for their supposed cognitive and gut benefits. While they do contain beta-glucan (a type of soluble fibre; page 39), the quantities in powders or capsules are often too small to meaningfully impact fibre intake. We need more research before anyone should be recommending them for gut health.

Colourful porridge and smoothie bowls
Aesthetically pleasing, often topped with fruit, seeds, and nut butters, these bowls can absolutely support fibre intake when made up of whole grains and with a variety of toppings. However, their benefit depends on the ingredients, not the "Instagrammability"! A colourful bowl is only as nutritious as what's in it.

The "plant points" trend

Encouraging a wide variety of plant foods each week (such as aiming for 30+ types) is a positive trend backed by research for the American Gut Project. Greater diversity in plant intake supports a more diverse gut microbiome especially when whole grains, legumes, vegetables, fruits, nuts, and seeds are involved. This one gets a tick! You can find out more about plant points on page 62 and we've even created our own tracker to help you keep a record of how you're doing on points every week (page 83).

Including any plant portion counts for a plant point, while dried herbs and spices each count for a quarter.

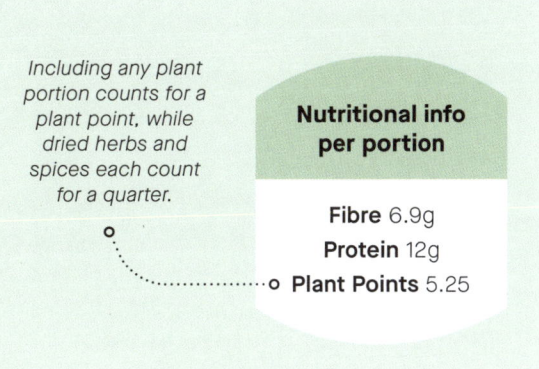

Nutritional info per portion

Fibre 6.9g
Protein 12g
Plant Points 5.25

How much fibre should I feed my children?

Fibre is not a nutrient that directly drives growth in the way protein, calcium, or essential fats do. However, it plays a supportive role in children's diets, shaping the environment in which healthy growth and development can occur. As a result, getting enough of it is really important for growing children.

At the simplest level, we know that a fibre-rich diet encourages healthy, regular bowel movements. That, in itself, helps children to maintain a healthy appetite, ensuring they are able to eat enough of the other nutrients that are essential for general growth and development. Nutritional needs throughout our lives, though, are not linear. During your child's first decades, adapting their intake appropriately for their age supports the growth of their bones, the development of their immune system, and their changing energy levels. The diagram below shows how those needs change from birth to adulthood.

Changing fibre needs in children

At birth, babies have all the nutrients they need from their mother's breast milk or from specially balanced formula milk. Once babies begin to eat solid foods, they need small amounts of fibre from the soft fruits, vegetables, and cereals we use in their purées. After that, the fibre needs of girls and boys change as they grow, including according to gender.

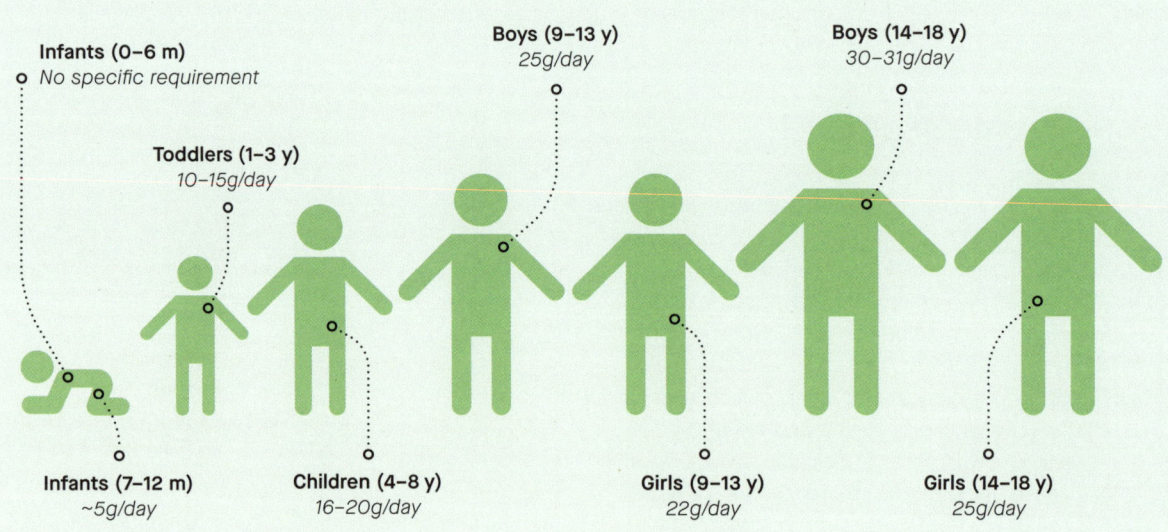

Fibre and growing bones

Over the years, a belief has emerged that eating a fibre-rich diet could impair bone health or limit growth in children. There has been a question as to whether foods rich in fibre also contain "anti-nutrients" such as phytates and oxalates. These are naturally occurring compounds found in fibre-rich foods that can bind to minerals such as calcium, iron, and zinc, theoretically reducing how much of those good nutrients the body absorbs. In practice, though, this is not the case. The European Food Safety Authority has concluded that the impact of phytates and oxalates on calcium absorption is negligible, and there is no evidence of adverse effects on bone health from eating fibre-rich foods. In fact, several studies suggest the opposite may be true: prebiotic fibres, which feed beneficial gut bacteria, may in fact improve calcium absorption and support bone-mineral density in children. This is particularly important as bone mass accumulates rapidly in childhood and adolescence, laying the foundation for lifelong bone health.

Fibre and a developing immune system

By supporting digestive health, fibre is essential for the development of the immune system. The gut microbiota, shaped partly by fibre intake (page 11), plays an important role in how minerals are absorbed and how the immune system develops. Evidence shows that children who consume adequate fibre benefit, like adults, from a more diverse gut microbiota and greater production of short-chain fatty acids, which help regulate immune function and inflammation. These effects are thought to reduce the risk of allergies and other immune-related conditions later in life.

Fibre and childhood energy needs

While they are growing, and particularly during growth spurts, children generally need more calories per kilogram of body weight than adults (note: that's not more calories overall – children's overall calorie needs are lower until they reach late teenagehood). For this reason, parents may be concerned that filling, high-fibre foods can reduce overall energy intake if consumed in large amounts. But, like everything, balance is key. Fibre should form a part of meals that are also rich in the healthy calories needed for energy (for all the running, playing, and learning – and for all the growing), and the nutrients needed to support growth. A bowl of porridge oats with nut butter and fruit, for example, provides fibre alongside protein, healthy fats – and healthy energy.

Top tips for parents

- **Start with small swaps** Making regular, fibre-rich swaps is a great way to get more fibre in to your children (page 66) – but make one swap at a time so the boost in fibre is gentle (and the changes are more likely to fall under the radar!).

- **Mix it up** Combine high-fibre options with familiar favourites to smooth the transition.

- **Make it fun** Get children involved in baking or topping their own yogurt bowls – they're more likely to eat what they help prepare.

- **Offer water** Encourage water alongside higher-fibre foods to avoid constipation.

- **Lead by example** Children copy what they see: if you eat fibre-rich foods, your children are more likely to follow!

- **Pair it with vitamin C** Serve fibre with vitamin C-rich foods to maximize iron absorption.

- **Look for a balanced plate** Include fibre in meals that also provide energy, protein, calcium, and healthy fats so as not to crowd out calories.

- **Think variety** A wide mixture of fruit, vegetables, pulses, and whole grains ensures children get many different types of fibre and a broad range of nutrients to support their growth and development.

- **Persevere** It can take up to 10 exposures before children accept vegetables or higher-fibre foods, especially those with slightly bitter flavours. Keep offering them in different ways and don't worry if they're rejected at first. A love for those new flavours will – most likely – come.

How do I get my child to eat more fibre?

Adding fibre-rich foods to your child's diet needn't be tricky (or a battle!) – sometimes it's about weaving them, little by little, into food children are already likely to recognize and love. Here are some ideas for every meal of the day. And don't forget to check out the parent-friendly tips on the previous page and the everyday swaps we can all make on page 66, too.

Breakfast

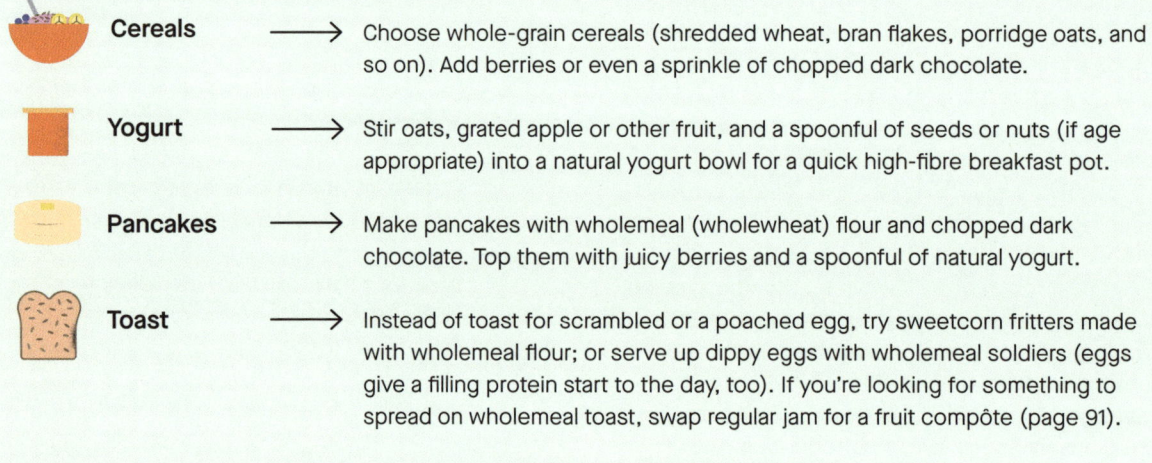

Cereals → Choose whole-grain cereals (shredded wheat, bran flakes, porridge oats, and so on). Add berries or even a sprinkle of chopped dark chocolate.

Yogurt → Stir oats, grated apple or other fruit, and a spoonful of seeds or nuts (if age appropriate) into a natural yogurt bowl for a quick high-fibre breakfast pot.

Pancakes → Make pancakes with wholemeal (wholewheat) flour and chopped dark chocolate. Top them with juicy berries and a spoonful of natural yogurt.

Toast → Instead of toast for scrambled or a poached egg, try sweetcorn fritters made with wholemeal flour; or serve up dippy eggs with wholemeal soldiers (eggs give a filling protein start to the day, too). If you're looking for something to spread on wholemeal toast, swap regular jam for a fruit compôte (page 91).

Lunch

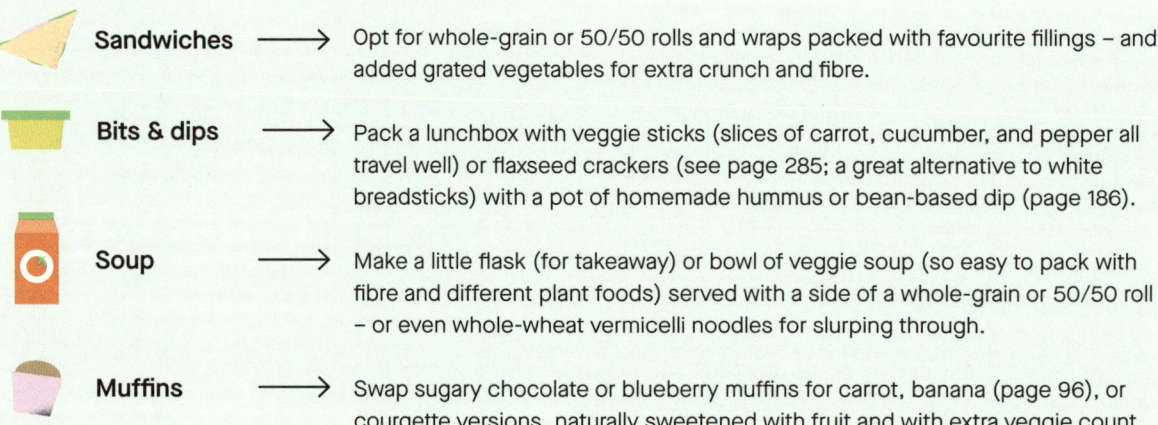

Sandwiches → Opt for whole-grain or 50/50 rolls and wraps packed with favourite fillings – and added grated vegetables for extra crunch and fibre.

Bits & dips → Pack a lunchbox with veggie sticks (slices of carrot, cucumber, and pepper all travel well) or flaxseed crackers (see page 285; a great alternative to white breadsticks) with a pot of homemade hummus or bean-based dip (page 186).

Soup → Make a little flask (for takeaway) or bowl of veggie soup (so easy to pack with fibre and different plant foods) served with a side of a whole-grain or 50/50 roll – or even whole-wheat vermicelli noodles for slurping through.

Muffins → Swap sugary chocolate or blueberry muffins for carrot, banana (page 96), or courgette versions, naturally sweetened with fruit and with extra veggie count.

Snacks

Fruit ⟶ A small handful of dried apricots, figs, or goji berries packs in the dietary fibre (add some nuts, if age appropriate and permitted); or dip some apple slices or orange segments in dark chocolate and leave to set. (Plus, remember, fresh fruit with the skin on – apples, pears, plums – is still the best and simplest form of fibre and the perfect snack!)

Beans ⟶ A handful of roasted chickpeas or fresh broad beans are crunchy, savoury, and naturally high in fibre.

Cookies ⟶ Homemade flapjacks or oat cookies (see page 193) instead of snack bars can be fibre superstars. Sweeten with pieces of dried fruit in the mixture if you like.

Supper

Burgers ⟶ Swap meat burgers for bean burgers with all the toppings (letting everyone stack their own makes the process fun) – and (of course) serve it all up in a whole-grain (or 50/50) bun!

Shepherd's or cottage pie ⟶ Try this with a topping of 50/50 potato mash (keep the skin on) and blitzed butter (lima) beans; sweet potato topping is a good option, too. Plus, you can use lentils in the filling, just as you can for Bolognese or chilli (page 165).

Fish fingers ⟶ Make homemade fish fingers or breaded chicken dippers with whole-wheat breadcrumbs.

Pizza ⟶ Make mini pizzas on wholemeal tortillas or pitta breads with all their favourite veggie toppings!

Sweet treats

Ice cream ⟶ Blend creamy Greek yogurt with a handful of frozen berries for an instant, fruit-packed "ice cream". Stir through some whole blueberries or raspberries at the end to keep some of the fibre intact.

Smoothies ⟶ Blend a handful of oats, chia seeds, or ground flaxseeds with fruit and yogurt. Blended fruit isn't as fibre-rich as whole fruit (page 51), but with the oats and seeds added to the mixture, you're winning here!

Banana split ⟶ Try a banana sliced lengthways with a filling of thick Greek yogurt (instead of cream). Scatter over some raspberries or chopped strawberries and sprinkle over some grated dark chocolate – add some seeds if your child is old enough.

The 30:30:30 fibre formula

Your weekly plant tracker

You now know that increasing the diversity of plants in your diet is one of the simplest ways to improve fibre intake. You also know that counting plant points will enable you to keep track of your fibre-fuelled nutrition every day. Here, we're giving you the tools to put that into practice.

A recap: the "Super Six" plant foods

Remember, the Super Six plant foods are not just limited to vegetables (page 62). They are made up of:

Vegetables

Fruit

Whole grains

Legumes

Nuts & seeds

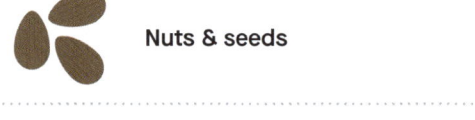

Herbs & spices

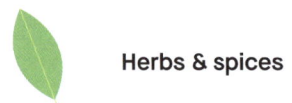

This weekly plant tracker is designed to help you to see at a glance how varied your weekly diet really is. Each time you eat a different plant food, simply tick the relevant box on the grid.

At first, you may find that you easily hit your varied vegetable or fruit quota, but need to up your legumes and nuts and seeds to bring some balance and variety. When you start out, embrace the challenge and don't let the goal hinder you. It's fine if some weeks you add in new plant foods and others you stick to established favourites. Over time, as you discover new recipes and new plant sources of fibre, hitting 30 different sources of plant fibre will become easier, more varied, and more enjoyable. Before you know it, the variety of plant foods you eat each week will simply be a natural part of your diet. Feel free to copy the grid from the book to keep it on hand wherever you are during mealtimes.

Of course, as an aside, the aim is not to stop eating, say, vegetables once you have ticked all the variety boxes in a week – the aim of the tracker is to encourage you to increase *types* of plant food that may be lacking in your diet, never to reduce the amount of those that you're already eating. More is definitely more!

10 plant foods for 5g of fibre

As a handy guide, each of the following will give you 5g of fibre. If you eat just six of them in one day, you've reached your goal of 30g of daily fibre!

- 250g (9oz) vegetables
- 1 tablespoon chia seeds
- 1½ tablespoons hemp seeds
- 80g (3oz) raspberries
- 100g (3½oz) frozen peas
- 75g (2¾oz) cooked lentils
- 100g (3½oz) avocado
- 1 thumb-sized piece of ginger (2.5cm/1in)
- 1 medium pear
- 70g (2½oz) black beans

Super-Six weekly tracker

Use this grid to track the variety of super-six foods in your diet. Score one point for every different kind of vegetable, fruit, whole grain, legume, nut, or seed you eat, ticking off the boxes as your points accumulate. Single herbs and spices count as one quarter point each. Once you're scoring at least 5 points each week in each super-six category, you're hitting your target of 30 different plant foods for the week.

The Super Six	Week commencing...	Bonus points
Vegetables — 1 vegetable type = 1 point	☐ ☐ ☐ ☐ ☐	☐ ☐
Fruit — 1 fruit type = 1 point	☐ ☐ ☐ ☐ ☐	☐ ☐
Whole grains — 1 grain type = 1 point	☐ ☐ ☐ ☐ ☐	☐ ☐
Legumes — 1 bean/pulse type = 1 point	☐ ☐ ☐ ☐ ☐	☐ ☐
Nuts & seeds — 1 type of nut, seed, or whole nut butter = 1 point	☐ ☐ ☐ ☐ ☐	☐ ☐
Herbs & spices — 1 herb or spice type = ¼ point (tick 4 small boxes to score 1 point)	(4×5 grid of small boxes)	(4×2 grid of small boxes)

The 30:30:30 fibre formula

Chapter Three

Recipes for a

This chapter brings everything together: the science, the habits, and the joy of food through recipes that fit real life. The dishes are designed not only to help you reach your target of 30g of fibre a day, but also to show that doing so needn't involve complicated cooking or endless hours at the stove – they are here both to nourish and to inspire confidence in the kitchen.

Each recipe comes with totals for plant points and fibre. Even the smallest ingredients contribute to your weekly totals. I have also included the protein to demonstrate how easy it is to achieve optimal protein count without trying.

Many of the recipes have been tested at home with my own family, so whether you're cooking for yourself, your children, or after a long working day, these dishes are not only healthy and delicious, but practical crowd-pleasers too.

Some recipes are air-fryer friendly. Look out for the symbol at the top of the page and refer to the recipe introduction or notes for alternative cooking instructions.

fibre-filled life

How the recipes work

These recipes are built around my 30:30:30 formula, aiming for around 30g fibre a day, 30 different plants a week, and chewing each bite about 30 times – which is more about how you eat than what you cook. There's also a chapter with meals that can be made in around 30 minutes. All the recipes aim to make reaching your daily fibre and plant-diversity targets as simple and enjoyable as possible.

Building up to 30g of fibre a day

Each recipe includes grams of fibre per portion or serving, so you can mix-and-match meals, snacks, and desserts to build toward 30g across the day. You don't need every recipe to be "perfect" on its own – think of your day as a whole:

- Breakfast + lunch + dinner: aim for around 6–10g fibre per meal
- Snacks + puds: use these as extra top-ups of fibre and plant points

Across the week, notice the variety too – different whole grains, pulses, nuts, seeds, fruit, and veg all count toward your 30 plants.

Understanding the nutrition panel

At the start of each recipe, you'll find a simple nutrition snapshot. For most recipes this will include:
- Fibre (g) – the star of the show, helping you track toward 30g a day
- Protein (g) – to support fullness, muscle maintenance, and steady energy
- Plant points – how many different plant ingredients that portion contributes

These figures are estimates, based on standard ingredients and typical supermarket values. They're there to guide, not to dictate, and they're not intended as a clinical or medical tool.

Servings, portions, and plant points

Some dishes are listed as "Serves 4–6" or similar. Where there's a range like this, the nutrition per portion has been calculated using the higher number of servings (that is, 6). That means the fibre and other nutrients shown are a conservative minimum, if you eat a larger portion (say it feeds 4 instead of 6), you'll get a little more than stated.

Similarly, plant points are calculated per portion, based on the recipe as written. If you're cooking for smaller or larger households, or stretching recipes with extra sides, your exact intake will naturally shift a little.

Ingredient swaps and variations

Real life doesn't always match a shopping list, and this book is going global, so I've given swaps and suggestions wherever I can.

- Can't find fresh herbs? Use dried and adjust to taste
- Can't find the right bean? Swap for another canned bean or a lentil
- Different whole grain available locally? Use what you can find

Any time you swap ingredients, use different brands, or follow a suggested variation, the fibre, protein, and energy values will change slightly, and your plant-point count may go up or down. That's completely normal, the important thing is to keep leaning toward whole, minimally processed plant foods most of the time.

Sides, serves, and extras

Unless clearly stated, the nutrition panel does not include sides or serving suggestions (for example, "serve with a rocket salad" or "add steamed greens"). These extras are a brilliant opportunity to boost fibre and plant points, but they will also alter the macro content positively.

Think of the nutrition panel as the fact-check for your base recipe. If you add:
- an extra handful of leafy greens,
- a spoonful of seeds, or
- a side of beans or lentils...

... you will increase both your nutritional intake and your plant points accordingly.

The Fibre Formula

Oils, fats, and a few kitchen notes

Where I've used oils, I recommend cold-pressed rapeseed oil or extra-virgin olive oil for everyday cooking and dressings. These provide unsaturated fats that support heart health and help you absorb fat-soluble vitamins from all those plants.

You don't need any fancy kit to cook from this book, basic pans, baking trays, and a decent knife will take you a long way. An air-fryer is sometimes offered as an option for speed and crispness, but it's never essential.

Use all of the recipes as a flexible framework, not a set of rules. The aim isn't perfection, it's to make high-fibre, plant-rich eating feel possible, pleasurable, and sustainable in the real world.

Equipment

You don't need a fancy kitchen to cook from this book, just a few basics you'll reach for again and again:
- Zester: for adding fine citrus zest to dressings, marinades, and bakes
- Grater: ideal for grating veg into sauces, fritters, and loaves, and for hard cheese
- Rolling pin: for rolling doughs and flattening things like breads or fibre-boosted snacks
- Potato masher: for mash, of course, but also for roughly crushing beans and pulses
- Small food processor: handy for blitzing nuts, seeds, dips, pestos, and quick crumb mixes
- Hand-held blender: perfect for blitzing soups and sauces straight in the pan
- Stand blender: useful for smoothies, sauces, and ultra-smooth soups
- Spatula: for folding batters, scraping every last bit from the bowl, and reducing food waste

Use what you already have. These bits and pieces for your kitchen will make high-fibre cooking faster and easier, but there is always a workaround.

Cook's notes

To keep things simple, the recipes in this book follow a few consistent assumptions:

Herbs and veg prep
- We use fresh herbs throughout, but you can substitute with dried: start with about 1 tsp dried per 1 tbsp chopped fresh and adjust to taste. All fresh parsley is flat-leaf.
- All onions and garlic are peeled, unless otherwise stated.
- Scrub vegetables, like carrots, sweet potatoes, and potatoes, but leave them unpeeled (to max the fibre).

Eggs and dairy
- All eggs are medium-sized.
- Butter is unsalted.
- In most baking, eggs can be swapped for flax eggs (1 tbsp ground flax + 3 tbsp water per egg, left to thicken).

Oils and fats
- Olive oil and rapeseed oil are the default, unless otherwise stated.
- Extra-virgin oils are best kept for finishing dishes or salad dressings, rather than high-heat cooking.

Nuts, seeds, and seasoning
- Store opened packets of nuts and seeds in sealed bags in the freezer to keep them fresh and reduce rancidity.
- Salt is fine sea salt. If you're using salt flakes, you'll need a little more by volume (season to taste).
- Chillies are with their seeds, unless otherwise stated.

Grains, legumes, pulses, and cans
- Soak dried pulses and legumes overnight before cooking, and rinse grains thoroughly before use.
- Many recipes use cans and pouches of grains and pulses for convenience, but cooking your own is even better.

Easy ingredient swaps
- Chickpea (gram) for yellow split pea flour, or vice versa.
- Marmite can be swapped for light soy sauce in some recipes to provide a similar umami depth (this will slightly alter the salt content).
- Any substitution or brand change will gently shift the fibre, protein, and energy values, and may nudge your plant-point count up or down. If you're keeping dishes largely wholefood and plant-rich, you're on the right track.

Recipes for a fibre-filled life

Breakfast represents a wonderful opportunity to boost fibre intake: cereals and grain-based foods contribute the majority of fibre to the average diet. Choosing wholegrain, plant-rich options that genuinely nourish makes this meal really count.

In this section, I've reimagined breakfast as achievable, exciting and, of course, fibre-rich. Whether it's a fig granola (my personal favourite) or carrot pancake with ginger, or a high-fibre smoothie blend, these recipes are designed to sustain energy, support gut health, and keep you fuller for longer. You'll also find air-fryer and prep-ahead options, because real life rarely allows for elaborate mornings.

Starting out with a fibre-rich breakfast supports digestion and blood-sugar balance, setting you up for a good day. It also helps to build a thriving microbiome, paving the way for lifelong health! Breakfast, then, when built on the right ingredients, isn't just the first meal of the day, it's your first opportunity to close the fibre gap.

Breakfasts

Nutty barley, cinnamon & dried fig granola

Nutritional info per 50g

Fibre 5.3g
Protein 5.2g
Plant Points 13.25

 Makes 800g   **Prep** 5 mins   **Cook** 40 mins

150g (5½oz) barley flakes

120g (4¼oz) spelt, rye, or jumbo oats (or use more barley flakes)

150g (5½oz) mixed nuts, roughly chopped (I use a mixture of almonds, hazelnuts, pecans, and walnuts)

35g (1¼oz) puffed quinoa (or use more barley flakes)

150g (5½oz) mixed seeds (I use 125g/4½oz pumpkin and sunflower, and the remainder sesame and flaxseeds)

2 tbsp psyllium husk

2½ tsp ground cinnamon

100g (scant ½ cup/3½oz) mild olive oil, coconut, or other mild oil

100g (⅓ cup/3½oz) maple syrup

150g (5½oz) dried organic figs, chopped

Sea salt

A wholesome, crunchy start to the day, this is a celebration of one of my favourite fruits. Figs are such an underrated ingredient in granolas; they add natural sweetness, a soft chew, and a lovely boost of calcium. Top tip: this isn't an overly sweet recipe, so if you prefer a little more sweetness, simply add an extra drizzle of maple syrup before baking.

1. Preheat the oven to 160°C/140°C fan/325°F and line your largest baking sheet with parchment paper.

2. Mix all the dry ingredients together in a large bowl until evenly combined.

3. In a jug, combine the oil and maple syrup, and stir through a pinch of salt. Pour the mixture over the dry ingredients and stir until everything is nicely coated.

4. Spread out the granola mixture in an even layer on the lined baking sheet and bake for 35–40 minutes, stirring occasionally so the granola cooks evenly, until golden.

5. Leave the granola to cool on the baking sheet, then stir in the figs. The granola will crisp up further as it cools.

6. Store it in an airtight container at room temperature for up to 1 week.

Note You can cook this in your air-fryer too. Heat the air-fryer to 160°C/325°F and air-fry for 10–12 minutes, tossing occasionally. You may need to cook the granola in a few batches, depending on the size of your air-fryer.

Grape & fennel seed baked oats

Nutritional info per serving

Fibre 10g
Protein 19g
Plant Points 6.25

 Serves 6   **Prep** 10 mins   **Cook** 45 mins

- 75g (2½oz) shelled pecans, raw almonds, walnuts, or hazelnuts, or a mixture
- 200g (7oz) jumbo oats
- 2 tbsp psyllium husk
- 1 tsp baking powder
- ½ tsp sea salt
- 425ml (scant 2 cups/15fl oz) milk of choice
- 3½ tbsp maple syrup or honey
- 1 tsp vanilla essence (optional)
- 2 flax eggs (2 tbsp ground flax with 6 tbsp water, soaked for 10 minutes) or regular eggs
- 3 tbsp olive oil, or melted coconut oil or butter
- 300g (10½oz) black seedless grapes or frozen blueberries
- 2 tsp fennel seeds
- 2 tsp demerara (turbinado) sugar
- Skyr, or Greek or coconut yogurt, to serve

This dish is beautifully versatile: it's perfect as a nourishing breakfast but it makes a great dessert too! Serve it with a spoonful of kefir for extra gut-friendly goodness.

1. Preheat the oven to 180°C/160°C fan/350°F and line a 20cm (8in) square brownie pan or baking dish with parchment paper.

2. Pop the nuts in the pan and toast them in the oven for 8–10 minutes until golden.

3. Meanwhile combine the oats, psyllium husk, baking powder, and salt in a bowl. Once the nuts are ready and cool enough to touch, chop them and add to the bowl.

4. In a separate bowl, whisk together the milk, maple syrup, vanilla (if using), flax eggs or eggs, and olive oil, then add this into the oats mixture.

5. Spread two-thirds of the grapes or blueberries on the bottom of the pan, then cover them in the oat mixture. Evenly distribute the remaining fruit on top, then sprinkle with the fennel seeds and the demerara. Place in the oven for 40–45 minutes until golden and firm, then allow to cool for a few minutes before slicing and serving with skyr or yogurt. Also delicious cold.

Blueberry & mango frozen smoothie bowl

Nutritional info per serving

Fibre 13g
Protein 22g
Plant Points 15

 Serves 2   **Prep** 10 mins

100g (3½oz) frozen blueberries (or choose your favourite)

100g (3½oz) frozen mango or frozen pineapple

1 fresh or frozen ripe banana

1 tbsp chia seeds and/or ground flaxseed

2 tbsp peanut butter, almond butter, or tahini

1 pitted date or 2 dried figs

150–175ml (scant ⅔ cup/ 5fl oz) milk of choice, or kefir (adjust for thickness)

To serve

1 kiwi, peeled and sliced, or ½ apple or pear, cored, and diced

2 tsp pumpkin seeds and/or sunflower seeds

2 tsp smooth or crunchy peanut butter

2 tsp chia, flaxseed, and/or hemp seeds

Optional extras

2 tbsp high-fibre granola (page 88) or puffed quinoa

1 tbsp coconut flakes

2 tsp chopped nuts (such as almonds, walnuts, hazelnuts, macadamia, or pecans)

2 tbsp skyr or Greek yogurt

The burst of colour in this smoothie bowl is a sign of its goodness – its vibrant purple hue comes from polyphenols, powerful plant compounds that support long-term health. You can, though, use whatever frozen fruit you have to hand (freezer staples are brilliantly cost effective in recipes like this one). Blackberries, raspberries, or mixed berries all work beautifully and provide good amounts of fibre. Have fun experimenting to find your favourite combo.

1. Blend all the smoothie ingredients together, adding more milk as needed until you have a thick and creamy mixture.

2. Top with kiwi, apple or pear, pumpkin and/or sunflower seeds, peanut butter, and chia, flaxseed or hemp seeds, and any of your chosen optional extras, and serve.

Prune & walnut banana muffins

Nutritional info per serving

Fibre 4.1g
Protein 7.8g
Plant Points 8.25

 Makes 12   **Prep** 15 mins   **Cook** 25 mins

1 orange
120g (4¼oz) pitted prunes
50g (1¾oz) raisins or sultanas
2 large ripe bananas
125g (½ cup/4½oz) skyr, or Greek or coconut yogurt
100g (3½oz) smooth peanut butter
4½ tbsp olive or rapeseed oil
30g (generous 2 tbsp) muscovado or coconut sugar
2 flax eggs (2 tbsp ground flax with 6 tbsp water, soaked for 10 minutes) or regular eggs
160g (1¼ cups/5¾oz) wholemeal (whole wheat) flour, spelt, or oat flour
1 tsp baking powder
½ tsp bicarbonate of soda (baking soda)
½ tsp sea salt
1 tsp mixed spice
50g (1¾oz) walnuts, finely chopped, plus 12 large halves, to decorate

We've all heard the classic advice: if you're struggling to get things moving... eat more prunes! That's because prunes contain sorbitol (a natural sugar alcohol) and insoluble fibre, both of which help keep the digestive system moving smoothly. In addition, they are a wonderfully versatile ingredient, adding natural sweetness, moisture, and richness to baking. Combined with fibre-rich flaxseeds (if you use flax eggs, which I recommend) and crunchy walnuts, these muffins are a delicious way to boost fibre without feeling like you're "being healthy" – even children love them!

1. Preheat the oven to 200°C/180°C fan/400°F. Line a 12-hole muffin pan with paper cases or grease generously.

2. Zest the orange into a blender, then cut the orange itself in half. Place the prunes in a bowl and squeeze over one orange half and top up with boiling water so that the prunes are just covered. Put to one side to soak for 10 minutes. Cover the raisins or sultanas in boiling water and put to one side for at least 5 minutes. Squeeze the other orange half into the blender with the zest.

3. Drain the prunes, then place them in the blender along with the bananas, skyr or yogurt, peanut butter, oil, sugar, and flax eggs or eggs. Blend until completely smooth.

4. In a large bowl, combine all the remaining ingredients (except the walnuts for decoration). Pour in the blended mixture and stir gently until just combined. Drain the raisins, add them to the batter, and fold through, being careful not to overmix.

5. Spoon the mixture into the muffin cases, then top each muffin with a piece of walnut. Bake for 20–25 minutes until risen and an inserted skewer comes out clean. Transfer to a rack to cool. Delicious warm, or will last 4 days in an airtight container.

Barley porridge with blackberry, apple & bay compôte

Nutritional info per serving

Fibre 13g
Protein 21g
Plant Points 6.5

 Serves 4   **Prep** 5 mins   **Cook** 12 mins

100g (3½oz) barley flakes

100g (3½oz) jumbo oats

1 tbsp chia seeds

500ml (2 cups/17fl oz) milk of choice

¼ tsp sea salt (optional)

¼ tsp ground nutmeg and/or ground cinnamon, plus extra to serve

4 tbsp almond or smooth or crunchy peanut butter, to serve

For the blackberry compôte

250g (9oz) fresh or frozen blackberries

1 small apple, cored and chopped into small chunks

1 bay leaf

2 tbsp maple syrup, plus extra to taste if needed

Barley works beautifully in porridge, offering a naturally nutty flavour and a slightly chewy texture. Although soaking oats overnight can increase their resistant starch, it isn't essential here: barley flakes cook quickly and deliver a creamy consistency in just 15 minutes. For an extra nutritional boost, stir chia seeds into the porridge, or add them to the compôte to create a lovely jam-like texture.

1. Soak the barley and oats in 500ml (2 cups/17fl oz) of water for at least 15 minutes, but ideally overnight if you have the time.

2. Place the soaked barley and oats (along with their soaking liquid) in a pan with the remainder of the porridge ingredients, except the almond or peanut butter, and bring the liquid to a rapid simmer. Turn down the heat to a gentle simmer, and cook the porridge for 10–12 minutes, stirring often, until it is tender and creamy.

3. Meanwhile, make the compôte. Place the blackberries, apple, bay, maple syrup, and 1½ tablespoons of water in a small pan and gently bring to the boil. Turn down the heat to a simmer and keep cooking until the apple is tender and the blackberries are defrosted (if using frozen) and beginning to break down. Crush a few berries to release their juice. Have a taste and add a little more maple syrup if you prefer. Set the compôte aside and keep it warm until the porridge is ready.

4. Divide the porridge between your serving bowls and spoon over a few tablespoons of the compôte. Top each serving with a tablespoon of almond or peanut butter and a little pinch of extra nutmeg or cinnamon, then serve.

Carrot pancakes with ginger, honey & turmeric yogurt

Nutritional info per serving

Fibre 8.5g
Protein 20g
Plant Points 10.5

 Serves 4   **Prep** 15 mins   **Cook** 15 mins

2½ tsp cider vinegar or lemon juice

315ml (scant 1⅓ cups/10¾fl oz) milk of choice

80g (2¾oz) raisins or sultanas

170g (scant 1⅓ cups/5¾oz) wholemeal (whole wheat) flour

60g (½ cup/2¼oz) plain (all-purpose) flour

1 tsp ground cinnamon

1 tbsp ground flaxseed or ground chia

about ½ tsp bicarbonate of soda (baking soda)

2 tsp baking powder

2 flax eggs (2 tbsp ground flax with 6 tbsp water, soaked for 10 minutes) or 2 small eggs

4 tsp melted coconut or olive oil

1 tsp maple syrup

1 large ripe banana, mashed

125g (4½oz) carrot, scrubbed and grated (shredded)

Sea salt

2 tbsp mixed seeds, to serve

For the spiced yogurt

300g (1¼ cups/10½oz) skyr, or Greek or coconut yogurt

½ tsp ground turmeric

2 tsp grated fresh ginger

2 tsp maple syrup or honey

I love experimenting with flavours, and this recipe was inspired by the abundance of carrots I always seem to have in the fridge. They are wonderful grated into pancake batter, bringing natural sweetness and a soft texture. If you're using flaxseeds rather than chia, you may need to add a little extra bicarbonate of soda to help the pancakes rise beautifully. Adding herbs or spices to a yogurt topping is an easy way to boost plant points.

1. Combine the vinegar and milk in a bowl and set it aside for 5–10 minutes until it begins to curdle (this will be less obvious with non-dairy milks). Separately, pour boiling water over the raisins in a bowl and leave to soak for 5 minutes.

2. Meanwhile, combine all the dry ingredients with a pinch of salt (you may need a touch more bicarbonate of soda if you're using flaxseeds over chia).

3. Whisk the flax eggs or eggs, 1 teaspoon of the oil and the maple syrup into the mashed banana and stir in the carrot.

4. Drain the raisins, then add these into the egg/banana mixture. Add this to the curdled-milk mixture. Fold the wet ingredients into the dry until just combined – try not to overmix. Rest the batter for 10 minutes to hydrate the flour.

5. While the batter is resting, make the spiced yogurt. Tip the yogurt into a bowl. Combine the turmeric, ginger, and honey and swirl the mixture through. Refrigerate until you're ready to eat.

6. Once the batter has rested, place a non-stick frying pan or skillet over a medium heat and add a drizzle of oil. Wipe it around with a paper towel to create a thin coating. Once hot, in batches, spoon the batter into the pan, about 2 tablespoons per pancake, leaving space between each pancake so they can spread slightly. Once small bubbles form after 2–3 minutes, gently flip each pancake over and cook the other side for 1–2 minutes. Keep warm in a low oven while you cook the rest, adding oil and wiping between batches as needed, then serve with the yogurt and sprinkled with the seeds. An extra drizzle of honey is nice, too.

Recipes for a fibre-filled life

Coconut, kale & turmeric-baked eggs with quinoa

Nutritional info per serving

Fibre 8.1g
Protein 26g
Plant Points 6.5

 Serves 2   **Prep** 15 mins   **Cook** 20 mins

70g (2½oz) white, black, or red quinoa, rinsed

1 tbsp coconut oil

½ tsp black mustard seeds

4–5 fresh or dried curry leaves (optional)

½ tsp cumin seeds

½ tsp fennel seeds

Thumb-sized piece of ginger, finely minced

1 small garlic clove, finely minced

½–1 green chilli (depending on heat), sliced

4 spring onions (scallions), sliced

150g (5½oz) kale, stems removed and chopped

2 tomatoes, chopped

¾ tsp ground turmeric

2 tbsp tamari or light soy sauce

200ml (scant 1 cup/7fl oz) coconut milk

4 eggs

Big handful of coriander (cilantro), leaves and stems chopped

Sea salt

Lime wedges, to serve

This breakfast is savoury-meets-sweet, and inspired by a trip abroad where I first tasted baked eggs infused with coconut and spice. It's packed with colour, flavour, and plant diversity, and you can easily make it vegan by leaving out the eggs. Save time by using a pouch of pre-cooked quinoa: mixed packs with red, black, and white seeds not only make life easier, but add extra plant points and a variety of fibres. If you want to make this vegan, swap out the eggs for tofu.

1. Place the quinoa in a pan with 160ml (⅔ cup/5¼fl oz) of water and a pinch of salt. Bring to a simmer and cook for 15 minutes until tender and the water has cooked away (add more if necessary). Cover with a tea towel and leave for at least 5 minutes to steam dry.

2. Meanwhile, place a large, wide oven-proof frying pan or skillet (with a lid) over a medium heat and melt the coconut oil. When hot, add the mustard seeds and as soon as they start popping, add the curry leaves (if using), cumin, and fennel seeds and fry for 30 seconds or until the curry leaves turn translucent.

3. Turn the heat down to low and add the ginger, garlic, chilli, and spring onions and a big pinch of salt. Fry for 2 minutes until the onion is softened. Stir in the kale, tomato, turmeric, tamari, and a splash of water and keep stirring until the kale begins to wilt, about 2–3 minutes.

4. Pour in the coconut milk and cooked quinoa and stir to combine. You want it to be quite saucy, so add a splash of water if it seems dry.

5. Heat up the grill (broiler) to high and make 4 small hollows in the mixture. Crack an egg into each hollow and cover with a lid. Simmer over a low heat for 2–3 minutes, then take off the lid and place under the grill for 2–3 minutes until the whites are set and the yolks are cooked to your liking. Scatter over the coriander and serve with lime wedges.

Chickpea pancakes with onion, tomatoes, coriander & coconut sambol

Nutritional info per serving

Fibre 8.5g
Protein 13g
Plant Points 6.25

 Serves 4   **Prep** 20 mins   **Cook** 10 mins

200g (1¾ cups/7oz) chickpea (gram) flour
½ tsp baking powder
¼ tsp ground turmeric
¾ tsp garam masala
¾ tsp sea salt
100g (3½oz) cherry tomatoes, chopped
¾ small red onion, chopped (remaining ¼ used below)
2 handfuls of coriander (cilantro), leaves and stems chopped, plus extra to serve
4 tsp coconut or olive oil, to fry

For the coconut sambol
¼ small red onion, chopped
¼ tsp hot chilli powder
1 green or red chilli, chopped
60g (2¼oz) desiccated (dried, shredded) coconut
Zest and juice of 1 lime
Sea salt and freshly ground black pepper

A coconut sambol is a vibrant Sri Lankan-style relish made with grated coconut, fresh herbs, and lime, the perfect partner for this savoury chickpea pancake. If you can't find fresh coconut, use desiccated or shredded instead. A fried egg on top will make it more substantial, or try sliced avocado if you're vegan or want more plant points. And if you like a bit of heat, feel free to add a touch of chilli.

1. Whisk together the chickpea flour, baking powder, spices, salt, and 250ml (generous 1 cup/9fl oz) of water and put to one side for 20 minutes to thicken up.

2. Meanwhile, prepare the sambol. Combine the sambol ingredients with 4 tablespoons of water, a good pinch of salt, and plenty of pepper. Mix well with your hands, scrunching them up a little, then put the mixture to one side.

3. Stir the chopped tomatoes, onion, and coriander into the rested batter.

4. Place a medium non-stick frying pan or skillet over a medium heat and warm 1 teaspoon of the oil. When hot, add a quarter of the batter and spread it around with the back of a spoon so it's about 3mm (⅛in) thick. Leave the pancake to cook for 2–3 minutes, or until you see small bubbles appearing on the surface. Then, gently flip it over. Cook the other side for 2–3 minutes, adding more oil if it feels like it needs it, until dark golden and a bit crunchy on the edges. Slide the pancake out of the pan on to a plate, and keep warm while you make the remainder.

5. Eat while nice and hot, with the sambol, a little extra coriander, and a fried egg if you want.

Potato farls with smashed avocado, feta & mint

Nutritional info per serving

Fibre 7.2g
Protein 9.8g
Plant Points 5.75

 Serves 4   **Prep** 15 mins + chilling   **Cook** 40 mins

- 450g (1lb) floury potatoes (such as Maris Piper), scrubbed
- 60g (2¼oz) butter, plus a little to grease the pan
- 100g (¾ cup/3½oz) wholemeal (whole wheat) flour, plus extra to dust
- 2 tbsp ground flaxseeds
- Sea salt and freshly ground black pepper

For the smashed avocado

- 2 avocados
- Juice of ½ lemon
- Small handful of mint leaves, chopped
- 70g (2½oz) feta, crumbled
- Pinch of dried chilli (red pepper) flakes, to serve (optional)

Soft and golden, these Irish griddle breads make a lovely alternative to toast. Prepare a batch at the weekend – they will keep beautifully for easy breakfasts throughout the week, and the cooling and re-heating increases the resistant starch. If you have leftover potatoes in the fridge, use those instead of boiling from scratch.

1. Cut the potatoes into large, even-sized chunks and place them in a pan of cold, salted water. Cover the pan with a lid and bring the water to the boil. Cook for about 12–15 minutes, or until the potatoes are tender, then drain them in a colander. Set the colander over the pan and leave the potatoes to dry for 10 minutes.

2. Return the dry potatoes to the pan and mash them until smooth. Ideally, refrigerate them for 12–24 hours at this point, but if you're short on time, spread the mash over a plate to help it cool quickly, then place it in the fridge until cold.

3. When you're ready to make and cook the farls, first stone and peel the avocados. Place the flesh into a bowl and crush it with a fork to a coarse consistency. Stir in the lemon juice, mint, and feta and season lightly to taste (it might not need salt – the feta is salty). Put to one side until you're ready to eat.

4. Melt the butter, then stir it with the flour and flaxseed into the cooled potato. Season with a little pepper, taste, and adjust the salt if necessary. Combine until you have a pliable and not-too-sticky dough.

5. Dust your hands with flour. Transfer the dough to a lightly floured surface and shape it into a ball. Cut the ball in half and set one half aside. Using a rolling pin, roll the other half into a rough circle approximately 15–17cm (6–6½in) in diameter. Cut the circle into 4 equal wedges.

6. Warm a large non-stick frying pan or skillet over a medium heat and grease it lightly with butter. When the butter is hot, add the farl quarters and cook them for 3 minutes until golden on the underside. Very gently turn over the wedges and cook on the other side for about 7–8 minutes, until heated through and golden. Transfer the cooked farls to a warm oven while you repeat with the remaining potato dough.

7. Divide the farls between 4 serving plates and serve with equal amounts of the smashed avocado and feta, and a pinch of chilli flakes, too, if you like.

Crispy chickpea fried eggs with garlic yogurt & herbs

Nutritional info per serving

Fibre 9.8g
Protein 33g
Plant Points 3.5

 Serves 2　　 **Prep** 5 mins　　 **Cook** 20 mins

- 1 × 400g (14oz) can chickpeas, drained and rinsed
- 1 tbsp sesame seeds
- 2 tbsp olive or rapeseed oil
- ¼ tsp dried oregano
- ½ tsp Turkish chilli flakes or pinch of chilli powder
- 4 eggs
- A few mint leaves, chopped, or a sprinkle of dried mint, to serve
- 1 tsp sumac (optional), to serve

For the garlic yogurt

- ½ small garlic clove, minced
- 150g (generous ½ cup/ 5½oz) skyr, or Greek or coconut yogurt
- Small handful of dill, chopped, to serve
- Sea salt and freshly ground black pepper

Using Turkish chilli flakes brings an authentic warmth to this Turkish twist on classic British fried eggs, but regular chilli works just as well, if that's what you have. Likewise, feel free to substitute dried mint for the fresh if that's easier. One tip: be patient before you start frying your chickpeas – make sure they're thoroughly dried, so that you get the desired crispy crunch in the finished dish.

1. Make the garlic yogurt. Combine the garlic and yogurt in a bowl and season well with salt and pepper. Put to one side.

2. Gently pat dry the chickpeas in a tea towel.

3. Warm a large non-stick frying pan or skillet (with a lid) over a medium-low heat and add the sesame seeds. Toast for 1–2 minutes until beginning to colour, then add the oil, chickpeas, and plenty of salt and pepper. Fry, stirring occasionally, for 7–9 minutes until the chickpeas begin to colour and turn crisp. Be patient as it will happen eventually.

4. Once the majority of chickpeas are crispy, stir in the oregano and chilli. Heat up the grill (broiler) to high and make 4 small hollows in the mixture. Crack an egg into each and cover with the lid. Simmer over a low heat for 2–3 minutes, then take off the lid and place the pan under the grill for 2–3 minutes until the whites are set and the yolks are cooked to your liking.

5. Transfer the dish to plates and spoon over the yogurt. Sprinkle over the herbs and sumac, then serve.

Super high-fibre seeded nut & raisin loaf

Nutritional info per serving

Fibre 13g
Protein 9.2g
Plant Points 9

 Makes 1 loaf   **Prep** 5 mins + resting   **Cook** 1 hour 20 mins

- 75g (2½oz) dried red lentils, finely ground
- 75g (2½oz) rolled oats
- 75g (2½oz) sunflower seeds
- 75g (2½oz) pumpkin seeds
- 75g (2½oz) flaxseeds
- 50g (1¾oz) almonds and/or hazelnuts, roughly chopped
- 75g (2½oz) raisins (optional)
- 2 tbsp chia seeds
- 4 tbsp psyllium husks
- 1¼ tsp sea salt
- 3 tbsp coconut oil, melted, plus extra to grease

I'm the biggest fan of loaves. From banana bread to seeded bakes, I'm obsessed with them, and I try to include at least one in every book I write. This high-fibre loaf is one of my favourites: packed with nuts and seeds, naturally sweetened with raisins, and flour-free, it's made entirely from store-cupboard staples. Soak the mixture overnight before baking to pop it straight in the oven in the morning. It keeps beautifully all week. Leave out the raisins if you want it less sweet.

1. Grease a 450g (1lb) loaf pan (or silicone loaf mould) with a little coconut oil and line it with parchment paper (base and sides).

2. Combine all the dry ingredients in a mixing bowl (with or without the raisins) and stir in the coconut oil so everything is nicely coated, then stir in 400ml (1¾ cups/ 14fl oz) of water. Transfer the mixture to the loaf pan and smooth the top.

3. Leave the loaf mixture to soak for at least 2 hours (and up to 12 hours), until it feels stiff and thick.

4. Preheat the oven to 180°C/160°C fan/350°F. Bake the bread for 1 hour 10 minutes– 1 hour 20 minutes until the top is golden and the loaf sounds hollow when you tap the bottom (briefly remove it to test, then return it to the pan). Leave the loaf to cool in the pan for
10 minutes, then transfer it to a rack to cool completely before slicing.

5. Store in an airtight container for up to 5 days. It's also delicious toasted.

With the juggle of work meetings, school runs, and otherwise packed schedules, it's all too easy to opt for something quick and processed for lunch. This chapter brings the joy back to practical, time-sensitive midday eating. Think hearty grain salads, the best sandwich I have ever made, soups that actually fill you up, and rolls layered with colour and crunch.

In our fast-paced lives, planning ahead is one of the simplest yet most powerful ways to look after both our health and our wallets. Preparing lunches in advance not only saves money but also helps us make more mindful choices, eat slowly, and digest properly. These recipes are designed to make that sequence easy: cook once, eat well all week.

Each ingredient adds something unique: from lentils offering resistant starch to nuts and seeds delivering healthy fats and prebiotic fibre. You'll also see that protein and fibre work best together, keeping hunger steady and energy balanced until suppertime.

Lunches

Vegetable summer rolls with mango & edamame beans

Nutritional info per serving

Fibre 13g
Protein 9.2g
Plant Points 9.75

 Makes 12
Serves 4

 Prep 30 mins

1 avocado, de-stoned, peeled, and sliced

1 not-too-ripe mango, peeled, de-stoned, and sliced

1 large broccoli stalk (about 100g/3½oz), peeled and cut into matchsticks

1 large carrot (about 125g/1½oz), scrubbed and cut into matchsticks

½ red (bell) pepper (about 75g/2½oz), deseeded and cut into matchsticks

100g (3½oz) red cabbage, shredded

115g (4oz) edamame beans, cooked

10g (¼oz) coriander (cilantro) and/or mint leaves

12 rice paper wrappers

Sea salt and freshly ground black pepper

For the dipping sauce

6 tbsp smooth or crunchy peanut butter

1 small garlic clove, minced

1 tbsp tamari or light soy sauce

Juice of 1 lime

1 tbsp maple syrup

A pinch of dried chilli (red pepper) flakes

This rainbow-tastic dish is as vibrant as it is versatile: it's perfect for showing off the beauty of fresh, colourful ingredients and, rolled up tightly, makes a stunning platter for entertaining. The creamy peanut-butter dipping sauce adds delicious richness – and even more plant points.

1. First, make the peanut butter dipping sauce by combining all the ingredients with 2–3 tablespoons of water. Stir until fluffy, then set aside.

2. Lay out all the prepared vegetables and herbs in front of you.

3. Pour some room-temperature water into a wide shallow bowl large enough to contain each wrapper.

4. One at a time, submerge each wrapper into the water for 5–10 seconds until soft, then use two hands to carefully transfer it to a clean work surface or plastic cutting board. Place a slice of avocado and a slice of mango about one-third of the way up from the bottom of the wrapper and pile equal amounts of the rest of the ingredients on top, leaving the top one-third free for wrapping. Pull up the bottom part of the wrapper over the veg, making sure everything is tightly tucked in. Fold in the edges and keep rolling all the way to the top. Slice the filled roll in half and place the halves on a plate (alternatively, you can keep the rolls whole, if you like).

5. Repeat with the rest of the ingredients, then serve with the dipping sauce.

Roast cauliflower & chickpeas with green tahini & pink onions

Nutritional info per serving

Fibre 14g
Protein 21g
Plant Points 7.75

 Serves 4   **Prep** 15 mins   **Cook** 35 mins

1 large or 2 small heads of cauliflower (about 850g/1lb 14oz altogether), stem trimmed

1 × 400g (14oz) can chickpeas, drained and rinsed

4 tbsp olive or rapeseed oil

1 tsp ground cumin

1 tsp ground coriander

½ tsp ground cinnamon

½ tsp smoked paprika

300g (10½oz) cherry tomatoes, halved

Sea salt and freshly ground black pepper

For the pickled onion

1 small red onion, sliced

Juice of ½ lemon

1 tsp caster (superfine) sugar

For the green tahini

1 garlic clove, roughly chopped

175g (6oz) tahini

Juice of 1 large lemon, plus extra if needed

3 tbsp olive oil

2 handfuls of parsley leaves, roughly chopped, plus extra to serve

Small handful of mint leaves, roughly chopped, plus extra to serve

Never let anyone tell you that cauliflower is bland. Roasting it with chickpeas brings out a gorgeous nuttiness. This simple vegetarian dish is perfect for sharing at the weekend, or for enjoying as a quick, nourishing weekday lunch.

1. Preheat the oven to 220°C/200°C fan/425°F.

2. Cut the cauliflower into large florets and slice the stem into large chunks, keeping any nice leaves. Place all the pieces, except the leaves, in a bowl along with the chickpeas, oil, and spices and season generously with salt and pepper. Use your hands to mix everything together until nicely coated, then spread out the mixture on your largest baking tray (you may want to use 2 if it looks crowded).

3. Roast the mixture in the oven for 15 minutes, stir, add the cauliflower leaves (if using), and roast for a further 15–20 minutes, until the edges of the cauliflower are golden and crisp and the chickpeas have firmed up.

4. Meanwhile make the pickled onion. Place the onion in a small bowl, sprinkle over the lemon juice and toss with the sugar and a pinch of salt. Put to one side to pickle while the cauliflower mixture finishes roasting.

5. Put all the tahini ingredients and 4 tablespoons of water in a blender or small food processor with a big pinch of salt and pepper and whizz until smooth. The mixture might initially be a little thick, so keep adding up to another 4 tablespoons) of water and whizzing until you have a lovely, fluffy dip. Adjust the seasoning. You may want to add more lemon juice, too.

6. Spread the tahini on the bottom of a big serving plate and tumble the roasted cauliflower and chickpeas on top. Arrange the tomatoes around the plate and scatter with the pickled onions and a few mint and parsley leaves. Serve warm or at room temperature.

Beetroot Waldorf grain salad

Nutritional info per serving

Fibre 11g
Protein 23g
Plant Points 7.75

 Serves 4 (as a main)　　 **Prep** 15 mins　　 **Cook** 10 mins

- 75g (2½oz) walnuts or pecans, halved
- 2 × 250g (9oz) mixed grain pouch (I like Merchant Gourmet 5 Glorious Grains)
- 3 tbsp walnut or olive oil
- Juice of 1 lemon
- 1 × 250g (9oz) cooked vac-packed beetroot, drained and chopped into 1.5–2cm (⅝–¾in) chunks
- 2 apples (I use Gala), scrubbed and chopped into 1.5–2cm (⅝–¾in) chunks
- 125g (4½oz) red or black seedless grapes, halved
- 3 celery sticks, finely sliced, any leaves roughly chopped
- 1 Little Gem lettuce, separated into leaves
- 100g (scant ½ cup/3½oz) skyr, or Greek or coconut yogurt
- 1 tbsp cider vinegar
- 1 tbsp Dijon or wholegrain mustard
- 2 tsp chopped tarragon leaves
- 200g (7oz) feta or vegetarian alternative, crumbled
- Sea salt and freshly ground black pepper

This vibrant twist on a classic Waldorf salad heroes earthy, sweet beetroot. It's a quick, throw-together option for busy days – just chop your ingredients and stir through a mixed grain pouch for ease. Toasted walnuts bring not only crunch and flavour, but also a boost of gut-nourishing omega-3 fatty acids.

1. Start by toasting the walnuts in a large dry pan over medium-low heat for 5–7 minutes until beginning to colour, then allow to cool.

2. Dress the grains with 1 tablespoon of the oil, the lemon juice, and some salt and pepper and spread them over the base of a large platter (or divide between 4 plates).

3. Pile the beetroot, apple, grapes, and celery on top of the grains and arrange the lettuce leaves around the edge of the salad.

4. Combine the remaining oil, along with the skyr or yogurt, cider vinegar, mustard, and tarragon in a small bowl and season lightly. Generously drizzle the dressing over the salad, tossing it if you wish, then scatter over the feta and toasted walnuts, and serve.

Turkish lentil & carrot soup with mint & chilli

Nutritional info per serving

Fibre 16g
Protein 17g
Plant Points 9

 Serves 4   **Prep** 10 mins   **Cook** 35 mins

5 tbsp olive or rapeseed oil

1 large onion, chopped

2 carrots, scrubbed and chopped

2 garlic cloves, chopped

1 tsp ground cumin

1 tsp sweet paprika

1½ tbsp tomato purée (paste)

200g (7oz) dried red lentils, rinsed

150g (5½oz) sweet potato, scrubbed and chopped

1.25 litres (5½ cups/2 pints) hot vegetable or chicken stock (bouillon)

1 tsp sea salt, plus extra to season

60g (2¼oz) bulgur wheat, rinsed

Juice of ½ lemon, plus wedges to serve

½ tsp Turkish chilli flakes, or ¼ tsp dried chilli (red pepper) flakes

Handful of mint leaves, finely chopped, or 1 tsp dried mint

Freshly ground black pepper

It's easy to fall into a soup rut, but this Turkish-inspired red lentil, carrot, and mint version is a brilliant way to keep things interesting and rack up plenty of plant points, too. Adjust the liquid at the end according to how thick you like your soup, and blend more or less, depending on your preference for texture. It's a great make-ahead – it keeps well in the fridge for two to three days in an airtight container.

1. Place a large, deep pan over a medium heat and warm 2 tablespoons of the oil. Add the onion, carrots, and a pinch of salt and cook, stirring, for 8–10 minutes until soft.

2. Add the garlic and, once fragrant (about 2–3 minutes), add the cumin, paprika, and tomato purée. Cook for a further 1–2 minutes before adding the lentils, sweet potato, stock, and 1 teaspoon of salt. Bring to a simmer and cook for 15–20 minutes until the lentils and sweet potato are soft.

3. Meanwhile, place the bulgur in a pan, cover in 150ml (scant ⅔ cup/5floz) of boiling water, add a pinch of salt and simmer for 8–10 minutes until the water has been absorbed. Add more water as needed. Stir in the lemon juice.

4. Combine the remaining oil, chilli, and mint in a small bowl and set aside to use as a garnish.

5. Once the lentils are soft, use an electric hand-held blender to purée the soup – either until smooth or stop halfway if you'd like a little texture. Stir in the cooked bulgur.

6. Check the seasoning, and transfer the soup to bowls. Spoon over the chilli-mint oil and serve each portion with a lemon wedge.

Caldo verde soup with smoky butter beans

Nutritional info per serving

Fibre 13g
Protein 12g
Plant Points 4.75

 Serves 4   **Prep** 10 mins   **Cook** 35 mins

3 tbsp olive oil

1 large leek, sliced

2 garlic cloves, sliced

1 × 570g (20oz) jar butter (lima) beans

350g (12oz) floury potatoes, such as Maris Piper, scrubbed and cut into 1.5–2cm (⅝–¾in) cubes

1 bay leaf

800ml (3½ cups/28fl oz) hot chicken or vegetable stock

300g (10½oz) dark leafy greens, such as spring greens or kale, chopped and thickest stems discarded

Sea salt and freshly ground black pepper

For the smoky butter beans

2 tbsp olive oil, plus extra to serve

2 garlic cloves, chopped

½ tsp smoked paprika, plus extra to serve

Big handful of parsley leaves, chopped, to serve

Caldo verde is Portuguese for "green broth" – a comforting, rustic soup traditionally made with potatoes, kale, and chorizo. My version keeps all that hearty flavour but swaps the meat for paprika-spiked butter beans, creating a wholesome vegan twist. I like using jarred butter beans for their rich, velvety liquid, which helps thicken the soup, but canned beans work just as well.

1. Warm the olive oil in a large deep pan over a medium heat and fry the leek and garlic with a pinch of salt for 5–7 minutes until soft and slightly coloured.

2. Add half the butter beans and all the liquid in the jar. Tip the remaining half of the butter beans into a colander and rinse, then drain on kitchen paper and set aside.

3. Add the potatoes, bay leaf, and stock to the pan. Season with salt and pepper, then bring the soup to a simmer and cook for 15–18 minutes until the potatoes are soft.

4. Meanwhile, make the smoky butter beans. In a small non-stick frying pan or skillet, warm the oil and garlic over a low heat and leave for 2–3 minutes to allow the garlic to infuse into the oil. Turn the heat up to medium, add the reserved, rinsed butter beans, along with the paprika, and some salt and pepper, and continue cooking, for another 4–5 minutes, stirring occasionally so they get a nice crust all over, then take the pan off the heat and keep the beans warm.

5. Remove the bay leaf and use an electric hand-held blender to purée the soup – either until smooth or stop halfway if you'd like a little texture. Add the greens and simmer for 5–6 minutes until tender but still bright green. Check the seasoning, then divide between your bowls to serve.

6. Top each bowl with smoky beans, a sprinkle of parsley, another pinch of paprika, and a drizzle of oil.

Crispy quinoa & kale salad with creamy cashew dressing

Nutritional info per serving

Fibre 11g
Protein 18g
Plant Points 10

 Serves 4   **Prep** 15 mins   **Cook** 45 mins

125g (4½oz) white, black, or red quinoa, rinsed

3 tbsp olive oil

150g (5½oz) kale, or cavolo nero, stems discarded

1 tbsp cider vinegar

200g (7oz) canned or frozen and defrosted, or fresh sweetcorn

200g (7oz) cherry tomatoes, halved

2 avocados, de-stoned, peeled, and chopped into 1cm (½in) cubes

1 red (bell) pepper, deseeded and chopped into 1cm (½in) cubes

50g (1¾oz) toasted pumpkin seeds

For the dressing

100g (3½oz) cashews, soaked for at least 2 hours

Juice of 2 limes

1 tbsp cider vinegar

2 tbsp olive or rapeseed oil

½ small garlic clove, chopped

10g coriander (cilantro) leaves and stems

½ green chilli, ideally jalapeño, deseeded

1 tsp maple syrup

Sea salt and freshly ground black pepper

This Mexican-inspired salad is substantial enough to enjoy for lunch or dinner. It holds up beautifully without going soggy, making it also perfect for packed lunches or picnics. You can use a pouch of pre-cooked quinoa to save time (if you can find it, black or red quinoa adds extra fibre and a lovely nuttiness). You'll need to soak the cashews for the dressing for at least 2 hours (or overnight) before you begin.

1. Preheat the oven to 190°C/170°C fan/375°F and line a large baking tray with parchment paper. Place the quinoa in a pan with 300ml (1¼ cups plus 1 tbsp/10½fl oz) of water, bring to a simmer and cook for 15 minutes until tender and the water has cooked away (add more water if necessary, until the quinoa is tender), then cover the pan with a tea towel for 5 minutes for the quinoa to steam-dry.

2. Stir in 2 tablespoons of the oil, spread the quinoa out in a thin layer on the tray, and place the tray in the oven. Bake, stirring once, for 25–30 minutes until the edges are golden and crisp. Leave to cool and get crispier.

3. Make the dressing. Drain the cashews from their soaking liquid and blitz with 100ml (7 tablespoons) of water and all the other dressing ingredients until bright green and smooth. Have a taste and adjust the seasoning with salt and pepper.

4. Place the kale in a large mixing bowl with the remaining tablespoon of oil, the cider vinegar, and a pinch of salt and use your hands to massage it until it begins to wilt, about 2–3 minutes.

5. Add the rest of the salad ingredients, season with salt and pepper and give everything a gentle toss. Transfer to a platter and scatter over the crispy quinoa. Generously drizzle the dressing over the salad, tossing it if you wish, then serve.

Coronation Brussels sprout salad with couscous & apricots

Nutritional info per serving

Fibre 9.5g
Protein 37g
Plant Points 6

 Serves 4   Prep 15 mins   Cook 20 mins

2 × 170g (6oz) chicken breasts or skinless, boneless thighs (at room temperature)

500g (1lb 2oz) Brussels sprouts, 400g (14oz) halved, 100g (3½oz) finely sliced

3 tbsp olive or rapeseed oil

120g (4¼oz) giant whole-wheat couscous

1½ tbsp cider vinegar

30g (1oz) chopped pecans or toasted almond flakes

60g (2¼oz) dried pitted apricots, thinly sliced

For the sauce

1½ tbsp mild curry powder

1 small garlic clove, minced

1 tbsp olive or rapeseed oil

250g (generous 1 cup/9oz) skyr, or Greek or coconut yogurt

1½ tbsp red or white miso

2 tsp maple syrup or honey

1½ tbsp cider vinegar

Sea salt and freshly ground black pepper

Handful of parsley leaves, chopped, to serve

A twist on the classic Coronation Chicken, this salad is easily made vegan by swapping out the chicken for tofu, or leaving it out altogether. If you can't find Brussels sprouts, chopped hispi (pointed) cabbage works perfectly, and fresh orange makes a lovely alternative to dried apricots, although with a little less fibre.

1. Preheat the oven to 220°C/200°C fan/425°F.

2. Meanwhile, combine all the sauce ingredients in a bowl and season with salt and pepper to taste. Use 5 tablespoons of the sauce to marinate the chicken – rubbing it generously over the meat. Set aside.

3. Tip the halved Brussels sprouts on to a large baking sheet and drizzle with 2 tablespoons of the oil. Toss well, spreading them out into an even layer. Add the chicken to the baking sheet (if it feels tight on space, place the chicken in a separate baking tray), season everything with salt and pepper and roast for 18–22 minutes, until the Brussels are dark, charred, and tender and the chicken is cooked through (70°C/158°F on a meat thermometer at the thickest part) – return the baking sheet to the oven if not. Once it's cooked, rest the chicken for 10 minutes, then slice.

4. While everything is in the oven, bring a pan of salted water to the boil and cook the couscous according to the packet instructions until tender. Drain it, then rinse it under cold water.

5. Toss the raw, sliced Brussels with the remaining oil and the cider vinegar and season with salt and pepper. Stir in the pecans or almond flakes and the apricots and put to one side.

6. Spread the remaining sauce over a big platter or divide it between your serving plates. Top with the cooked couscous, then the charred Brussels sprouts and the chicken. Finish with the shredded Brussels salad and a good sprinkling of parsley.

Note You can cook the chicken in an air-fryer at 180°C/350°F for 18–20 minutes until a meat thermometer registers 74°C/165°C.

Roast beetroot, carrot & blackberry salad with halloumi

Nutritional info per serving

Fibre 13g
Protein 25g
Plant Points 7.5

 Serves 4   **Prep** 15 mins   **Cook** 50 mins

- 500g (1lb 2oz) bunch of beetroot (beet), scrubbed, cut into 2–3cm (1in) wedges
- 400g (14oz) sweet potatoes, scrubbed, cut into 2–3cm (1in) pieces
- 4 shallots, quartered, or 2 red onions, cut into eighths
- 2 tbsp thyme leaves
- 6 tbsp olive or rapeseed oil
- 3 thick slices (about 300g/10½oz) stale rye bread, torn into 2–3cm (1in) pieces
- 225g (8oz) halloumi, cut into 1.5cm (⅝in) chunks
- 150g (5½oz) fresh or defrosted frozen blackberries
- 1 tsp maple syrup or honey
- 2 tsp cider vinegar
- 2 carrots, scrubbed and shaved into ribbons with a peeler
- 60g (2¼oz) rocket (arugula)
- Sea salt and freshly ground black pepper

This recipe showcases the incredible anthocyanins found in dark-coloured fruits and vegetables (like beetroot and blackberries). Anthocyanins are powerful plant compounds that support brain health and help protect against inflammation. For a vegan option, swap the halloumi for a handful of toasted mixed nuts, which add crunch and extra plant protein. You can use pre-cooked beetroot to save time. Soaking the halloumi helps reduce saltiness and keeps it tender during cooking. You won't need oil, as a non-stick pan works perfectly.

1. Preheat the oven to 200°C/180°C fan/400°F. Scatter the beetroots, sweet potatoes, shallots, and thyme into a roasting pan and toss with 3 tablespoons of the oil. Roast for 35–45 minutes, turning once or twice.

2. Meanwhile, toss the rye bread in a tablespoon of oil, spread it out on another lined tray and toast on the shelf under the veg for the final 20 minutes of the vegetable cooking time.

3. While the bread is baking, place the halloumi in a bowl, cover with boiling water, and leave for 20 minutes to soften.

4. Make the dressing next. Roughly crush 40g (1½oz) of blackberries with a fork and stir in the maple syrup or honey, vinegar, and remaining 2 tablespoons of oil. Put to one side.

5. Once the veg is golden and the rye bread is crisp, allow them to cool slightly on the tray. Prepare a platter or 4 plates with the shaved carrots, rocket, and remaining blackberries.

6. Place a non-stick frying pan or skillet over a medium heat. Drain the halloumi and pat it dry with paper. Once the pan is hot, add the halloumi (you won't need any oil) and leave for 2 minutes before turning and cooking the other side for a further 2 minutes until nicely golden all over and hot through.

7. Transfer the roasted veg, rye croûtons, and halloumi to the prepared platter or plates. Drizzle over the dressing and serve immediately while the halloumi is still hot.

Crispy rice salad with prawns, broccoli & avocado

Nutritional info per serving

Fibre 7.9g
Protein 21g
Plant Points 9.5

 Serves 4   **Prep** 10 mins   **Cook** 25 mins

2 × 250g (9oz) pouch of cooked long-grain brown rice, or leftover rice

3 tbsp sesame oil or rapeseed or mild olive oil

1 tbsp tamari or light soy sauce

½ head (about 200g/7oz) broccoli, head, and stem roughly chopped

100g (3½oz) edamame beans

1 ripe avocado, de-stoned, peeled, and diced

12 radishes, sliced

3 spring onions (scallions), sliced

Big handful of mint leaves, shredded

150g (5½oz) cooked prawns or medium tofu

40g (1½oz) roasted peanuts, chopped, to serve

For the dressing

1½ tbsp sesame oil

1 tbsp sesame seeds, toasted

2 tbsp mild olive oil

2 tbsp tamari

1 tbsp maple syrup

Juice of 1½ limes

Sea salt and freshly ground black pepper

This vibrant salad is all about texture: crisp rice, creamy avocado, and tender prawns. Make it vegan by swapping the prawns for baked tofu, which soaks up the dressing beautifully. This recipe scales effortlessly too – for smaller portions, skip the oven and crisp the rice in a hot pan with a drizzle of oil. Just don't overcook it if you want to keep that lovely chew.

1. Preheat the oven to 200°C/180°C fan/400°F and line a baking sheet with parchment paper. Toss the rice in the oil so it's evenly coated and spread it out in an even layer on the lined baking sheet. Bake it in the oven for 20–25 minutes, stirring occasionally until golden and crisp, but with a little bite. Once golden, drizzle over the tamari or soy sauce and toss well before leaving to cool.

2. Place the chopped broccoli and edamame in a steamer (or in a bowl in the microwave, and cover with cling film/plastic wrap). Cook them for 4–5 minutes until the broccoli is al dente and the edamame are tender, then leave to cool.

3. When the vegetables are cool, place them in a bowl along with the avocado, radishes, spring onions, mint, and prawns or tofu. Combine the dressing ingredients and season with salt and pepper. Add the dressing and the crispy rice, and season to taste with salt and pepper. Toss gently to combine.

4. Divide the mixture between your serving plates, sprinkle with the peanuts, and serve.

Recipes for a fibre-filled life

Baked chickpea & carrot falafels with tahini sauce

Nutritional info per serving

Fibre 12g
Protein 15g
Plant Points 10.5

 Serves 4   **Prep** 15 mins + chilling   **Cook** 30 mins

75g (2½oz) carrots, scrubbed and coarsely grated

1 × 400g (14oz) can chickpeas, drained, rinsed, and thoroughly dried

1 onion, chopped

3 garlic cloves, chopped

Handful of parsley, chopped

Handful of coriander (cilantro), chopped

1 tsp ground cumin

1 tsp ground coriander

1 tsp sea salt

½ tsp baking powder

2–4 tbsp chickpea (gram) flour or plain (all-purpose) flour

4 tbsp olive or rapeseed oil

For the tahini sauce

100g (3½oz) tahini

½ small garlic clove, minced

Juice of 1 lemon

1 tbsp olive oil

For the salad

1 tbsp pomegranate molasses or juice of ½ lemon

1½ tbsp olive oil

Seeds from ½ pomegranate

1 cucumber, chopped

400g (14oz) cherry tomatoes, halved

Sea salt and freshly ground black pepper

These are a lighter, more delicate take on traditional falafels, which are made with soaked dried chickpeas. They are ideal for children or adults on the go, as they make a great lunchbox option with that creamy whipped tahini sauce in a pot for dipping.

1. Place the carrot in some kitchen paper and wring out all the liquid. Set aside.

2. Tip all the remaining falafel ingredients except the flour and oil into a blender and blitz until finely chopped – you want plenty of texture but the mixture needs to be fine enough that it will stick together.

3. Transfer the mixture to a bowl and stir in the carrots and 2 tablespoons of the flour. Grab a handful of the mixture and if it feels like it's not sticking together, add a little more flour. Test again, and keep adding up to another 2 tablespoons of flour until you are satisfied the mixture will hold. Chill and rest the mixture in the fridge for 30 minutes.

4. Meanwhile, preheat the oven to 200°C/180°C fan/400°F and line a baking sheet with parchment paper. Grease the paper generously with 2 tablespoons of the oil.

5. About 1 tablespoon at a time, scoop out portions of the chilled mixture and form each one into a patty. You should get 16 patties altogether. Place them on a baking tray as you go. Use a pastry brush to brush the top and side of each patty with the remaining 2 tablespoons of oil.

6. Bake the falafels for 12–15 minutes until golden, then gently turn them over and cook the other side for 10–12 minutes, until they are cooked through and golden. Leave to rest and firm up for 5 minutes.

7. Meanwhile, to make the tahini sauce, stir together the tahini, garlic, lemon juice, and oil. It will seize up, but slowly start whisking in 4–5 tablespoons of water until you get a lovely, creamy sauce, the texture of thick yogurt. Season to taste and add more lemon if you want it perkier or more oil if you want it richer.

8. To make the salad, whisk together the molasses or lemon juice and oil, then add the other ingredients. Season lightly and toss.

9. Serve the warm falafel with the tahini for dipping or drizzling, and the salad on the side. On top of warm flatbreads is delicious.

Green goddess avocado sandwich

Nutritional info per serving

Fibre 7.7g
Protein 21g
Plant Points 9

 Makes 2   **Prep** 5 mins

- 4 slices wholemeal (whole wheat) or rye bread
- 1 large ripe avocado, de-stoned, peeled, and thinly sliced
- Handful of sprouts, cress, or microgreens
- Handful of baby spinach
- 8–10 slices cucumber
- 2 tbsp sauerkraut (or pickled onions; see page 114)
- 4 romaine, Little Gem, or butter lettuce leaves

For the sauce

- ½ tbsp capers in brine, well-drained
- A few pinches of parsley leaves
- A few pinches of dill leaves
- ½ small garlic clove, peeled
- ½ tsp Dijon mustard
- 1 tbsp olive oil
- 5 tbsp skyr, or Greek or coconut yogurt
- Sea salt and freshly ground black pepper

I can honestly say this is one of the best sandwiches I've ever made; it's also one my clients have loved for years. The magic lies in the sauce: a silky blend of avocado, parsley, dill, garlic, and Dijon mustard. Use dried herbs if that's what you have – the result is still wonderfully creamy, tangy, and packed with flavour.

1. Make the sauce first. Chop the capers and herbs together and sweep them into a bowl. Grate in the garlic and stir in the mustard, oil and skyr or yogurt. Season to taste.

2. To assemble, thickly spread all the slices of bread with the sauce, then top 2 slices of bread with the avocado, sprouts, spinach, cucumber, sauerkraut, and finally the lettuce. Place the other bread slices on top (sauce side downward) and firmly press together before cutting in half and eating immediately.

This chapter celebrates real, everyday meals built around the simple goal of getting more plants, more fibre, and more colour on to your plate in around just 30 minutes – these recipes are the "Bonus 30" we introduced on page 57. They demonstrate that nutritious cooking doesn't have to be complicated or time-consuming. Rather, they prove that wholesome, homemade food can be about quick, clever fixes without cutting any nutritional corners: adding tofu to a pasta sauce, blending beans into mac 'n' cheese, and so much more.

Each speedy meal supports balanced nutrition, combining fibre and protein with healthy fats and slow-release carbohydrates for sustained energy, steady appetite, and positive mood.

30-minute dinners

Green butterbean mac & fibre cheese

Nutritional info per serving

Fibre 18g
Protein 34g
Plant Points 4.75

 Serves 4   **Prep** 10 mins   **Cook** 20 mins

- 150g (5½oz) cavolo nero, kale, or spinach, stems removed as necessary
- 300g (10½oz) whole-wheat macaroni
- 2 tbsp olive or rapeseed oil
- 1 large leek, sliced
- 2 garlic cloves, sliced
- 2 × 400g (14oz) cans butter (lima) beans
- ¼ nutmeg, grated
- 150g (5½oz) Cheddar, Red Leicester, Gouda, and/or Gruyère (ideally a mixture), grated (shredded)
- 75g (2½oz) Parmesan (or vegan substitute), grated
- Sea salt and freshly ground black pepper

Made with whole-wheat macaroni, a blend of butterbeans, and healthy greens, this recipe boosts fibre without compromising the classic cheesy flavour you'd expect from such a guaranteed family favourite. It's delicious proof that comfort food can still be wonderfully nutritious.

1. Bring a pan of salted water to the boil and cook the green leaves for 5–6 minutes until tender. Scoop them out of the water into a large blender. Add the macaroni to the boiling water and cook according to the packet instructions until al dente. Drain, reserving a cupful of the cooking water.

2. While the pasta is cooking, warm the oil in a pan over a medium heat and fry the leek and garlic for 5–7 minutes, until softened and beginning to colour.

3. Reserve 120g (4¼oz) of the beans, then transfer the rest, including their liquid, to the blender with the greens. Add the nutmeg and plenty of salt and pepper and blitz until you have a completely smooth, vibrant green sauce. Pour the sauce into a baking dish.

4. Heat your grill (broiler) to medium. Combine the Cheddar and/or other cheeses with the Parmesan and set aside. Stir the drained pasta into the baking dish along with all but 2 big handfuls of the mixed cheeses. Tip in the reserved beans and the cooked leek and garlic mixture, then stir well to combine, adding a few splashes of cooking water until the mixture reaches your desired consistency. Scatter over the reserved cheese mixture.

5. While the mixture is still hot, place the dish under the grill for 4–6 minutes, until the cheese is melted and delicious and the sauce is bubbling.

Grilled mackerel fillet with herby rice

Nutritional info per serving

Fibre 12g
Protein 44g
Plant Points 8.25

 Serves 4   **Prep** 10 mins   **Cook** 15 mins

- 4 × 150g (5½oz) skin-on mackerel fillets
- 1½ tbsp tamari or light soy sauce
- 1½ tbsp maple syrup or honey

For the salad

- 75g (2½oz) desiccated (dried, shredded) coconut
- 1 small red onion, finely chopped
- 250g (9oz) green beans, cut into 2cm (¾in) pieces
- 2 × 250g (9oz) pouches of cooked basmati and wild rice
- 20g (¾oz) coriander (cilantro), leaves and stems chopped
- 20g (¾oz) Thai basil, leaves picked and chopped
- 15g (½oz) mint, leaves picked and chopped
- 15g (½oz) dill, tender fronds chopped
- 75g (2½oz) roasted peanuts, roughly chopped
- Zest and juice of 3 limes
- Sea salt and freshly ground black pepper
- ½ cucumber, thickly sliced on the diagonal, to serve

This grilled mackerel comes with *nasi ulam*, a traditional Malaysian herby rice salad. It's the kind of recipe that rewards you with every mouthful. And, as a bonus, your gut bacteria will love the incredible plant diversity it brings to the table.

1. Marinate the mackerel. Pat the fillets dry with kitchen paper, then make several shallow diagonal cuts, being sure to only score the skin and not to cut into the flesh. Place the fillets in a small container, and rub with the tamari or soy sauce and maple syrup or honey. Leave the fish to marinate in the fridge while you get on with everything else.

2. Place the coconut in a small dry pan over a medium-low heat and toast it, stirring often, until it begins to turn golden, about 3–4 minutes. Transfer the coconut to a plate and leave it to cool.

3. Place the onion in a small bowl and cover with cold water – this takes the edge off.

4. Bring a small pan of salted water to the boil and cook the beans until al dente (about 3–4 minutes). Drain them and rinse under cold water until cool.

5. Combine the cooled toasted coconut, green beans, drained onion, and the rest of the salad ingredients (except the cucumber to serve) in a salad bowl and season with salt (it will need a bit) and pepper.

6. Heat up your grill (broiler) until very hot (alternatively, you can cook the fish in an oiled frying pan or skillet). Place the mackerel fillets on a foil-lined tray, skin-side up. Spoon over any leftover marinade, then place them under the grill for 2–4 minutes until the skin is crispy and bubbly. Gently turn the fillets over and cook the other side for 1–2 minutes, until the flesh is opaque (check if you're unsure).

7. Serve the mackerel alongside the rice salad and the slices of cucumber.

Harissa-spiced hispi wedges with date & almond tabbouleh & mint yogurt

Nutritional info per serving

Fibre 15g
Protein 19g
Plant Points 9

 Serves 4   **Prep** 10 mins   **Cook** 30 mins

1 tsp cumin seeds
1 tsp coriander seeds
1 tsp caraway seeds
½ tsp dried chilli (red pepper) flakes
1 small garlic clove, minced
1 tsp sea salt
2 tbsp tomato purée (paste)
2 tbsp olive or rapeseed oil
1 tbsp maple syrup or honey
Zest of 1 lemon, plus wedges
2 hispi cabbages, quartered

For the bulgur wheat
180g (6¼oz) bulgur wheat
20g (¾oz) parsley, leaves and stems chopped
60g (2¼oz) roasted skin-on almonds, chopped
2 spring onions (scallions), chopped
60g (2¼oz) dried pitted dates or apricots, chopped
Juice of 1 lemon
2 tbsp olive oil
Sea salt and freshly ground black pepper

For the mint yogurt
½ small garlic clove, minced
Handful of mint leaves, chopped
200g (generous ¾ cup/7oz) skyr, or Greek or coconut yogurt

This dish is a flavour explosion: smoky, sweet, nutty, and fresh all at once. It might sound elaborate, but it is wonderfully simple to bring together and a fantastic way to transform humble cabbage into something special. For meat eaters, the recipe is equally delicious made with a roasted chicken leg in place of the cabbage.

1. Preheat the oven to 220°C/200°C fan/425°F. Line a baking sheet with parchment paper.

2. Place all the seeds in a small frying pan or skillet over a medium heat and dry-fry, stirring often, for 2–4 minutes until they begin to smell fragrant. Tip them into a pestle and mortar (or spice grinder) along with the chilli flakes and grind until fine. Add the garlic with a big pinch of salt and grind to a paste, then stir in the tomato purée, oil, maple syrup or honey, and lemon zest. Season with pepper, then rub the mixture over the hispi quarters.

3. Transfer the cabbage to the lined baking sheet and roast for 20–25 minutes until the edges are nicely charred and the centre is tender but still has a little bite.

4. While the cabbage is in the oven, bring a pan of salted water to the boil. Rinse the bulgur and add it to the pan, cooking until tender (about 9–12 minutes; check the packet for exact timings). Drain it into a sieve and place it over the hot pan to steam dry so it's nice and fluffy once cooled (still a little warm is fine, too).

5. Once the bulgur is ready, transfer it to a mixing bowl and add the rest of the salad ingredients. Season to taste with salt and pepper.

6. To make the mint yogurt, combine all the yogurt ingredients in a bowl and season to taste with salt and pepper.

7. Divide the cabbage wedges equally between your serving plates and serve alongside the tabbouleh and a spoonful of mint yogurt. Add lemon wedges for squeezing over.

Creamy artichoke, green olive & parsley pasta

Nutritional info per serving

Fibre 14g
Protein 20g
Plant Points 5

 Serves 4   **Prep** 10 mins   **Cook** 15 mins

400g (14oz) whole-wheat rigatoni (or pasta shape of choice)

2 × 280g (10oz) jars of artichokes in oil, quarters or halves, drained (oil reserved if you like)

1 small lemon

3 tbsp olive oil (or use reserved artichoke oil, if it's 100% oil)

2 garlic cloves, finely chopped

A pinch of dried chilli (red pepper) flakes, plus extra to serve

15g (½oz) parsley, leaves and stems chopped

50g (1¾oz) pitted green olives, roughly chopped

45g (1½oz) Parmesan (or vegan substitute), grated, plus extra to serve

Sea salt and freshly ground black pepper

This is a really elegant pasta – not only full of fibre, but full of flavour, too. Artichokes preserved in oil rather than brine will taste best – and if yours have vinegar added, reduce the amount of lemon to compensate. Try not to keep heating the sauce after you've added the Parmesan as it will become lumpy.

1. Bring a large pan of salted water to the boil and cook the pasta according to the packet instructions until al dente.

2. Meanwhile, place a large non-stick frying pan or skillet over a medium-high heat (you'll be adding your pasta to it, so the bigger the better). When the pan is very hot, add the artichokes cut side down (no need to add extra oil), and cook untouched for 4–5 minutes, turning once until they are nicely browned and a little crispy.

3. Zest the lemon into a blender and cut the lemon in half. Turn the heat under the artichokes down to medium and add the oil to the pan along with the garlic and chilli flakes. Cook, stirring gently, for 1–2 minutes until the garlic begins to smell fragrant and feel sticky, then squeeze in the lemon juice from both halves of the lemon to stop the garlic cooking. Turn off the heat and season generously with salt and pepper.

4. Transfer half the artichokes to the blender with the zest. Add 6½ tablespoons of water and whizz until you have a smooth purée. Scoop the purée into the pan with the rest of the artichokes.

5. Drain the pasta, reserving a generous cup of the cooking water. Return the artichoke pan to a very low heat and stir in the parsley, olives, and drained pasta. Toss gently to combine. Take the pan off the heat, stir in the Parmesan (or alternative) and a few good splashes of the reserved pasta water and keep stirring – the cheese will melt and emulsify with the oil and water into a silky sauce. Add more pasta water as needed until the sauce is glossy and coats the pasta beautifully. Transfer the pasta to your serving plates, and top with a little extra Parmesan (or alternative), if you like.

Kimchi fried spelt with sesame fried eggs

Nutritional info per serving

Fibre 16g
Protein 23g
Plant Points 8

 Serves 2   Prep 10 mins   Cook 10 mins

- 2 tbsp mild olive or rapeseed oil
- 100g (3½oz) kale, thick stems discarded, shredded
- 3 spring onions (scallions), thinly sliced, white and green parts separated
- 1 large carrot, scrubbed and coarsely grated
- ½ sweet potato (about 115g/4oz), scrubbed and coarsely grated
- 75g (2½oz) frozen peas, defrosted
- 3 tbsp kimchi, roughly chopped, plus 1 tbsp kimchi juice (and optional extra juice to serve)
- 1 × 250g (9oz) pouch of cooked pearled spelt (or use a mixture of grains, pearled barley, and brown or black rice)
- 1 tbsp tamari or light soy sauce

For the eggs

- 2 tbsp sesame seeds
- 2 tsp sesame oil
- 2 eggs

Kimchi is a wonderfully beneficial fermented food that supports gut health. If you think you're not a fan, this dish – with its balance of tangy, savoury, and nutty flavours – is here to convert you. The recipe makes a satisfying weekend brunch or a quick midweek dinner.

1. Warm the oil in a large frying pan or skillet over a medium heat and stir-fry the kale for 2–3 minutes, adding a few tablespoons of water to help it along, until it begins to wilt.

2. Add the spring-onion whites, along with the carrot, sweet potato, peas, and kimchi and stir-fry for another 2–3 minutes until the carrot and sweet potato are beginning to soften.

3. Add the tablespoon of kimchi juice, and the grains and tamari or soy sauce and keep cooking and stirring until the grains are hot and everything is nicely combined. Turn off the heat and keep warm while you cook your eggs.

4. Warm up a small non-stick frying pan or skillet over a medium-low heat. Sprinkle in the sesame seeds and toast for 1–2 minutes or so until they begin to colour. Pour the sesame oil over the seeds, then crack in the eggs and fry them until they are cooked to your liking.

5. Divide the spelt between your serving plates and spoon them over with a teaspoon of kimchi juice if you like. Top each portion with an egg and a sprinkling of the spring-onion greens.

Gigli with red pesto & tofu sauce

Nutritional info per serving

Fibre 13g
Protein 26g
Plant Points 5.5

 Serves 4   **Prep** 2 mins   **Cook** 15 mins

450g (1lb) spelt gigli or other whole-wheat pasta shape

225g (8oz; drained weight) roasted and skinned jarred red (bell) peppers (in brine)

75g (2½oz) sundried tomatoes

300g (10½oz) silken tofu

40g (1½oz) skin-on or blanched almonds or sunflower seeds

1 garlic clove, minced

4 tbsp olive oil

4 tbsp nutritional yeast, plus extra to serve

Sea salt and freshly ground black pepper

Handful of basil leaves, to serve (optional)

Tofu is such an underrated ingredient and, in this dish, it makes the sauce luxuriously smooth while adding a great source of plant-based protein. The homemade red pesto is quick to blend, and bursting with extra plant points and fibre. Even my children adore this one!

1. Bring a pan of salted water to the boil and cook the pasta according to the packet instructions until al dente.

2. Meanwhile, place all the other ingredients except for the basil in a blender with plenty of salt and pepper and blitz until smooth. Have a taste and adjust the seasoning if you like.

3. Drain the pasta and return it to the pan. Over a low heat, pour over the sauce and stir well to combine.

4. Divide the pasta between your serving plates, tear over a few basil leaves, and sprinkle with a little extra nutritional yeast to serve.

Cod en papillote with rocket & sunflower seed pesto

Nutritional info per serving

Fibre 14g
Protein 41g
Plant Points 6.75

 Serves 4   **Prep** 10 mins   **Cook** 25 mins

- 4 tbsp extra-virgin olive oil, plus extra to grease
- 4 × 150–160g (about 5½oz) cod (or other meaty white fish) fillet, skin removed
- 1 lemon
- 2 × 400g (14oz) cans cannellini (navy) or other white beans, drained and rinsed
- 1 × 280g (10oz) jar of artichokes, in oil or brine, drained and quartered
- 240g (8½oz) cherry tomatoes, halved, larger ones roughly chopped
- A few rosemary or thyme sprigs

For the rocket and sunflower seed pesto

- ½ small garlic clove, minced
- 60g (2¼oz) rocket (arugula)
- 60g (2¼oz) sunflower seeds
- 4 tbsp olive oil
- Zest and juice of ½ lemon
- ¼ tsp sea salt, plus extra to season
- Freshly ground black pepper

"En papillote" simply means cooking in parchment paper, a gentle method that locks in flavour and moisture. You can easily swap the cod for other fish, or make it vegan with hispi (pointed) cabbage (just allow a little extra cooking time). Serve the dish simply – with spinach or kale – and save any leftover pesto for spreading over bread to make sandwiches the next day.

1. Preheat the oven to 200°C/180°C fan/400°F. Cut 4 squares of foil, each 40cm (16in) square. Place a sheet of parchment paper (also 40cm/16in square) on top of each foil square to make double-layered bases. Lightly grease the parchment with a little oil.

2. Sit a piece of fish in the middle of each piece of oiled parchment and season with salt and pepper. Zest some lemon over each piece. Thinly slice the lemon into rounds and divide the rounds between the cod pieces.

3. Divide the rest of the ingredients between the cod portions, finishing with a tablespoon of olive oil over each. Season generously, then pull up the edges of the paper to make a dome and crimp the edges of the foil – you want to trap the cooking steam. Place the parcels on a tray and pop them in the oven for 20–25 minutes, by which time the fish should be cooked through.

4. Meanwhile, place all the ingredients for the pesto in a blender or small food processor with 1–2 tablespoons of water and pulse until finely chopped. Season with pepper and more salt to taste.

5. Carefully open the cod parcels (don't delay in opening as the fish will overcook) and transfer the fish to serving plates. Spoon over the pesto according to taste, and serve with some kale or spinach on the side.

Persian herb & grain stewed lentils with caramelized onions

Nutritional info per serving

Fibre 14g
Protein 14g
Plant Points 7.25

 Serves 4   **Prep** 15 mins   **Cook** 20 mins

2 tbsp olive or rapeseed oil

1 onion, chopped

2 carrots, scrubbed and chopped

2 tsp sea salt, plus extra to season

3 garlic cloves, chopped

½ tsp ground cumin

½ tsp ground coriander

¼ tsp ground turmeric

½ tsp freshly ground black pepper, plus more to taste

1 × 250g (9oz) pouch of mixed grains, barley, or long-grain brown rice

1 × 400g (14oz) can cannellini (navy), kidney, or pinto beans, or lentils, drained and rinsed

1 litre (4⅓ cups/1¾ pints) hot vegetable or chicken stock (bouillon)

200g (7oz) fresh or frozen spinach

20g (¾oz) parsley, leaves and stems chopped

20g (¾oz) coriander (cilantro), leaves and stems chopped

20g (¾oz) dill, chopped

Skyr, or Greek or coconut yogurt, to serve

For the caramelized onions

2 tbsp olive or rapeseed oil

2 onions, thinly sliced

1½ tsp dried mint

Perhaps more a soup than a stew, this is a bowl packed with vibrant greens. Use any grains or pulses you have to hand – pre-cooked mixed-grain pouches make it even easier, but if you have only dried lentils in the cupboard, they will, of course, work too – simply add them as for the pre-cooked, but with a little extra water, then simmer until tender before adding the herbs and spinach. Don't be put off by the long ingredient list – the dish is simple to pull together and feels like a hug in a bowl.

1. Warm the oil in a deep pan over a medium-low heat and add the onion, carrots, and 1 teaspoon of the salt. Fry for 10–12 minutes, then add the garlic and fry for another 2 minutes until fragrant.

2. Add the spices and cook, stirring, for 30 seconds to toast them, then add the grains, pulses, stock, and remaining teaspoon of salt and bring to a simmer for 5–8 minutes. Add the spinach and herbs and continue simmering for another 2 minutes until the spinach has wilted. Taste and adjust the seasoning.

3. While the onion and carrot are cooking, make the caramelized onions. Put a frying pan or skillet over a medium-low heat and add the oil, onions, and a pinch of salt. Cook very slowly, for about 20 minutes, stirring only occasionally to prevent sticking, until dark golden and caramelized, adding a splash of water if they stick. Stir through the mint. Set aside.

4. Transfer the stew to bowls, and serve with a big spoonful of yogurt and the caramelized onions.

Eating more fibre doesn't mean leaving your all-time favourites behind. These classics are the dishes so filled with nostalgia they never fail to sustain, comfort, and bring a smile. From a bubbling fish pie to a plate of perfectly sauced meatballs or a hearty burger on a Friday night, these are the recipes that connect us to family, tradition, and memory. And, with a few simple tweaks, they can also be fibre-fuelled to support your gut health!

There is something for everyone in this chapter, including plenty of meat-free options: a vibrant chickpea ratatouille bursting with Mediterranean flavour; a chunky chilli packed with antioxidants; a luxurious mushroom spelt "risotto"; and my beloved wholemeal baked aubergine Milanese with its golden, crisp coating. They are all wholesome twists on well-loved favourites.

Fibre favourites

Stuffed potato skins with cashew sauce

Nutritional info per serving

Fibre 12g
Protein 24g
Plant Points 8.75

 Serves 4   **Prep** 10 mins + soaking   **Cook** 1 hour 10 mins

6 potatoes (about 150–170g/5½–6oz; such as Maris Piper)

2 tbsp olive or rapeseed oil

Freshly ground black pepper

½ tsp sea salt

2 tbsp toasted pumpkin seeds, to serve

For the sweetcorn filling

300g (10½oz) frozen sweetcorn, defrosted

2 spring onions (scallions), chopped

1 green chilli (ideally jalapeño), chopped

Big handful of coriander (cilantro), leaves and stems chopped

50g (1¾oz) feta, crumbled, or vegetarian alternative (optional)

2½ tbsp skyr, or Greek or coconut yogurt

Juice of 1 lime

1 tbsp olive or rapeseed oil

For the cashew sauce

100g (3½oz) cashews

1 tbsp cider vinegar

2 tbsp olive or rapeseed oil

½ garlic clove, chopped

½ tsp garlic granules

1 tsp smoked paprika, plus extra to garnish

1½ tbsp nutritional yeast

1 avocado, de-stoned, peeled, and chopped, to serve

These stuffed skins are inspired by *elotes*, a Mexican streetfood. You'll need to soak the cashews for at least 2 hours in advance, ideally overnight, to get a beautiful creaminess in the sauce. Speed up the cooking by air-frying or microwaving the potatoes, then roasting them; or air-frying at 200°C/400°F for 5–8 minutes on each side. The recipe is also delicious made with sweet potatoes.

1. Soak the cashews for the sauce in 125ml (generous ½ cup/4fl oz) water for at least 2 hours, or ideally overnight.

2. When you're ready to cook, preheat the oven to 200°C/180°C fan/400°F. Prick the potatoes all over with a fork, rub in ½ tablespoon of the oil and place them on a baking sheet. Bake for 1 hour (or for 35–40 minutes at 200°C/400°F in your air-fryer; or 8–10 minutes on full power in your microwave), turning them once during cooking.

3. Meanwhile, drain the cashews from their soaking liquid, and place them in a blender along with the rest of the sauce ingredients. Blitz for 1–2 minutes until completely smooth, then put to one side while you make the remainder of the dish.

4. Remove the potatoes from the oven and increase the temperature to 240°C/220°C fan/475°F. When the potatoes are cool enough to touch, halve each one and scoop out the flesh, leaving a 5mm (¼in) layer around the inside (reserve the flesh for making mash, gnocchi, or the potato farls on page 104). Return the skins to the baking sheet, cut-side down and roast for 5 minutes, then turn them over, brush the cut side with the remaining olive oil, season with salt and pepper and roast for another 5–8 minutes, or until crispy.

5. While the skins are in the oven, make the sweetcorn filling by combining all the ingredients in a bowl. Season with salt and pepper to taste. Put to one side until the skins are ready.

6. Once the potato skins are crispy, pile each one with the sweetcorn salad, divide the avocado between them, then spoon over the cashew sauce. Sprinkle with the pumpkin seeds, garnish with paprika, then serve with extra sauce on the side.

Creamy white bean fish pie

Nutritional info per serving

Fibre 13g
Protein 38g
Plant Points 6.5

 Serves 4 generously   **Prep** 10 mins   **Cook** 1 hour

- 40g (1½oz) butter
- 2 small leeks, sliced
- 30g (¼ cup/1oz) white spelt flour
- 1 bay leaf
- 450ml (scant 2 cups/16fl oz) whole milk
- 1½ tsp Dijon or English mustard
- Zest and juice of 1 small lemon
- 350g (12oz) fish-pie mix (cod, smoked haddock, and salmon), cut into large chunks
- 1 × 400g (14oz) can white beans, such as cannellini (navy), butter (lima) beans, or flageolet
- 150g (5½oz) frozen peas
- Small bunch of parsley, chopped

For the potato mash

- 1kg (2lb 4oz) floury potatoes (such as Maris Piper), scrubbed and cut into large (3–4cm/1¼in) even-sized chunks
- 40g (1½oz) butter
- Sea salt and freshly ground black pepper

Fish pie is so perfect that I didn't want to tamper with it too much – it just needed a gentle nudge to increase the fibre. Blending in creamy white beans – cannellini, butter, or flageolet – add that extra goodness, as well as a beautiful texture to complement the flaky fish. I leave the skins on the potatoes, too, because that's where much of the fibre and so many of the nutrients are held.

1. Make the mash first to allow it time to cool. Place the potatoes in a large, deep pan of plenty of salted water and bring the water to the boil. Boil the potatoes for about 12–15 minutes, until tender, then drain them, reserving a cupful of the cooking water, and tip them back into the pan. Mash well, stirring in 75–100ml (4–6½ tbsp/ 2¼fl oz–3½fl oz) of the reserved potato cooking water, along with the butter, at the end. Season to taste with salt and pepper and leave to cool.

2. Preheat the oven to 200°C/180°C fan/400°F. Melt the butter in a wide pan over a medium heat. When hot, add the leeks and fry for 6–8 minutes, until sweet, softened, and beginning to colour. Add the flour and the bay leaf and cook for a minute or two, stirring, then slowly add the milk, stirring constantly until you have a smooth roux.

3. Bring the roux to a simmer, stirring until it begins to thicken. Add the mustard, some salt and pepper to taste, and the lemon zest and juice. Add the fish, pushing it under the surface to submerge. Cook gently for 1–2 minutes, then gently fold through the beans, peas, and parsley, taking care not to break up the fish. Remove the pan from the heat and transfer the mixture to a 26cm (10in) baking dish.

4. Spoon the cooled mash over the fish, smooth the surface and score it all over with a fork. Place the dish in the oven and bake the fish pie for 25–30 minutes until the sauce is bubbling and the topping is golden.

Persian-style chicken with walnut, pomegranate & saffron rice

Nutritional info per serving

Fibre 9g
Protein 71g
Plant Points 6.25

 Serves 4   **Prep** 10 mins   **Cook** 1 hour 10 mins

200g (7oz) walnuts

2 tbsp olive or rapeseed oil, plus extra if needed

6–8 bone-in, skinless chicken thighs

2 onions, chopped

Seeds from 4 cardamom pods, ground

½ tsp ground turmeric

1 cinnamon stick or ½ tsp ground cinnamon

120g prunes, de-stoned and halved

500ml (2 cups/17fl oz) pomegranate juice

Seeds from ½ pomegranate, to serve

Big handful of parsley leaves, chopped, to serve

For the saffron rice

300g (10½oz) brown basmati rice, soaked for 30 minutes

3 cardamom pods, lightly split

Pinch of saffron threads, soaked in 2 tbsp hot water (optional)

Fesenjān (the inspiration for this dish) is a traditional Persian stew made with a rich, tangy-sweet sauce of walnuts and pomegranate molasses (often known as "pheasant jam"). For a vegan twist, you can swap the chicken for roasted celeriac, which soaks up the flavours just as well.

1. Start by toasting the walnuts in a large dry pan over a medium-low heat for 5–7 minutes until beginning to colour. Leave to cool, then transfer to a food processor and blitz until they form a fine-breadcrumb texture. Make them as fine as you can, but be sure not to over-blitz as you don't want a paste.

2. Warm the oil in a large heavy-based pan over a medium heat. Pat the chicken dry with kitchen paper, season, then add the thighs to the hot pan, taking care not to overcrowd the space (cook in batches, if necessary). Sauté the chicken, untouched, for 6–8 minutes, turning once during that time, then remove to a plate. (Repeat for remaining batches, as needed.)

3. Add the onions and a big pinch of salt to the pan, scraping up any delicious stuck bits, and adding a dash more oil if the pan is too dry.

4. Fry the onions for about 10 minutes until soft and golden. Add the blitzed walnuts and cook for another couple of minutes, stirring constantly so they take on a little colour. Stir in the spices, prunes, and pomegranate juice. Return the chicken to the pan, then pour in just enough water to cover the chicken. Season well.

5. Reduce the heat to very low – you should see only fine, gentle bubbles – and simmer for 35–45 minutes, stirring occasionally to prevent sticking, until the chicken is tender and falling off the bone.

6. While the chicken is cooking, make the rice. Tip the rice into a deep pan with the cardamom pods and a pinch of salt and cover with 700ml (3 cups/24fl oz) of water. Bring to the boil and simmer for 35–45 minutes (adding more water if needed), until the water has been absorbed and the rice is tender. Remove from the heat, pour over the saffron and its soaking liquid, stir, then cover with a lid for 10 minutes.

7. Run a fork through the rice and divide it between your serving plates. Top with the chicken and sauce, and sprinkle with the pomegranate seeds and parsley to serve.

Pasta e fagioli with squash

Nutritional info per serving

Fibre 16g
Protein 16g
Plant Points 10

 Serves 4–6   **Prep** 10 mins   **Cook** 35 mins

- 3 tbsp olive oil, plus extra to serve
- 1 carrot, scrubbed and chopped
- 1 onion, chopped
- 2 celery sticks, chopped
- 250g (9oz) butternut or any variety of squash, peeled, deseeded, and chopped into 1cm (½in) cubes
- 2 tsp sea salt, plus extra to season
- 3 garlic cloves, chopped
- 1 rosemary sprig, leaves roughly chopped
- 1 bay leaf
- ¼–½ tsp dried chilli (red pepper) flakes (optional)
- 750ml (3¼ cups/26fl oz) boiling water, vegetable or chicken stock (bouillon), plus about another 250ml (generous 1 cup/9fl oz) water to cover
- 1 × 400g (14oz) can plum tomatoes, rinsed and chopped; or 3 tomatoes, chopped
- 2 × 400g (14oz) can borlotti (cranberry) or cannellini (navy) beans, drained and rinsed
- 200g (7oz) cavolo nero or kale, stems discarded, chopped
- 160g whole-wheat macaroni or other small pasta shape
- Freshly ground black pepper
- Handful of parsley, chopped, to serve (optional)

Fagioli (pronounced fah-joh-lee) is the Italian word for beans – so, this is, quite simply, "pasta and beans". If you're cooking with the intention of having leftovers or eating later, cook the pasta separately and add it to the bowls as you serve. This prevents the pasta from soaking up all the broth and becoming mushy, and also makes the dish quicker to pull together when you want to eat.

1. In a large, deep pan, warm the oil over a medium heat. Add the carrot, onion, celery, squash, and 1 teaspoon of the salt and fry for 10–12 minutes until soft. Add the garlic, herbs, and chilli (if using) and cook for 2 minutes until the garlic is tender.

2. Add the water or stock, tomatoes, and 1⅔ cans of beans. Use a hand-held blender to whizz the remaining beans into a purée, then add these to the pan. I like to also crush some of the squash against the side of the pan to thicken the sauce. Simmer for 10 minutes to allow the flavours to mingle, then add the cavolo nero, pasta, remaining teaspoon of salt, some pepper to taste, and enough boiling water to just cover the soup (I used 250ml/generous 1 cup/9fl oz).

3. Simmer, stirring often, for approximately 8–10 minutes, until the cavolo is tender and the pasta is al dente (check the pasta packet for exact timings). The soup should be thick and delicious, but do add more water to loosen if you like. Check the seasoning (it will need a lot), then transfer to bowls. Scatter over some parsley if you wish, drizzle with oil, and serve. The soup will continue to thicken as it sits, so add a little more water if you're not serving immediately.

Pork, lentil & ricotta meatballs in tomato sauce

Nutritional info per serving

Fibre 13g
Protein 34g
Plant Points 6

 Serves 4   **Prep** 10 mins   **Cook** 45 mins

40g (1½oz) wholemeal (whole wheat) breadcrumbs soaked in 4 tbsp water for 10 minutes; or 30g (1oz) rolled oats soaked in 4–5 tbsp water, to soften

200g (7oz) lean pork mince (ground pork)

150g (5½oz) cooked green or brown lentils, drained thoroughly if from a can

75g (2½oz) ricotta

1 garlic clove, minced

1½ tbsp ground flaxseed

1 egg, beaten

15g (½oz) parsley, leaves and stems finely chopped; or 1 tsp fennel seeds or dried oregano

30g (1oz) Parmesan, grated, plus extra to serve

For the tomato sauce

3 tbsp olive or rapeseed oil

2 garlic cloves, finely sliced

2 × 400g (14oz) can chopped tomatoes

1 × 400g (14oz) can borlotti (cranberry) beans, drained and rinsed

Parmesan rind (optional)

Big handful of basil leaves, plus extra to serve

Sea salt and freshly ground black pepper

Thinking of ways to keep much-loved classics on the menu, just with a little extra nourishment, is what makes my job so interesting. These meatballs are my lighter, higher-fibre take on a family favourite. The lentils boost both the fibre and plant diversity, while the ricotta keeps everything tender and juicy.

1. Squeeze the water from the breadcrumbs (or drain the oats), then place all the ingredients for the meatballs in a mixing bowl and mix with your hands to combine. Shape them into 20 large walnut-sized balls. Place them in the fridge to chill while you prepare the tomato sauce.

2. For the sauce, place a wide pan (with a lid) over a medium-low heat. Add the oil and the garlic and warm them together until the garlic begins to feel sticky and is colouring on the edges (don't let it burn), then add the tomatoes and borlotti beans. Half-fill the tomato can with water, give it a swirl and add the tomato-y water too. Then, pop in the Parmesan rind if you have one, and season with salt and pepper. Simmer the sauce for 20–25 minutes, until slightly reduced and tasting delicious.

3. Reduce the heat to low, add the meatballs to the sauce, and partially cover the pan with the lid – you want the sauce to simmer very gently. Simmer for 20 minutes, carefully turning the meatballs after 10 minutes until they are evenly tender and cooked through. Cut one open if you're unsure. Tear in some basil leaves, and serve with extra grated Parmesan. Whole-wheat pasta, mashed potato, or brown rice are good on the side.

My champion chunky veg & chocolate chilli

Nutritional info per serving

Fibre 17g
Protein 16g
Plant Points 14

 Serves 4–6   **Prep** 15 mins   **Cook** 1 hour 10 mins

300g (10½oz) sweet potatoes, scrubbed

2 red (bell) peppers, deseeded

250g (9oz) chestnut (brown) mushrooms

6 tbsp olive or rapeseed oil

3 tsp smoked paprika

3 tsp ground cumin

1 onion, chopped

1 celery stick, chopped

1 carrot, chopped

3 garlic cloves, chopped

1 × 400g (14oz) can red kidney beans, drained

1 × 400g (14oz) can black beans, drained

1 × 400g (14oz) can chopped tomatoes

1 tsp dried oregano

1 bay leaf

1 tsp chilli powder

4 tbsp tamari or light soy sauce

½ tbsp maple syrup

25g (1oz) 70% dark (semisweet) chocolate

For the guacamole

2 ripe avocados

1 small garlic clove, minced

1 tomato, chopped

1 spring onion (scallion), chopped

Juice of 2 limes

Handful of coriander (cilantro), chopped

Sea salt and freshly ground black pepper

My kids love this dish so much that I make it again and again. It's packed with beans, pulses and whatever veg I have to hand and it freezes well for up to three months. To save time, you can roughly blitz the onion, celery, and carrot in a food processor. Add a tablespoon of Marmite or miso for a gut-friendly umami kick.

1. Cut the sweet potatoes and red peppers into 2–3cm (1in) chunks and quarter the mushrooms. Preheat the oven to 200°C/180°C fan/400°F.

2. Put the mushrooms, sweet potatoes, and peppers in your largest baking pan and pour in 4 tablespoons of the oil. Sprinkle in the paprika and cumin, season with salt and pepper, and toss everything together to nicely coat. Bake the vegetables for 25–30 minutes until tender.

3. About halfway through the vegetables' cooking time, warm the remaining oil in a large, deep pan and fry the onion, celery, carrot, garlic, and a big pinch of salt for 10–12 minutes until the onion is soft and sweet. Crush one quarter of the kidney beans, with a fork, then add all the beans to the pan with the rest of the ingredients, except for the chocolate. Fill one of the cans with water and add that too.

4. When the vegetables are ready, add them to the pan and simmer for 30–40 minutes, until the sauce is thickened and everything is soft and delicious, adding the chocolate for the final 10 minutes. Season with salt, pepper, and more chilli powder if you want it spicier, or more maple syrup if you'd like it sweeter.

5. While the chilli is cooking, make the guacamole. Peel and de-stone the avocados, then crush the flesh in a bowl with a fork until you reach your desired texture (or use a hand-held blender if you want it really smooth). Stir in the other guacamole ingredients and season with salt and pepper.

6. Serve the chilli with brown rice, or jacket potatoes and coleslaw, and spoonfuls of the guacamole on top.

Chickpea ratatouille

Nutritional info per serving

Fibre 10g
Protein 9.5g
Plant Points 8.25

 Serves 4   **Prep** 15 mins   **Cook** 1 hour 15 mins

6 tbsp olive or rapeseed oil

1 large or 2 red small onions, thinly sliced

3 garlic cloves, thinly sliced

1 yellow (bell) pepper, deseeded and thinly sliced

1 red (bell) pepper, deseeded and thinly sliced

1 tsp sweet paprika

1 × 400g (14oz) can chopped tomatoes

1 × 400g (14oz) can chickpeas, drained and rinsed

1 tbsp sherry or cider vinegar

Small bunch of basil, leaves picked

500g (1lb 2oz) tomatoes, sliced into 4mm- (¼in-) thick rounds

1 aubergine (eggplant), sliced into 4mm- (¼in-) thick half-moons

300g (10½oz) courgettes (zucchini), sliced into 4mm- (¼in-) thick rounds

1 tsp dried oregano

Sea salt and freshly ground black pepper

A vibrant twist on a classic ratatouille, this version uses chickpeas to make it more filling and higher in fibre, without losing that silky, slow-cooked feel. The key is slicing the veg thinly so they soften at the same pace, creating a rich, tomato-based stew packed with colour and flavour. Finish with a drizzle of good olive oil.

1. Preheat the oven to 220°C/200°C fan/425°F.

2. Warm 3 tablespoons of the oil in a wide saucepan (ideally with a lid) over a medium heat and fry the onion for 5–6 minutes until soft, then add the garlic, peppers and a pinch of salt and cook for another 5 minutes, until the peppers are soft. Add the paprika, tomatoes, and chickpeas and simmer for 5 minutes. Stir in the vinegar, tear in the basil leaves, and season with salt and pepper to taste.

3. Transfer the chickpea mixture to a 30 × 20cm (12 × 8in) baking dish. Arrange the tomato, aubergine, and courgette slices, in overlapping rows, in the baking dish, alternating between vegetables. Sprinkle the top with oregano, salt and pepper, and finish with the remaining 3 tablespoons of oil. Cover with foil and bake for 45–50 minutes, removing the foil after 30 minutes, until the veg is tender and coloured on the edges (check that the aubergine is tender by inserting a sharp knife – it should glide through).

4. Let the ratatouille sit for 5–10 minutes to absorb its juices before eating it warm or at room temperature. It would also be delicious with the rocket and sunflower seed pesto from page 150.

Pearl spelt & mushroom "risotto"

Nutritional info per serving

Fibre 11g
Protein 21g
Plant Points 11

 Serves 4   **Prep** 15 mins   **Cook** 1 hour 10 mins

20g (¾oz) dried porcini mushrooms

1 litre (4 cups/35fl oz) boiling water

1 vegetable or chicken stock cube (bouillon)

1½ tsp Marmite (optional)

3 tbsp olive or rapeseed oil

1 celery stick, chopped

1 leek, sliced

2 garlic cloves, chopped

200g (7oz) chestnut (brown) or button mushrooms, chopped

200g (7oz) oyster mushrooms, chopped (or use more chestnut)

250g (9oz) pearl spelt or pearl barley, rinsed

1 tsp sea salt

150g (5½oz) spinach leaves

40g (1½oz) Parmesan (or vegan substitute), grated (shredded), plus extra to serve

Freshly ground black pepper

For the pesto

80g (2¾oz) watercress

1 small garlic clove, roughly chopped

40g (1½oz) roasted hazelnuts, almonds, or pistachios

25g (1oz) Parmesan (or vegan substitute), grated

5 tbsp olive oil

Juice of ½ small lemon

This is an absolute winner – rich, comforting, and full of flavour. Using spelt or barley grains rather than rice is a wonderful way to bring more plant diversity – and more fibre – into a traditional dish. To speed up the cooking, you can roughly blitz the mushrooms in a food processor and soak the grains either the night before, as this helps speed up the cooking. Always check the packet for cooking times, as some spelt varieties vary.

1. Place the porcini in a large jug or bowl, cover in the boiling water, crumble in the stock cube, stir in the Marmite (if using), and leave the porcini to soak for at least 10 minutes.

2. Meanwhile, warm the oil in a large pan over a medium heat. Add the celery, leek, and garlic and cook for 5 minutes, until the celery and leek are just softened. Add all the chopped fresh mushrooms and fry for 5–8 minutes until the mushrooms have softened. Scoop out the porcini from their soaking water (reserve the water), roughly chop them, and add them to the pan.

3. Add the spelt or barley, along with the mushroom soaking water and salt. Season with pepper, then cook for 40–50 minutes, stirring occasionally, and ensuring the grains are always covered in liquid (add more water, if needed) until they are tender.

4. Meanwhile, make the pesto. Place the watercress, garlic, and roasted nuts in the bowl of a small food processor and blitz until finely chopped. Add the Parmesan (or alternative), oil, and lemon juice and season with salt and pepper. Blitz again briefly, to combine, then transfer the pesto to a small bowl.

5. Once the spelt or barley is tender, add the spinach, stirring to wilt. Take the pan off the heat, stir in the Parmesan (or alternative), and check the seasoning, adjusting as necessary. Serve the "risotto" in bowls with a big dollop of pesto and a sprinkle of extra Parmesan, if you wish.

Black bean & beetroot burgers

Nutritional info per serving

Fibre 17g
Protein 21g
Plant Points 11.25

 Serves 4   Prep 20 mins   Cook 30 mins

1 tbsp ground flaxseed

1 tbsp flaxseeds

about 3 tbsp olive or rapeseed oil

1 small leek, finely chopped

2 garlic cloves, finely chopped

2 tsp Marmite

1 × 400g (14oz) can black beans

1 beetroot (beet), scrubbed and coarsely grated

½ sweet potato, scrubbed and coarsely grated

50g (1¾oz) dried wholemeal (whole wheat) breadcrumbs

2 tbsp chickpea (gram) flour

60g (2¼oz) defrosted sweetcorn

1 tsp smoked paprika

½ tsp ground cumin

4 wholegrain burger buns and toppings, to serve

For the burger sauce

½ garlic clove, minced

1½ tsp Dijon or American mustard

1 tbsp cider vinegar

100ml (scant ½ cup/3½fl oz) mild olive oil

1 tbsp tomato purée (paste)

¼ tsp smoked paprika

1 tsp maple syrup

1 small gherkin (pickled cucumber), chopped

Sea salt and freshly ground black pepper

A brilliant alternative to processed meat, the beans and beetroot in these burgers create a rich, satisfying texture, and they're just as good topped with melted cheese as any burger with beef (use vegan cheese, if you need). Cook the burgers slowly over a medium heat to ensure they cook through – if the heat is too high, the outsides will burn before the insides are ready.

1. First, make a flaxseed "egg". Mix the ground flaxseed with 3 tablespoons of water and leave to soak for at least 10 minutes. Stir in the flaxseeds and set aside.

2. Meanwhile, warm 1 tablespoon of the oil in a small pan over a medium heat and fry the leek and garlic with a pinch of salt for 4–5 minutes until softened. Stir in the Marmite and leave it to melt in.

3. Drain the black beans, reserving the liquid. Tip the beans into a bowl and mash them lightly, leaving them with a little texture. Squeeze dry the beetroot and sweet potato, then stir them into the bowl with beans. Add the remaining burger ingredients, season well with salt and pepper and mix with your hands so everything is nicely incorporated. The mixture can be refrigerated and stored for up to 5 days at this point, or frozen in an airtight freezer bag for up to 3 months.

4. Shape the burger mixture into 4 equal balls, then flatten them into patties about 2–3cm (1in) thick. Place them in the fridge to firm up for at least 20 minutes while you prepare the burger sauce.

5. To make the sauce, first measure out 5 teaspoons of the reserved liquid from the black beans. Add this with the garlic, mustard, vinegar, and a big pinch of salt to a tall jug and blitz with a hand-held blender on the highest setting for 15 seconds until blended and frothy. Very slowly and with the blender still running, drizzle in the oil until fully incorporated. Move the blender up and down to get as much air into the mixture as possible. You'll soon find the sauce begins to thicken. Once thick, stir in the other ingredients and season with salt and pepper, and adding a little extra maple syrup or cider vinegar as needed. Refrigerate until you're ready to serve.

6. To cook the burgers, warm the remaining 2 tablespoons of oil in a large non-stick frying pan or skillet over a medium-low heat. Once the oil is hot, add the burgers and cook on each side for 6–7 minutes without moving, until a dark crust has formed (add more oil if you need to). Transfer each burger to a split burger bun and serve immediately drizzled with the sauce and loaded with the toppings of your choice (I like sliced tomato, sliced gherkin, and sliced cheese).

Wholemeal baked aubergine Milanese

Nutritional info per serving

Fibre 16g
Protein 25g
Plant Points 6.75

 Serves 4   **Prep** 20 mins + salting   **Cook** 30 mins

2 large aubergines (eggplants), cut lengthways into 1.5cm (⅝in) slices (you should get about 8 slices)

3 tbsp olive or rapeseed oil

150g (5½oz) wholemeal (whole wheat) breadcrumbs

40g (1½oz) Parmesan (or vegan substitute), grated, plus extra to serve

2 eggs, beaten with 1 tbsp milk, or 4 tbsp oat cream

40g (⅓ cup/1½oz) wholemeal (whole wheat) flour, generously seasoned

280g wholemeal (whole wheat) spaghetti

Sea salt and freshly ground black pepper

Lemon wedges, to serve

Rocket (arugula) salad, to serve

For the tomato sauce

3 tbsp olive or rapeseed oil

3 garlic cloves, sliced

2 × 400g (14oz) can chopped tomatoes

Big handful of basil leaves, plus extra to garnish

Inspired by my love of aubergine parmigiana, this version has a light, crispy twist – like a classic Milanese! Make your own breadcrumbs by pulsing day-old wholemeal bread in a food processor. You could skip the salting step, but it really does help the coating stay crisp. For a quicker option, cook the Milanese in an air-fryer at 180°C (350°F) until golden.

1. Spread some sheets of kitchen paper on plates or chopping boards, salt both sides of the aubergine slices and leave them to drain on the kitchen paper for 30 minutes.

2. Meanwhile, prepare the tomato sauce. Warm the oil and garlic in a pan over a medium-low heat. Gently fry the garlic for 4–5 minutes until sticky and beginning to colour on the edges. Add the tomatoes, and some seasoning, and bring to a simmer. Cook gently until reduced – the time it takes you to cook the aubergine should be long enough (add splashes of water to the pan if it ever looks dry).

3. Preheat the oven to 200°C/180°C fan/400°F and line a baking sheet with parchment paper. Drizzle with 1½ tablespoons of the oil. Once the aubergine has released some liquid (you'll see droplets on the surface of the slices), rinse under the tap and pat the slices dry with kitchen paper. Mix the breadcrumbs with the Parmesan and spread them out on a plate. Tip the egg mixture into a shallow bowl and then the flour mixture on to another plate.

4. One by one, lightly coat the aubergine slices in the flour mixture, then gently dip them into the egg, and then into the breadcrumbs, pressing each slice to help the breadcrumbs stick. Place the slices on the oiled baking sheet and spray (or brush) the remaining oil over each one. Bake for 20–25 minutes, turning after 15 minutes, until the aubergine is golden and crisp on both sides.

5. While the aubergine slices are in the oven, bring a pan of salted water to the boil and cook the pasta according to the packet instructions until al dente. Drain the pasta, reserving a cupful of the cooking liquid.

6. Rip the basil into the tomato sauce, then toss the sauce through with the cooked pasta, adding just enough pasta water to loosen – you want it nice and saucy.

7. Transfer the pasta to plates, sit a couple of aubergine slices on the side, and serve each portion with a lemon wedge, and some extra grated Parmesan (or alternative) and basil leaves over the top. A rocket salad is good with this, too.

Recipes for a fibre-filled life

Mushroom & bean stroganoff

Nutritional info per serving

Fibre 7.6g
Protein 13g
Plant Points 10

 Serves 4   **Prep** 15 mins   **Cook** 20 mins

- 300g (10½oz) chestnut (brown) mushrooms, halved, or quartered if large
- 200g (7oz) mixed mushrooms, such as oyster, shiitake, eryngii and chanterelle, portobello, or more chestnut (brown) mushrooms, cut into large chunks
- 1 tbsp tamari or light soy sauce
- 3 tbsp olive oil
- 1 large leek or onion, sliced
- 2 garlic cloves, chopped
- 1 tsp thyme leaves
- 1 bay leaf
- 2 tsp smoked paprika
- 2 tbsp tomato purée (paste)
- 2 tsp cider vinegar
- 1 × 400g (14oz) can kidney beans, drained and rinsed
- 1 × 400g (14oz) can black beans, drained and rinsed
- 350ml (1½ cups/12fl oz) hot mushroom, vegetable, or chicken stock (bouillon)
- 1½ tsp Dijon mustard
- 1 tsp red or white miso, or Marmite
- 2–3 tbsp cream or crème fraîche (oat alternatives can be used, too)
- Sea salt and freshly ground black pepper
- Handful of parsley, chopped, to serve
- 200g (7oz) brown basmati rice, cooked, to serve

I've suggested canned beans here, but, if you can get them, jarred will add extra depth. For the best final flavour, I'm frying the mushrooms without oil first – it helps drive off moisture and intensify the results.

1. Place a very wide frying pan, skillet, or saucepan over a medium-high heat and, once hot, add the chestnut mushrooms, cooking them untouched for 2 minutes. Stir, and cook for another 2 minutes until nicely browned. Scrape the mushrooms on to a plate and repeat with the mixed mushrooms – cooking them for less time or until brown. Then, return the chestnut mushrooms to the pan, add the tamari or soy sauce and simmer for 20–30 seconds until it bubbles away and is absorbed by the mushrooms. Scrape them all on to the plate and wipe out the pan.

2. Turn the heat down to medium and add the oil, leek or onion, and garlic and cook for a further 4–5 minutes, scraping up any delicious stuck bits, until the leek or onion is softened. Stir in the herbs, paprika, tomato purée, vinegar, beans, and stock. Season with salt and pepper to taste, then simmer for 5 minutes before returning the mushrooms to the pan along with the mustard and the miso or Marmite. Add a splash of water if the sauce seems a bit dry and simmer for a further 5 minutes to give the mushrooms some time to absorb the sauce.

3. Swirl the cream through the pan, sprinkle over the parsley, and serve with brown basmati rice.

Chicken & quinoa meatballs with white bean broth

Nutritional info per serving

Fibre 12g
Protein 51g
Plant Points 6.5

 Serves 4   Prep 15 mins   Cook 20 mins

For the meatballs

120g (4¼oz) cooked white quinoa

400g (14oz) chicken mince (ground chicken)

60g (2¼oz) Parmesan, grated, plus extra to serve

1 egg, beaten

Big handful of parsley leaves, chopped

1 tsp fennel seeds

1 small garlic clove, minced

1 tsp sea salt, plus extra to season

2 tbsp olive oil

Freshly ground black pepper

For the broth

2 tbsp olive oil

2 small leeks or 1 large onion, chopped

1 large or 2 small fennel bulbs, finely chopped

2 garlic cloves, chopped

1 Parmesan rind (optional)

200g (7oz) frozen peas

2 × 400g (14oz) cans cannellini (navy) beans, drained and rinsed

1.25 litres (5½ cups/2 pints) chicken stock (bouillon)

2 big handfuls of mint leaves, chopped

2 big handfuls of parsley leaves, chopped

1 head of Little Gem lettuce, roughly shredded

Adding quinoa to these meatballs makes them so much lighter than using chicken alone. When in season, add asparagus or any fresh greens you have on hand to the broth – nourishing and endlessly versatile and comforting.

1. Combine all the meatball ingredients except the oil in a bowl, seasoning generously with pepper. Then, shape the mixture into 20 ping-pong-sized balls. Place these in the fridge while you prepare the broth.

2. In a large deep pan, warm the olive oil and fry the leeks, fennel, and a pinch of salt for 8 minutes, until the vegetables are softened. Add the garlic and cook for another 2 minutes until fragrant, then add the Parmesan rind (if using), peas, beans, and stock and bring to a simmer. Season generously with salt and pepper.

3. Warm the oil for the meatballs in a large frying pan or skillet over a medium heat and fry, turning, for 8–10 minutes, until deep golden and crisp all over, and juicy inside (you may need to fry in batches). Check that the meatballs are cooked through by cutting one in half if you're unsure. Divide the meatballs between 4 serving bowls.

4. Stir the herbs and lettuce through the broth, simmer for a minute or so until the lettuce wilts. Ladle the broth equally over the meatballs and top with a little extra Parmesan to serve.

When it comes to The Fibre Formula, rather than restricting foods in our diet, we need to make the foods we do eat work harder. For snacks that means choosing ingredients that balance fibre, protein, and healthy fats to support steady energy, better blood-sugar control, and long-term gut health. And it's perfectly possible! Think popcorn – light, crunchy, and full of wholegrain goodness; baked crisp vegetable bhajis; homemade crackers with veg-packed dips; prune and date crumble flapjacks; and cookies made with rye. These are small, smart upgrades that make a big difference.

Sweet and savoury snacks

Popcorn (3 ways)

Popcorn is a wonderfully high-fibre snack, providing around 15g of fibre per 100g. Experiment with seasonings to rack up the plant points.

1. Pour the oil into a large, heavy-based pan over a medium-high heat. Once hot, add the corn and shake gently to coat the kernels and distribute them in a single layer.

2. Cover the pan with a lid and leave it over the heat, shaking the pan gently every 30 seconds. The popcorn is ready when the pops slow down and are about 2–3 seconds apart – it should take about 3 minutes altogether. Tip the popcorn into a large bowl ready for coating.

 Makes 150g (5½oz)   **Prep** 5 mins   **Cook** 3–8 mins (depending on coating)

For a Marmite coating

3 tbsp rapeseed or sunflower oil
120g (4¼oz) popping corn
50g (1¾oz) butter or mild olive oil
4 tsp Marmite

1. Preheat the oven to 150°C/130°C fan/300°F. Cover a baking tray with parchment paper. Melt the butter in a small pan over a low heat (or heat the oil) and stir in the Marmite until you have a smooth, glossy liquid. Pour the Marmite mixture over the popcorn and stir to coat thoroughly.

2. Spread the popcorn over the lined baking tray and bake for 3–4 minutes to crisp up a little (skip this step if you don't mind Marmite fingers).

Nutritional info per serving

Fibre 4.8g
Protein 6.9g
Plant Point 1

For a spicy cheese coating

3 tbsp rapeseed or sunflower oil
120g (4¼oz) popping corn
4 tbsp nutritional yeast
1½ tsp smoked paprika
1½ tsp garlic powder
½–¾ tsp chilli powder (depending on heat)
1 tsp sea salt
A little butter, melted (optional), for drizzling

1. Place the ingredients in a clean spice grinder and blitz until you have a fine powder, then toss the mixture through the hot popcorn. Add a drizzle of hot butter, if you like.

Nutritional info per serving

Fibre 7.7g
Protein 9g
Plant Points 1.75

For a cinnamon sugar coating

3 tbsp rapeseed or sunflower oil
120g (4¼oz) popping corn
2 tbsp dark brown soft sugar
1 tsp ground cinnamon
½ tsp sea salt
A little butter, melted (optional), for drizzling

1. Place the ingredients in a clean spice grinder and blitz until you have a fine powder, then toss the mixture through the hot popcorn. Add a drizzle of hot butter, if you like.

Nutritional info per serving

Fibre 5.1g
Protein 3g
Plant Points 1.25

Broccoli, carrot & celeriac bhaji with coriander chutney

Nutritional info per serving

Fibre 9.5g
Protein 12g
Plant Points 8.75

 Makes 12
Serves 4

 Prep 15 mins

 Cook 30 mins

- 8 tsp olive, rapeseed, or coconut oil
- 100g (3½oz) broccoli, including the peeled stalk, roughly chopped
- 1 red onion, finely sliced, slices separated
- 100g (3½oz) carrot, scrubbed and coarsely grated
- 80g (2¾oz) celeriac, peeled and coarsely grated
- 150g (1¼ cups/5½oz) chickpea (gram) or yellow split pea flour
- ½ tsp bicarbonate of soda (baking soda)
- 2 tsp black mustard seeds
- ½ tsp ground turmeric
- ½ tsp ground coriander
- ¾ tsp sea salt, plus extra
- 2 tbsp lemon or lime juice

For the coriander chutney

- 75g (2½oz) coriander (cilantro) leaves
- 50g (1¾oz) desiccated (dried, shredded) coconut, or raw cashews or peanuts
- Juice of 1 large lemon or 2 limes
- ½–1 small green chilli (depending on heat), deseeded
- 1 garlic clove
- ½ tsp ground cumin
- ½ tsp sea salt

My love of Indian food inspired this colourful, veggie-packed bhaji snack featuring broccoli, carrot, and celeriac for plant points and fibre. A fresh coriander chutney adds the perfect finishing touch.

1. Preheat the oven to 200°C/180°C fan/400°F. Prepare a 12-hole muffin pan by adding ½ teaspoon of oil to each hole.

2. In a large bowl, combine the vegetables so they're nicely mixed, then sprinkle in the flour, bicarbonate of soda, spices, and salt. Toss with your hands to combine, then stir in the remaining 2 teaspoons of oil and the citrus juice. Add 3–4 tablespoons of cold water (you want just enough moisture to help the flour stick to the vegetables).

3. Divide the mixture between the holes in the pan, trying not to compress them too much – you want them nice and crinkly on top. Bake for 25–30 minutes, turning them gently after 15 minutes, until dark golden and crisp.

4. While the bhajis are in the oven, place all the chutney ingredients in a blender and blitz until smooth. You may need to add a few tablespoons of water to get it going. Transfer to a small bowl and adjust the seasoning to taste.

5. Remove the tray of cooked bhajis from the oven and leave them to cool for a moment (just until they are a little firmed up and cool enough to touch). Then, remove them from the muffin pan and serve immediately with the chutney.

Za'atar chickpea crackers

Nutritional info per serving

Fibre 1.1g
Protein 1.8g
Plant Points 7

 Makes About 30   **Prep** 5 mins   **Cook** 30 mins

- 125g (1¼ cups/4½oz) chickpea (gram) or yellow split-pea flour
- 15g (½oz) sesame seeds
- 10g (¼oz) chia seeds
- 30g (1oz) sunflower seeds
- 20g (¾ oz) ground flaxseeds
- ½ tsp sea salt
- 2 tbsp nutritional yeast
- 1½ tsp nigella seeds
- 2 tsp za'atar
- 2 tbsp olive oil

Za'atar is a fragrant Middle Eastern spice blend made with herbs, sesame seeds, and sumac, giving a nutty, citrusy flavour to these chickpea-based crackers. If you can't find it, though, you can experiment with other flavours to make the crackers your own: cumin, fennel, paprika, rosemary, turmeric, or even miso would all work well. Serve them with any veggie dip you fancy (see page 186 for ideas).

1. Preheat the oven to 180°C/160°C fan/350°F and line a large baking sheet with parchment paper.

2. Combine all the ingredients in a mixing bowl with 120ml (½ cup/4fl oz) of water and mix well – you should have a thick paste.

3. Spread the paste on to the lined baking sheet. Use a spatula to evenly smooth it out into a rectangle measuring approximately 30 × 28cm (12 × 11¼in). Score the rectangle into rough squares with a knife (without cutting all the way through). You're aiming for 30 individual crackers altogether. Then, bake for 25–30 minutes until the single, scored piece is golden and firm to the touch. Remove the baking sheet from the oven and leave the cracker to cool at room temperature (it will harden as it cools).

4. Break the cracker along the score lines, then store in an airtight container for up to 2 weeks.

Dips (3 ways)

Making your own dips is a quick way to add more fibre, flavour, and plant points to your diet. Pair these with the crackers on page 185, or crunchy vegetable sticks.

Bean, miso & tahini dip

1 tbsp white miso paste
3 tbsp olive oil
2 onions, sliced into eighths
3 garlic cloves, skin on
½ tsp sea salt, plus extra to taste
1 × 400g (14oz) can pinto, borlotti (cranberry), or cannellini (navy) beans
1½ tbsp cider vinegar
1 tbsp tahini
Freshly ground black pepper
Snipped chives, to serve

1. Preheat the oven to 180°C/160°C fan/375°F. Mix half the miso with 1 tsp water. Stir in 2 tbsp oil and toss with the onions. Bake on a lined baking sheet, with the garlic, for 25–30 minutes. Peel the garlic and blitz with the onions. Add the other ingredients and 75ml (5 tbsp/2¼fl oz) water. Season, purée, and sprinkle with chives to serve. Store for up to 5 days.

Nutritional info per 100g
Fibre 3.9g
Protein 5g
Plant Points 3.75

Green whipped tofu & butterbean dip

300g (10½oz) silken tofu, drained
1 × 400g (14oz) can butter (lima) or cannellini (navy) beans, drained and rinsed
60g (2¼oz) spinach leaves
½ garlic clove, finely chopped
Big handful of dill, plus extra to serve
Big handful of parsley
Big handful of chives
1–2 tsp white wine or cider vinegar
75g (2½oz) olive oil, plus extra to serve
Zest and juice of 1 lemon
1 tsp sea salt
Freshly ground black pepper

1. Whizz everything together in a blender until completely smooth. Check the seasoning, and adjust with more vinegar or lemon juice until the dip is bright and perky. Transfer to a bowl and drizzle with oil before serving. Store for up to 5 days.

Nutritional info per 100g
Fibre 3.1g
Protein 4.1g
Plant Points 5.25

Muhammara

125g (4½oz) walnuts
1 tsp cumin seeds
1 small garlic clove, finely chopped
275g (9½oz; drained weight) roasted red (bell) peppers from a jar, rinsed
2 tsp Turkish chilli flakes or ¼ tsp dried chilli (red pepper) flakes
½ tsp smoked paprika
1 tbsp pomegranate molasses; or 1 date and 1 tsp red wine vinegar
1 tsp sea salt, plus extra to taste
75ml (5 tbsp/2½fl oz) olive oil
½ tbsp ground psyllium (optional)
Freshly ground black pepper

1. Toast the walnuts in a dry pan on medium-low heat for 5–7 minutes. Set aside. Toast the cumin for 30 seconds. Add the cumin, walnuts, and all the other ingredients to a processor. Pulse for texture or whizz until smooth. Season, then store for up to 7 days.

Nutritional info per 100g
Fibre 4.1g
Protein 4.4g
Plant Points 4.25

Roast split peas with peanuts, coconut & crispy kale chaat

Nutritional info per 275g

Fibre 7.8g
Protein 9.6g
Plant Points 6

 Makes about 275g   **Prep** 10 mins + overnight soaking   **Cook** 20 mins

150g (5½oz) yellow split peas, soaked for at least 8 hours, ideally overnight

3 tbsp melted coconut oil

½ tsp sea salt

75g (2½oz) kale, stem removed, chopped

60g (2¼oz) roasted peanuts or cashews

30g (1oz) coconut flakes

1½ tbsp chaat masala powder

Chaat masala powder

½ tsp ground coriander seeds

½ tsp ground fennel seeds

½ tsp ground cardamom

½ tsp ground ginger

1 tsp ground cinnamon

½ tsp amchur (sour mango powder)

Pinch of asafoetida

Pinch of chilli powder

Chaat is a traditional Indian streetfood known for its bold, tangy, and spicy flavours. This version brings that same lively balance with roasted split peas, crunchy peanuts, toasted coconut, and crisp kale. If you don't have time to soak the split peas overnight, simply rinse and boil them first for 6–7 minutes until tender but still holding their shape. You can cook the kale in an air-fryer at 190°C (375°F) for 4–5 minutes, turning once, to make sure it's completely dry for maximum crispiness.

1. Combine all the chaat masala ingredients in a bowl and set aside.

2. Preheat the oven to 200°C/180°C fan/400°F. You'll need two baking sheets – one lined with parchment paper, the other with a rack set above it.

3. Drain the split peas, tip them into a clean tea towel and pat them dry. The more dry they are, the more crispy they'll get.

4. In a mixing bowl, toss the dried split peas with 2 tablespoons of the melted coconut oil and the salt and spread them out over the lined baking tray, making sure they have plenty of space. Roast for 10 minutes.

5. While the split peas are in the oven, toss the kale with the remaining tablespoon of oil, massaging it gently into the leaves so each leaf is lightly coated. Spread these out over the wire rack, making sure each piece has plenty of space (do this in batches, if necessary).

6. After 10 minutes, the split peas should be pale golden (don't let them get too dark as they get very crunchy). Stir them, and place the rack with the kale on the shelf beneath the split peas. Continue roasting for 10 minutes.

7. Sprinkle the peanuts and coconut flakes on top of the split peas and roast for a final 5 minutes until everything is golden and the kale is crisp.

8. Allow the split peas, peanuts, and coconut to cool slightly, then transfer to a bowl and toss with the chaat. Taste for salt, adjusting as necessary. Scatter over the kale, then gently toss everything together and eat immediately. The kale may not stay crispy for more than a day or two, but the rest of the mixture will last up to 2 weeks.

Prune & date crumble flapjacks

Nutritional info per square

Fibre 5.5g
Protein 9.8g
Plant Points 13.25

 Makes 9   **Prep** 15 mins   **Cook** 35 mins

2 tbsp ground flaxseed

200g (7oz) jumbo oats or rolled oats

50g (scant ½ cup/1¾oz) wholemeal (whole wheat) or wholemeal spelt flour

75g (2½oz) mixed seeds (such as 65g/2¼oz pumpkin and sunflower and the remaining flaxseed and sesame)

1½ tsp ground ginger

½ tsp sea salt

3 tbsp maple syrup or honey or 75g (6½ tbsp/2½oz) light brown soft sugar

6½ tbsp melted coconut or olive oil

3 tbsp smooth or crunchy peanut butter

50g (1¾oz) mixed nuts (such as almonds, walnuts, hazelnuts, macadamias, or pecans), chopped

For the filling

100g (3½oz) dates, pitted

100g (3½oz) prunes, pitted

Zest and juice of 1 orange

I'm the self-proclaimed biggest crumble-lover in the world – it's my all-time favourite dessert, and now I can eat it on the go! These flapjacks combine the digestive-friendly goodness of prunes with naturally sweet dates for perfect chewy-meets-crunchy texture. Medjool dates add extra stickiness. This is the most delicious, fibre-packed crumble-posing-as-flapjack you'll ever make.

1. First, mix the ground flaxseed with 6 tablespoons of water and leave to soak for 10 minutes (this is your flax "egg"). Set aside.

2. Preheat the oven to 180°C/160°C fan/350°F. Line a 20cm (8in) square brownie pan with parchment paper.

3. In a bowl, combine the oats, flour, seeds, ginger, and salt. In a separate bowl, whisk together the honey, maple syrup or sugar, prepared flax "egg", oil, and peanut butter. Pour the wet ingredients over the dry ingredients and use your hands to mix them together until fully combined.

4. Transfer two-thirds of the mixture to the prepared pan and push it down firmly with the back of a spoon until you have an even layer. Pop it in the oven for 15 minutes until golden on the edges.

5. Meanwhile, make the filling. Place the dried fruit and orange zest and juice in a small pan and bring the mixture to a simmer. Simmer for 2–3 minutes to soften, then transfer the mixture to a blender or small food processor and blitz until smooth-ish (a few chunks are fine). Add a few splashes of water if it needs help to blend properly.

6. Spoon the filling mixture over the baked base and smooth it out into an even layer. Combine the chopped nuts with the remaining flapjack mixture, then scatter this over the filling. Press down firmly again.

7. Return the pan to the oven for 15–18 minutes until the topping is golden. Leave the flapjack to cool completely, then lift out the parchment and cut the flapjacks into 9 equal squares (for smaller treats, you can cut into 12, but note the fibre and protein will be slightly less per square). The flapjacks will store in an airtight container for 5 days.

Dark chocolate, date & rye cookies

> **Nutritional info per serving**
>
> **Fibre** 2.5g
> **Protein** 3.1g
> **Plant Points** 3

 Makes 12   **Prep** 15 mins + resting   **Cook** 15 mins

- 200g (7oz) 75%–85% dark (semisweet) chocolate, broken into pieces
- 25g (1oz) unsalted butter or coconut oil, softened
- 60g (2¼oz) pitted dates
- 45g (⅓ cup/1½oz) rye flour
- ½ tsp baking powder
- ¼ tsp sea salt
- 2 eggs
- 100g (½ cup) dark brown soft or muscovado sugar
- ½ tsp vanilla extract (optional)

Rye flour not only gives these cookies an extra fibre boost but also a subtle nuttiness, making them both wholesome and moreish. They're quick to whip up and guaranteed to please. Top tip: if your dates are on the dry side, soak them in boiling water for 10 minutes to soften before blending.

1. Place the chocolate and butter or oil in a heatproof bowl set over a pan of barely simmering water and stir until melted and combined. Alternatively, heat in a microwave on the lowest setting in 30-second blasts, stirring between each, until just melted. Set aside to cool for 10 minutes.

2. Using a blender, blitz the dates to a purée, then stir them into the melted chocolate.

3. Combine the flour, baking powder, and salt in a bowl and set aside.

4. In a mixing bowl, use an electric whisk to mix the eggs and sugar for 2–3 minutes until lighter in colour and increased in volume. Fold in the melted chocolate mixture and the vanilla, followed by the flour mixture. Cover the bowl and refrigerate for at least 30 minutes.

5. Preheat the oven to 180°C/160°C fan/350°F and line 2 large baking sheets with parchment paper. Divide the mixture into 12 spoonfuls and roll each one into a ball. Arrange the 12 balls on the baking sheet, leaving plenty of space between each one. Sprinkle with a little salt, then place in the oven for 12–15 minutes until firm on the edges and a little crinkly on top.

6. Leave the cookies to cool on the tray for 15–20 minutes, then transfer them to a wire rack to cool completely. Store in an airtight container for 1 week.

Quinoa & dark chocolate bark with cranberry & fig

Nutritional info per serving

Fibre 5.3g
Protein 7.3g
Plant Points 12

 Makes 12–14 pieces   **Prep** 15 mins   **Cook** 25 mins + chilling

- 100g (3½oz) mixed nuts such as pecans, walnuts, hazelnuts, almonds, pistachios, or peanuts, roughly chopped
- 30g (1oz) pumpkin seeds
- 40g (1½oz) sunflower seeds
- 1 tbsp chia seeds
- 3 tbsp ground flaxseed
- 100g (3½oz) white, red, or black quinoa, rinsed
- 75g (3½ tbsp) maple syrup or honey
- 2 tbsp melted coconut oil
- ¼ tsp sea salt
- 200g (7oz) 70% dark (semisweet) chocolate, broken into pieces

For the bark toppings
- 40g (1½oz) dried cranberry or sour cherries, chopped
- 40g (1½oz) dried figs, sliced
- 30g (1oz) any nut (see above), chopped

Using dark chocolate for this bark not only gives it an intense flavour but also increases the fibre content. Decorate it however you like – it's a really impressive, "healthier" treat for the whole family.

1. Preheat the oven to 180°C/160°C fan/350°F and line a large baking sheet with parchment paper.

2. In a mixing bowl, combine the nuts, seeds, flaxseed, quinoa, maple syrup, 1 tablespoon of the melted coconut oil and the salt in a bowl. Spread the mixture on to the lined baking sheet, then use the back of a spoon to smooth it to 1–1.5cm (½–⅝in) thick. Bake for 20–25 minutes until golden and firm to the touch. Allow to cool.

3. Add the chocolate and remaining coconut oil to a heatproof bowl set over a pan of barely simmering water. Heat until just melted, stirring to combine. Alternatively, heat in a microwave on the lowest setting in 30-second blasts, stirring between each until just melted. If you have a cooking thermometer, the chocolate is ready when the thermometer reading is 45–50°C (113–122°F).

4. Using a spatula, spread the chocolate over the bark to create a smooth surface. Scatter over your choice of toppings, then transfer the bark to a fridge or freezer for at least 20 minutes, until firm.

5. Break the bark into pieces to serve. Store it in the fridge or freezer.

Frozen peanut butter & banana-stuffed dates

Nutritional info per serving

Fibre 2.5g
Protein 3.5g
Plant Points 4

 Makes 12

 Prep 5 mins
+ freezing

12 Medjool dates

6 tbsp natural peanut butter, ideally crunchy

1 banana, cut into 12 slices

15g (½oz) 70% dark (semisweet) chocolate, finely chopped

Pinch of sea-salt flakes

These are an absolute treat – like a homemade version of a popular peanut and caramel chocolate bar (you know the one). They are indulgent, but they are also packed with fibre, healthy fats, and plant points – and that makes them nourishing too!

1. Slice each date down one side and remove the stone, making a pocket and keeping the date intact.

2. Spoon ½ tablespoon of peanut butter into each date pocket and sit a piece of banana in the peanut butter.

3. Sprinkle each stuffed date with a little chocolate and salt, then place the dates on a tray in the freezer for at least 1 hour or until frozen solid. They are best eaten straight out of the freezer.

Recipes for a fibre-filled life

In this chapter, indulgence and nourishment sit side by side – a host of tempting desserts that quietly boost your fibre and improve the plant diversity of your diet too. You'll find warming puddings alongside others that are fresh and fruity. Best of all, they are easy to make. The mango and coconut chia pudding, so naturally creamy and refreshing, takes minutes from fridge to table; a new take on rice pudding – with brown rice, salted pear compôte, and dark chocolate – is far simpler to rustle up than its decadent name suggests; soft and flavourful vegan bread-and-butter pudding takes just 15 minutes to prepare, then the oven does the work. And then there's a sticky toffee pudding, because no dessert chapter, no matter how fibre-fuelled, would be complete without it.

Desserts

Chickpea blondies with tahini, dark chocolate & raspberries

Nutritional info per blondie

Fibre 4.1g
Protein 5.3g
Plant Points 5

 Makes 12   **Prep** 5 mins   **Cook** 25 mins

- 1 × 400g (14oz) can chickpeas, drained and thoroughly dried
- 125g (4½oz) tahini, peanut, or almond butter, plus 1 tbsp to drizzle
- 55g (scant ½ cup/2oz) oat flour
- 150g (scant ½ cup/5½oz) maple syrup
- ¼ tsp bicarbonate of soda (baking soda)
- ¼ tsp baking powder
- ½ tsp sea salt
- 2 tsp vanilla extract
- 100g (3½oz) 70% dark (semisweet) chocolate, cut into small chunks
- 75g (2½oz) fresh or frozen raspberries

A nutritionist I may be, but I'm also a firm believer in everything in moderation – and a gooey blondie-style treat is not for compromise. Made with chickpeas, tahini, and dark chocolate, these are high in fibre and protein yet taste every bit as indulgent as you would expect from a blondie. At the photoshoot for the book, everyone in the studio couldn't get enough of them.

1. Preheat the oven to 180°C/160°C fan/350°F and line a 20cm (8in) square brownie pan with parchment paper.

2. Place everything except the tahini for drizzling, the chocolate, and the raspberries in a blender and blitz until smooth. Stir through the chocolate, then pour the mixture into the pan and smooth the surface.

3. Evenly dot the raspberries over the top of the mixture, then drizzle with the tablespoon of tahini. Bake for 23–26 minutes until an inserted skewer comes out pretty clean. (A few crumbs are fine, you just don't want it to be sticky.)

4. Leave the blondies to cool completely in the pan, then cut them into 12 equal pieces. Store them in an airtight container in the fridge for up to 5 days.

Mango & coconut chia pudding

 Serves 4   **Prep** 10 mins + resting

Nutritional info per serving

Fibre 6.9g
Protein 4.2g
Plant Points 4.25

2 ripe mangoes, de-stoned and peeled

Zest and juice of 1 lime

1 × 400ml (14fl oz) can full-fat coconut milk

Seeds from 3 cardamom pods, ground (optional)

2–3 tbsp maple syrup or honey, depending on the ripeness of your mangoes

40g (1½oz) chia seeds

40g (1½oz) flaked or desiccated (dried, shredded) coconut, toasted, to serve

I love chia seeds – their texture, consistency and versatility make them one of my favourite ingredients. They're a great source of fibre, protein, and omega-3 fats, all essential for long-term health. This mango and coconut chia pudding is creamy, refreshing, and naturally sweet. At home, my son adores adding pistachios on top for a lovely crunch and extra plant points.

1. Place the flesh of 1 mango in a blender along with the lime zest and juice and blitz until smooth.

2. Add the coconut milk, cardamom, and maple syrup or honey, and blitz again briefly. Transfer the mixture to a mixing bowl (or keep in the blender jug) and add the chia seeds. Stir well, then transfer the mixture to the fridge for 15 minutes for the seeds to hydrate.

3. Stir the hydrated mixture again to make sure the chia seeds are well distributed, then spoon it equally into 4 glasses or small bowls. Refrigerate for 30 minutes for the pudding to firm up.

4. Meanwhile, cut the remaining mango flesh into small chunks. Once the chia pudding is set, spoon over the chunks and top with some toasted coconut. Serve immediately.

Autumnal crumble with apples, pears & blackberries

Nutritional info per serving

Fibre 7.9g
Protein 9.9g
Plant Points 10.25

 Serves 4   **Prep** 20 mins   **Cook** 45 mins

2 firm apples (such as Braeburn or Granny Smith), cored and chopped into 2cm (¾in) chunks

1 large not-too-ripe pear, cored and chopped into 2cm (¾in) chunks

150g (5½oz) fresh or frozen blackberries or raspberries

3 tbsp maple syrup or honey

½ tsp ground cinnamon

1 tsp cornflour (cornstarch)

Skyr, or Greek or coconut yogurt, crème fraîche, or oat cream, to serve

For the topping

70g (generous ½ cup/2½oz) wholemeal (whole wheat) flour or wholemeal spelt flour

30g (1oz) rolled oats

30g (1oz) barley oats, or more rolled oats

1 tsp ground psyllium husk (optional)

25g (2 tbsp) light brown soft sugar

70g (2½oz) mix of pumpkin, sunflower, and sesame seeds

1½ tsp white miso (optional)

75g (2½oz) coconut oil or cold butter

Sea salt

Autumnal crumble reminds me so much of childhood. This version is all about maximizing fibre while keeping that homely, nostalgic feel. The miso adds a gorgeous salted-caramel note to the fruit – if you don't have it, nuts or desiccated coconut make a lovely alternative. You can also play around with warming spices, like cardamom, nutmeg, and ginger if you like. If you're using frozen berries, allow a little longer (40–50 minutes) for everything to bake beautifully.

1. Preheat the oven to 180°C/160°C fan/350°F.

2. Combine the fruit, maple syrup, cinnamon, cornflour, and 2 tablespoons of water in a small baking dish (about 20cm/8in) square.

3. In a mixing bowl, for the topping, combine the flour, oats, psyllium husk (if using), sugar, and seeds with a pinch of salt. Separately stir the miso into the coconut oil, then add the mixture to the dry ingredients. Rub them together briefly with your fingertips until the mix resembles breadcrumbs.

4. Sprinkle the topping over the fruit and bake for 35–45 minutes (a little longer if you're using frozen berries) until the fruit is bubbling and tender and the topping is dark golden – check halfway through the cooking time and cover with parchment paper or foil if the top is getting dark too quickly or before the fruit is cooked through.

5. Serve with yogurt, crème fraîche, or oat cream.

Vegan bread & butter pudding

Nutritional info per serving

Fibre 10g
Protein 20g
Plant Points 5.5

 Serves 4   Prep 15 mins   Cook 45 mins

- 4 tbsp ground flaxseed
- 225g (8oz) stale wholemeal (whole wheat) bread (ideally sourdough), crusts removed, sliced into thick triangles
- 40g (1½oz) dairy-free spread, melted if a firm "butter", plus extra to grease
- 60g (2¼oz) raisins or sultanas
- 60g (2¼oz) dried pitted apricots, roughly chopped (or use more raisins)
- 1 lemon
- 100g (⅓ cup/3½oz) maple syrup, or 100g (½ cup/3½oz) light brown soft sugar
- 1 tsp ground cinnamon
- 1½ tsp vanilla essence
- 600ml (generous 2½ cups/21fl oz) dairy-free milk (ideally oat milk)
- 250ml (generous 1 cup/9fl oz) whippable oat cream, plus optional extra to serve
- ¼ tsp grated nutmeg
- Dairy-free yogurt, to serve (optional)

This vegan bread-and-butter pudding is a wonderful way to use up bread that's just past its best, and a simple way to boost your fibre intake. The result is rich, comforting, and full of flavour, proving that plant-based versions of traditional desserts can be every bit as delicious.

1. First, make the flax eggs. Tip the flaxseed into a bowl and cover with 125ml (generous ½ cup/4fl oz) of water. Leave to soak for at least 10 minutes.

2. Preheat the oven to 180°C/160°C fan/350°F. Lightly grease a 1.5-litre (2¾-pint) ovenproof dish (preferably ceramic or glass). Spread one side of each of the bread slices with the dairy-free spread and arrange the slices around the base of the dish.

3. Place the raisins or sultanas and the apricots in a small bowl. Zest the lemon into a mixing bowl or jug, then squeeze the lemon juice over the dried fruit, and top up with just-boiled water so they're just covered. Set aside for 10 minutes to plump up.

4. Combine the maple syrup or sugar, cinnamon, vanilla, milk, and oat cream with the lemon zest and stir in the fully hydrated flax eggs.

5. Drain the dried fruit and evenly scatter it over the buttered bread. Pour over the milk mixture, then sprinkle over the nutmeg. Place the pudding in the oven for 40–45 minutes until golden on top but with a light wobble in the middle (it will continue to set as it cools). Serve warm with more oat cream or with dairy-free yogurt.

Brown rice pudding, salted pear compôte & dark chocolate

Nutritional info per serving

Fibre 5.5g
Protein 11g
Plant Points 4.25

 Serves 4   **Prep** 10 mins   **Cook** 1 hour

150g (¾ cup/5½oz) brown risotto or short-grain rice

750ml (3¼ cups/26fl oz) whole milk or oat milk, plus extra if needed

3 tbsp maple syrup, or 75g (2½oz) light brown soft or coconut sugar

1 tsp vanilla extract

Seeds from 5 cardamom pods, ground

1 tbsp ground flaxseed

40g (1½oz) 70% dark (semisweet) chocolate, chopped, to serve

For the compôte

350g (12oz) pears, skin on, cored and diced

1½ tbsp mild olive or coconut oil

1½ tbsp maple syrup

¾ tsp sea salt

Pears are such an easy ingredient, and they work especially beautifully with dark chocolate. In this rice pudding, I've used pears to make a salted pear compôte that adds a touch of elegance – as well as extra fibre and plant points – to the whole dish. Soak the rice beforehand to help it cook faster. I've used brown risotto or short-grain rice, but if you have only long-grain rice in the cupboard, that's fine – just soak it for at least 2 hours before you begin.

1. Place the rice in a small pan and cover with plenty of water. Bring to the boil and cook for 10 minutes to soften the outside of the grains. Drain, then return the rice to the pan with the rest of the pudding ingredients, except the flaxseed and chocolate. Bring everything to a simmer and cook for another 1 hour, or until the rice has plumped up and is tender. Stir in the flaxseed, and simmer for another 5 minutes until the pudding is lovely and thick. Add more milk or water if you feel it's looking dry.

2. To make the compôte, combine all the ingredients in a medium pan over a medium heat. Bring to the boil, then turn down the heat and simmer for 8–10 minutes until the pear is just tender and you have a delicious syrup. Put to one side for a moment.

3. To serve, spoon the rice pudding into bowls and top with the compôte. Sprinkle with the chopped chocolate to finish.

Baked pears with walnuts & bitter chocolate

Nutritional info per serving

Fibre 5.4g
Protein 10g
Plant Points 4

 Serves 4   **Prep** 5 mins   **Cook** 50 mins

2 large, slightly underripe pears, halved

50g (1¾oz) walnuts, coarsely chopped

50g (1¾oz) 70% dark (semisweet) chocolate, coarsely chopped

2 tbsp tahini

2 tbsp maple syrup or honey

½ tsp sea salt

1 tbsp olive oil or coconut oil

Skyr, or Greek or coconut yogurt, crème fraîche, or oat cream, to serve

This elegant dessert combines the natural sweetness of pears with the rich depth of dark, bitter chocolate. The contrast is divine, and the addition of walnuts brings a chewy crunch, along with omega-3s and extra plant points. It's a simple yet sophisticated pudding that feels really special.

1. Preheat the oven to 180°C/160°C fan/350°F. Place the pear halves, cut-side up, in a baking dish and use a teaspoon to scoop out the cores, making a generous, deep hole in each.

2. Combine the walnuts, chocolate, tahini, half the maple syrup or honey, and the salt in a small bowl. Stuff the mixture into the pear holes, piling it high until it's all used up.

3. Combine the remaining maple syrup or honey and the oil and use a pastry brush to generously brush over the cut side of the pears. Cover the baking dish with foil and bake for 30 minutes, then remove the foil and bake for a further 15–20 minutes until the pears are tender, lightly coloured at the edges, and you can easily insert a sharp knife into the flesh.

4. Serve warm with yogurt or oat cream.

Almond & berry pudding

Nutritional info per serving

Fibre 8.9g
Protein 11g
Plant Points 9

 Serves 4–6   **Prep** 20 mins   **Cook** 40 mins

- 400g (14oz) frozen berries, such as raspberries, blueberries, strawberries, or blackcurrants
- 4 pitted dates, finely chopped
- 3 tbsp maple syrup or honey
- 2 tsp cornflour (cornstarch)
- 2 tbsp chia seeds
- Juice of ½ lemon (optional)

For the sponge

- 75g (2½oz) room temperature unsalted butter or coconut oil
- 75g (6½ tbsp/2½oz) light brown soft or coconut sugar
- 2 eggs
- 75g (2½oz) smooth almond or peanut butter
- 1 tsp vanilla extract
- 75g (generous ½ cup/2½oz) wholemeal (whole wheat) flour or wholemeal spelt flour
- 1½ tsp baking powder
- ½ tsp sea salt
- 45g (1½oz) flaked almonds, salted peanuts, or seeds, to sprinkle
- Skyr, or Greek or coconut yogurt, crème fraîche, or oat cream, to serve

I'm obsessed with the texture of this soft, gorgeous pudding. If you've chosen tart berries, like blackcurrants, you can skip the lemon, if you prefer; and feel free to use slices of peach, apple, or pear for a little variety. Make it vegan by swapping the eggs for flax eggs.

1. Preheat the oven to 180°C/160°C fan/350°F and grease a 20cm (8in) square or 18 × 25cm (7 × 10in) baking dish.

2. Place the berries, dates, maple syrup or honey, and 2 tablespoons of water in a small pan and simmer for 8–10 minutes, stirring occasionally, until slightly reduced and the berries are beginning to soften. Remove a large tablespoon of the syrup into small bowl, stir in the cornflour to make a slurry, then return the mixture to the pan. Stir in the chia seeds and the lemon, if using. Tip the mixture into the baking dish and set aside while you prepare the sponge.

3. In a mixing bowl, whisk the butter or oil and sugar and with an electric whisk for 2–3 minutes until pale and fluffy, then, one at a time, beat in the eggs until fully incorporated. Beat in the almond butter and vanilla.

4. In a separate bowl, combine the flour, baking powder, and salt, then fold the dry ingredients through the wet, being careful not to overmix.

5. Spoon the sponge on top of the fruit, spreading it out with a spatula until smooth. Sprinkle with the almonds, gently pushing them into the batter so they stick.

6. Bake the pudding for 25–30 minutes until the sponge and almonds are golden – check halfway through and cover with parchment paper or foil if the almonds are burning, then test with a skewer before removing from the oven (it should come out clean) and give the pudding a little longer if necessary. Cool for 5 minutes and serve warm with yogurt, crème fraîche, or oat cream.

Sticky date pudding with figs

Nutritional info per serving

Fibre 8.2g
Protein 10g
Plant Points 6.75

 Serves 6   **Prep** 10 mins   **Cook** 35 mins

150g (5½oz) pitted dates, quartered

100g (3½oz) dried figs, quartered

1 large orange

3½ tbsp rapeseed, mild olive, or coconut oil or melted butter

80g (4 tbsp) maple syrup or honey

2 flax eggs (2 tbsp ground flax mixed with 6 tbsp water, and soaked for 10 minutes) or 2 eggs

100g (¾ cup/3½oz) wholemeal (whole wheat) or wholemeal spelt flour

1½ tsp baking powder

1 tsp bicarbonate of soda (baking soda)

50g (1¾oz) ground almonds

1 tsp ground cinnamon

½ tsp ground ginger

¼ tsp ground nutmeg

50g (1¾oz) oat bran or oats, whizzed to a flour

¼ tsp sea salt

Skyr, or Greek or coconut yogurt, crème fraîche, or oat cream, to serve

For the sauce

1¼ tbsp cornflour (cornstarch)

200ml (scant 1 cup/7fl oz) oat, almond, or whole milk

150ml (½ cup + 2 tbsp/ 5fl oz) maple or date syrup

1 tsp vanilla extract

¼ tsp sea salt

1 tbsp melted coconut oil or butter

I've avoided putting a sticky toffee pudding in my books for years, but it's my husband's absolute favourite, and I couldn't resist creating a version that's a little more nourishing while keeping every bit of that nostalgic charm. The figs add a lovely jammy texture and pair beautifully with the dark, toffee-like sauce. This pudding is simple to make, endlessly adaptable, and a wonderful reminder that even the most indulgent traditional puddings can be given a wholesome twist.

1. Place the dates and figs in a bowl. Zest in the orange and squeeze in the orange juice, then pour over 200ml (scant 1 cup/7fl oz) of boiling water. Leave for 10 minutes to soften.

2. Preheat the oven to 180°C/160°C fan/350°F and grease a 20cm (8in) square baking dish or pan with a little extra oil or butter.

3. Using a hand-hand blender, blitz the soaked fruit and its soaking liquid to a smooth purée. In a bowl, whisk the oil and maple syrup or honey into the eggs, then stir this mixture into the fruit purée.

4. In a mixing bowl, combine all the dry ingredients, then stir in the wet mixture. Pour the lot into the prepared baking dish or pan and bake for 30–35 minutes until golden on top.

5. While the pudding is in the oven, make the sauce. Stir the cornflour into 3 tablespoons of the milk to make a slurry, then combine everything except the coconut oil in a saucepan over a medium-low heat. Stir constantly and bring to a rolling boil – you should see the sauce thicken slightly. Turn the heat down a little, add the coconut oil and keep gently simmering until the pudding is ready.

6. Use a skewer to make a few holes in the pudding. Pour the sauce over the top and leave it for a few minutes to sink in.

7. Scoop the pudding into bowls and serve with yogurt, crème fraîche, or oat cream.

Baked banana split with berries & toasted seeds

Nutritional info per serving

Fibre 9.2g
Protein 10g
Plant Points 10.25

 Serves 4   **Prep** 5 mins   **Cook** 25 mins

For the bananas

4 ripe bananas

½ tsp ground cinnamon

1 tbsp maple syrup or honey

150g (5½oz) raspberries, blackberries, and/or blueberries

For the toasted seeds

2 tbsp pumpkin seeds

2 tbsp sunflower seeds

2 tbsp sesame seeds

1 tbsp poppy seeds

2 tbsp desiccated (dried, shredded) coconut

1 tbsp psyllium husks (optional)

1 tbsp maple syrup

1 tbsp coconut oil or butter

150–200g (generous ½ cup/5½–7oz) skyr, or Greek or coconut yogurt, to serve

Sea salt

This is a playful, fibre-rich update on a nostalgic classic. If you don't have any fresh berries to hand, the bananas are delicious topped with a quick berry chia jam instead; or use frozen, quickly defrosted in the microwave.

1. Preheat the oven to 200°C/180°C fan/400°F and line a baking sheet with parchment paper.

2. Lay out a large piece of foil, then place a large piece of parchment paper on top. Hinge open the bananas by splitting them lengthways in half (in the skins). Sit them in the middle of the parchment paper, sprinkle with cinnamon and maple syrup, then seal the parcels tightly by folding over the edge of the paper, then crimping the edge of the foil to trap in the steam. Place on a tray and pop in the oven to bake for 25 minutes.

3. Meanwhile, in a small bowl, combine all the ingredients for the toasted seeds, add a pinch of salt and tip out the mixture on to the lined baking sheet. Spread out the seeds in an even layer, then bake for 10 minutes, stirring once, until golden brown. Remove from the oven and leave to cool.

4. Remove the bananas from their packages and transfer them to serving plates. Spoon some yogurt along the middle, top with a big spoonful of berries, and sprinkle generously with the toasted seeds. Eat immediately, drizzled with the syrup from the baked bananas, if you like.

Index

1-2-3 plant-based plate 64
30-minute meals 57

A
acacia fibre 65
adaptogenic mushrooms 75
age: benefits of fibre 37, 48–49
    daily fibre recommendations 58
almonds 33
    almond & berry pudding 212
    date & almond tabbouleh 141
appetite 13, 21, 41, 42, 43
apples 43
    autumnal crumble 205
    beetroot Waldorf grain salad 117
    blackberry, apple & bay compôte 97
apricots: Coronation Brussels sprout salad 125
artichokes: creamy artichoke, green olive & parsley pasta 142
aubergines (eggplants): chickpea ratatouille 166
    wholemeal baked aubergine Milanese 173
autumnal crumble 205
avocados: crispy rice salad with prawns, broccoli & avocado 129
    green goddess avocado sandwich 133
    guacamole 165
    potato farls with smashed avocado, feta & mint 104

B
bananas 13, 79
    baked banana split 216
    frozen peanut butter & banana-stuffed dates 197
    prune & walnut banana muffins 94
bark, quinoa & dark chocolate 194
barley 39, 43, 47
    barley porridge 97
    nutty barley, cinnamon & dried fig granola 88
beans 30, 63, 79
    bean, miso & tahini dip 186
    creamy white bean fish pie 157
    mushroom & bean stroganoff 174
    white bean broth 177
    see also individual types of beans
beetroot: beetroot Waldorf grain salad 117
    black bean & beetroot burgers 170
    roast beetroot, carrot & blackberry salad 126
berries 43
    almond & berry pudding 212
    baked banana split with berries 216
beta-glucan 38, 39, 43, 53
bhaji, broccoli, carrot & celeriac 182
bile acids 24, 38, 39
black beans: black bean & beetroot burgers 170
    mushroom & bean stroganoff 174
blackberries: autumnal crumble 205
    blackberry, apple & bay compôte 97
    roast beetroot, carrot & blackberry salad 126
bloating 34, 35, 44, 55, 59, 73
blondies: chickpea blondies with tahini, dark chocolate & raspberries 201
blood-glucose 10, 13, 24, 39, 41, 43, 44, 50, 51
blood pressure 11, 39
blueberry & mango frozen smoothie bowl 93
bone health 32, 46, 48, 49, 77
bowel cancer 11, 24, 36
bowel movements 10, 26–27, 43, 44, 73
the brain 25, 34, 37, 42, 53
bread 12, 59, 61, 66, 78
    green goddess avocado sandwich 133
    super high-fibre seeded nut & raisin loaf 108
bread & butter pudding, vegan 206
Bristol Stool Chart 27
broccoli: broccoli, carrot & celeriac bhaji 182
    crispy rice salad with prawns, broccoli & avocado 129
broth, white bean 177
Brussels sprouts: Coronation Brussels sprout salad 125
bulgur wheat: date & almond tabbouleh 141
burgers 79
    black bean & beetroot burgers 170
butter (lima) beans 33
    caldo verde soup with smoky butter beans 121
    green butterbean mac & fibre cheese 137
    green whipped tofu & butterbean dip 186

C
cabbage: harissa-spiced hispi wedges 141
caldo verde soup with smoky butter beans 121
cancer 11, 24, 36
cannellini (navy) beans: green whipped tofu & butterbean dip 186
    Persian herb & grain stewed lentils 151
    white bean broth 177
carbohydrates 10, 12, 34, 40, 45
    fuelling sport 44
    quality of 41
    simple carbs 12, 44, 45
cardiovascular health 12, 24, 38–39, 44
carrots: baked chickpea & carrot falafels 130
    broccoli, carrot & celeriac bhaji 182
    carrot pancakes 99
    roast beetroot, carrot & blackberry salad 126
    Turkish lentil & carrot soup 118
cashews: creamy cashew dressing 122
    stuffed potato skins with cashew sauce 154
cauliflower: roast cauliflower & chickpeas with green tahini & pink onions 114
cavolo nero: green butterbean mac & fibre cheese 137
    pasta e fagioli with squash 160
celeriac: broccoli, carrot & celeriac bhaji 182
chaat, crispy kale 189
cheese: beetroot Waldorf grain salad 117
    green butterbean mac & fibre cheese 137
    potato farls with smashed avocado, feta & mint 104
    roast beetroot, carrot & blackberry salad 126
cheese, vegan 67
chewing 55, 57, 59
chia seeds 33, 34, 35, 47, 59
    chia-seed water 75
    mango & coconut chia pudding 202
chicken 30
    chicken & quinoa meatballs with white bean broth 177
    Coronation Brussels sprout salad 125
    Persian-style chicken 159
chickpea (gram) flour: chickpea pancakes 103
    za'atar chickpea crackers 185
chickpeas 33, 47
    baked chickpea & carrot falafels 130
    chickpea blondies with tahini, dark chocolate & raspberries 201
    chickpea ratatouille 166
    crispy chickpea fried eggs 107
    roast cauliflower & chickpeas with green tahini & pink onions 114
chicory root 71
children 76–79
chillies: my champion chunky veg & chocolate chilli 165
    Turkish lentil & carrot soup 118
chocolate 66
    baked pears with walnuts & bitter chocolate 211
    brown rice pudding, salted pear compôte & dark chocolate 209
    chickpea blondies with tahini, dark chocolate & raspberries 201
    dark chocolate, date & rye cookies 193
    dark chocolate hot chocolate 69
    frozen peanut butter & banana-stuffed dates 197
    my champion chunky veg & chocolate chilli 165

quinoa & dark chocolate bark 194
cholesterol 10, 24, 38, 39, 46
chromosomes 49
chutney, coriander 182
coconut: coconut sambol 103
    roast split peas with peanuts, coconut & crispy kale chaat 189
coconut milk: coconut, kale & turmeric-baked eggs 100
    mango & coconut chia pudding 202
coffee 68
colorectal (bowel) cancer 11, 24, 36
colour, adding to your plate 64
compôtes: blackberry, apple & bay compôte 97
    brown rice pudding, salted pear compôte & dark chocolate 209
constipation 27, 34, 59, 65, 73, 75
cookies, dark chocolate, date & rye 193
coriander (cilantro): chickpea pancakes with onion, tomatoes & coriander 103
    coriander chutney 182
Coronation Brussels sprout salad 125
courgettes (zucchini): chickpea ratatouille 166
couscous, Coronation Brussels sprout salad with 125
crackers, za'atar chickpea 185
cranberries: quinoa & dark chocolate bark 194
crumble: autumnal crumble 205
    prune & date crumble flapjacks 190

D
dates: dark chocolate, date & rye cookies 193
    date & almond tabbouleh 141
    frozen peanut butter & banana-stuffed dates 197
    prune & date crumble flapjacks 190
    sticky date pudding with figs 215
diabetes, Type-2 11, 13, 24, 43, 50–51
diet business 72
dips 78
    bean, miso & tahini dip 186
    green whipped tofu & butterbean dip 186
    muhammara 186
dressing, creamy cashew 122
drinks 68–69, 79

E
eating 57, 59
edamame beans 30, 33
    vegetable summer rolls 113
eggs: coconut, kale & turmeric-baked eggs 100
    crispy chickpea fried eggs 107
    kimchi fried spelt with sesame fried eggs 145

energy 21, 24, 40, 41, 77
environment: environmental toxins 52–53
    fibre and the environment 16
enzymes 30
equol 46
exercise 44–45, 59

F
falafels, baked chickpea & carrot 130
farls, potato 104
fasting, intermittent 72
fats, healthy 64
fennel seeds: grape & fennel seed baked oats 90
fermented foods 28, 29
fibre: adjusting to eating more 59
    amount consumed globally 18–21
    eating too much 73
    and the environment 16
    fibre gap 6, 9, 17, 22
    fibre tables 60–61
    history of fibre intake 14–17
    how much is in your food 58–61
    insoluble fibre 10, 26, 43
    recommended daily intake 6, 13, 56, 58
    soluble fibre 10, 26, 38, 39, 43, 59
    trends and myths 74–75
    what it is 10–13
    why the gut needs fibre 24–25
figs: nutty barley, cinnamon & dried fig granola 88
    quinoa & dark chocolate bark 194
    sticky date pudding with figs 215
fish 30, 79
    cod en papillote with rocket & sunflower seed pesto 148
    creamy white bean fish pie 157
    grilled mackerel fillet with herby rice 138
flapjacks, prune & date crumble 190
flaxseeds 34, 47
FODMAPs 34, 35
FOS (inulin-type) 65
fructooligosaccharides (FOS) 28, 34
fruit 79, 80–81
    30:30:30 fibre formula 60, 62, 63, 64
    eating whole fruit 51
    fruit smoothies 68
    leaving skin on 67

G
garlic yogurt 107
ginger, honey & turmeric yogurt 99
GLP-1 42, 57
gluten-free foods 13
grains 60, 62, 63, 64, 73, 80–81
    beetroot Waldorf grain salad 117
    Persian herb & grain stewed lentils with caramelized onions 151

granola, nutty barley, cinnamon & dried fig 88
grapes: beetroot Waldorf grain salad 117
    grape & fennel seed baked oats 90
green butterbean mac & fibre cheese 137
green goddess avocado sandwich 133
green powders 74
green whipped tofu & butterbean dip 186
greens 64
    caldo verde soup with smoky butter beans 121
guacamole 165
the gut: benefits of a high-fibre diet 24
    diabetes and 51
    effect of weight-loss drugs on 42, 43
    fibre and hormonal balance 47
    Gut-Brain axis 25, 34, 37
    Gut-Skin axis 48
    heavy metals and 53
    IBS and fibre 34–35
    microplastics and 53
    why fibre is needed 24–25
gut bacteria (microbiome) 11, 41, 48, 62
    children's 77
    benefits of fibre 12, 24–25, 55
    diabetes and 51
    heavy metals and 52, 53
    prebiotics and probiotics 28, 29, 34, 37, 41, 77
gut-cleansers 74

H
Hadza people 6, 15
harissa-spiced hispi wedges 141
heart health 11, 24, 38–39
heavy metals 52–53
herbs 62, 63, 80–81
    crispy chickpea fried eggs with garlic yogurt & herbs 107
    grilled mackerel fillet with herby rice 138
    Persian herb & grain stewed lentils 151
honey: ginger, honey & turmeric yogurt 99
hormones 31, 42, 46, 52
    and gut functions 24, 25, 26, 47
hot chocolate, dark chocolate 69
hydration 26, 45, 59, 73
    and fibre absorption 68
    and IBS 35
    stools and 27

I
immune system 10, 12, 24, 25, 31, 77
inflammation 12, 24, 37, 46, 49
insulin 31, 41
    insulin sensitivity 13, 32, 51
intermittent fasting 72
inulin 28, 34, 35, 65, 71
irritable bowel syndrome (IBS) 25, 26, 27, 34–35, 73

Index

J
juice diets 72

K
kale: coconut, kale & turmeric-baked eggs 100
   crispy quinoa & kale salad 122
   green butterbean mac & fibre cheese 137
   roast split peas with peanuts, coconut & crispy kale chaat 189
kefir 28, 29
ketogenic diets 72
kimchi 28, 29
   kimchi fried spelt with sesame fried eggs 145
kiwi fruit 26
kombucha 28, 29

L
labels 23, 70–71
legumes 60, 62, 63, 80–81
lentils 33, 47
   Persian herb & grain stewed lentils 151
   pork, lentil & ricotta meatballs in tomato sauce 162
   super high-fibre seeded nut & raisin loaf 108
   Turkish lentil & carrot soup 118
lettuce: beetroot Waldorf grain salad 117
   green goddess avocado sandwich 133
linseeds 35
long-chain fatty acids (LCFAs) 11

M
mango: blueberry & mango frozen smoothie bowl 93
   mango & coconut chia pudding 202
   vegetable summer rolls 113
marketing 72
Marmite popcorn 181
matcha tea 68
meat 64, 66
meatballs: chicken & quinoa meatballs with white bean broth 177
   pork, lentil & ricotta meatballs in tomato sauce 162
Mediterranean diet 46
medium-chain fatty acids (MCFAs) 11
men, fibre intake 21
menopause 32, 46–47
mental health 10, 13, 24, 37
microplastics 52
Milanese, wholemeal baked aubergine 173
milks, plant-based 68
   vegan bread & butter pudding 206
mindful eating 57
mint: mint yogurt 141
   potato farls with smashed avocado, feta & mint 104
Turkish lentil & carrot soup 118
miso: bean, miso & tahini dip 186
muffins 78
   prune & walnut banana muffins 94
muhammara 186
muscles 30, 31, 32, 40, 44, 46
mushrooms: adaptogenic 75
   mushroom & bean stroganoff 174
   pearl spelt & mushroom 'risotto' 169
myths 74–75

N
nutritional yeast: spicy cheese popcorn 181
nuts 43, 47
   30:30:30 fibre formula 59, 61, 62, 63, 73, 80–81
   nutty barley, cinnamon & dried fig granola 88
   prune & date crumble flapjacks 190
   quinoa & dark chocolate bark 194
   super high-fibre seeded nut & raisin loaf 108

O
oat milk 68
oats 13, 33, 39, 43, 47
   barley porridge with blackberry, apple & bay compôte 97
   grape & fennel seed baked oats 90
   IBS-friendly diets 34, 35
   nutty barley, cinnamon & dried fig granola 88
   oat beta-glucan 59, 65
   prune & date crumble flapjacks 190
   super high-fibre seeded nut & raisin loaf 108
olives: creamy artichoke, green olive & parsley pasta 142
onions: caramelized onions 151
   chickpea pancakes with onion, tomatoes, coriander & coconut sambol 103
   roast cauliflower & chickpeas with green tahini & pink onions 114

P
pancakes 78
   carrot pancakes 99
   chickpea pancakes 103
pancreas 42, 50
pasta 12, 13, 66
   creamy artichoke, green olive & parsley pasta 142
   gigli with red pesto & tofu sauce 147
   green butterbean mac & fibre cheese 137
   pasta e fagioli with squash 160
   wholemeal baked aubergine Milanese 173
peanut butter: blueberry & mango frozen smoothie bowl 93
frozen peanut butter & banana-stuffed dates 197
   prune & walnut banana muffins 94
peanuts 30
   roast split peas with peanuts, coconut & crispy kale chaat 189
pears 43
   autumnal crumble 205
   baked pears with walnuts & bitter chocolate 211
   salted pear compôte 209
pectin 28, 43, 53, 65
peppers: chickpea ratatouille 166
   muhammara 186
Persian herb & grain stewed lentils 151
Persian-style, chicken 159
pesto: gigli with red pesto & tofu sauce 147
   rocket & sunflower seed pesto 148
phytates 73, 77
phytochemicals 12, 13
phytoestrogens 46, 47
pickled onion 114
pie, creamy white bean fish 157
plant-based milks 68
plant foods: eating 30 per week 56, 62–65
   energy-dense 40
   how plant-based nutrition boosts fibre 11–12
   plant points 62, 75
   weekly plant tracker 80–81
plastics, dietary 52–53
polyphenols 12, 24, 48
pomegranate, Persian-style chicken with walnut & 159
popcorn (3 ways) 181
pork, lentil & ricotta meatballs in tomato sauce 162
porridge 75
   barley porridge with blackberry, apple & bay compôte 97
portion sizes 21
posture 59
potatoes 12, 13, 67
   caldo verde soup 121
   creamy white bean fish pie 157
   potato farls with smashed avocado, feta & mint 104
   stuffed potato skins with cashew sauce 154
prawns: crispy rice salad with prawns, broccoli & avocado 129
prebiotics 12, 13, 24, 28–29, 37, 47, 77
   and diabetes 51
   psyllium husk 26
   side effects of 73
probiotics 28–29
processed food 15, 16, 17, 22, 23, 41
protein 30–33, 40, 41
prunes: prune & date crumble flapjacks 190
   prune & walnut banana muffins 94
psyllium husk 26, 27, 34, 35, 38, 65

Q

quinoa 33
- chicken & quinoa meatballs with white bean broth 177
- coconut, kale & turmeric-baked eggs with quinoa 100
- crispy quinoa & kale salad 122
- quinoa & dark chocolate bark 194

R

raisins: super high-fibre seeded nut & raisin loaf 108
- vegan bread & butter pudding 206

raspberries, chickpea blondies with tahini, dark chocolate & 201
ratatouille, chickpea 166
resistant starch 13, 28, 41, 53
rice 12, 13, 66
- brown rice pudding, salted pear compôte & dark chocolate 209
- crispy rice salad 129
- herby rice 138
- saffron rice 159

ricotta: pork, lentil & ricotta meatballs in tomato sauce 162
"risotto", pearl spelt & mushroom 169
rocket & sunflower seed pesto 148
rye 47, 59
- dark chocolate, date & rye cookies 193
- nutty barley, cinnamon & dried fig granola 88

S

saffron rice 159
salads 64
- beetroot Waldorf grain salad 117
- Coronation Brussels sprout salad 125
- crispy quinoa & kale salad 122
- crispy rice salad with prawns, broccoli & avocado 129
- date & almond tabbouleh 141
- roast beetroot, carrot & blackberry salad 126

sambol, coconut 103
sandwiches 78
- green goddess avocado sandwich 133

satiety 24, 41, 55, 57
sauces: cashew sauce 154
- tahini sauce 130
- tomato sauce 162, 173

sauerkraut 28, 29
sea moss 74
seeds 43, 73, 80-81
- 30:30:30 fibre formula 59, 61, 62, 63
- baked banana split with berries & toasted seeds 216
- nutty barley, cinnamon & dried fig granola 88
- prune & date crumble flapjacks 190
- super high-fibre seeded nut & raisin loaf 108
- za'atar chickpea crackers 185

serotonin 37
sesame seeds 47
- kimchi fried spelt with sesame fried eggs 145

short-chain fatty acids (SCFAs) 13, 37, 41
and the gut 11, 12, 24, 25, 28, 39, 48, 49, 51
skin health 48
sleep 10, 37
smoothie bowls 75
- blueberry & mango frozen smoothie bowl 93

smoothies 68, 79
soups 78
- caldo verde soup with smoky butter beans 121
- Turkish lentil & carrot soup 118

soybeans 46, 47
spelt: kimchi fried spelt with sesame fried eggs 145
- nutty barley, cinnamon & dried fig granola 88
- pearl spelt & mushroom 'risotto' 169

spices 62, 63, 80-81
spicy cheese popcorn 181
spinach: green butterbean mac & fibre cheese 137
split peas: roast split peas with peanuts, coconut & crispy kale chaat 189
sporting performance 44-45
sprouts: Coronation Brussels sprout salad 125
squash, pasta e fagioli with 160
sticky date pudding with figs 215
stools 26-27, 32, 43, 73
strength, building 32
stress 25, 26, 34
stroganoff, mushroom & bean 174
summer rolls, vegetable 113
sunflower seeds: rocket & sunflower seed pesto 148
super high-fibre seeded nut & raisin loaf 108
Super Six 62, 63, 80-81
supplements 29, 65
swaps 66-67, 77, 84
sweetcorn: stuffed potato skins 154
synbiotics 29

T

tabbouleh, date & almond 141
tahini: bean, miso & tahini dip 186
- chickpea blondies with tahini, dark chocolate & raspberries 201
- roast cauliflower & chickpeas with green tahini & pink onions 114
- tahini sauce 130

tea 68
telomeres 49
tempeh 33
tofu 30, 33
- gigli with red pesto & tofu sauce 147
- green whipped tofu & butterbean dip 186

tomatoes: chickpea pancakes with onion, tomatoes, coriander & coconut sambol 103
- chickpea ratatouille 166
- pasta e fagioli with squash 160
- tomato sauce 162, 173
- wholemeal baked aubergine Milanese 173

traffic-light systems 70
trends 74-75
Turkish lentil & carrot soup 118
turmeric: coconut, kale & turmeric-baked eggs 100
- ginger, honey & turmeric yogurt 99

U

ultra-processed foods (UPFs) 16, 17, 22-24, 36, 41, 58

V

vegetables 43
- 30:30:30 fibre formula 60, 62, 63, 64, 80-81
- leaving skin on 67
- my champion chunky veg & chocolate chilli 165
- vegetable summer rolls with mango & edamame beans 113
- *see also individual types of vegetables*

W

Waldorf grain salad, beetroot 117
walnuts: baked pears with walnuts & bitter chocolate 211
- Persian-style chicken with walnut & pomegranate 159
- muhammara 186
- prune & walnut banana muffins 94

weight-loss drugs 42-43
weight management 11, 13, 24, 32, 39, 40-41, 49
wheat bran 26
women: fibre intake 21
- menopause 32, 46-47

Y

yogurt 78
- baked banana split 216
- garlic yogurt 107
- ginger, honey & turmeric yogurt 99
- mint yogurt 141

Z

za'atar chickpea crackers 185

Resources and bibliography

Books

The Science of Nutrition by Rhiannon Lambert
The Science of Plant-Based Nutrition by Rhiannon Lambert
The Unprocessed Plate by Rhiannon Lambert

Podcasts

The Wellness Scoop with Ella Mills and Rhiannon Lambert
Food for Thought with Rhiannon Lambert
ZOE Science and Nutrition with Jonathan Wolf

Reports

Romanello, Marina et al. (2025). Countdown on health and climate change: climate change action offers a lifeline. *The Lancet*

The Food Foundation (2025). The Broken Plate 2025

Find all scientific references for the information provided in this book here:

www.dk.com/blogs/resources/the-fibre-formula-bibliography

The publisher would like to thank the following for their kind permission to reproduce their data:

(a) above; (b) below/bottom; (c) centre; (l) left; (r) right; (t) top

27 (r) Copyright Clearance Center – Rightslink: Illustration based on Fig. 1 Bristol Stool Scale from the *Scandinavian Journal of Gastroenterology*, "Stool Form Scale as a Useful Guide to Intestinal Transit Time" (1966; Lewis, S. J., Heaton, K. W.) reprinted by permission of Informa UK Limited, trading as Taylor & Francis Group, www.tandfonline.com, https://www.tandfonline.com/loi/igas20. **37 (br) Elsevier:** © 2022 The Authors. Published by Elsevier Inc. / Graph based on Konstantinos Prokopidis, Panagiotis Giannos, Theocharis Ispoglou, Oliver C. Witard, Masoud Isanejad, "Dietary Fiber Intake is Associated with Cognitive Function in Older Adults: Data from the National Health and Nutrition Examination Survey", *The American Journal of Medicine*, Volume 135, Issue 8 (pp.e257-e262), 2022, ISSN 0002-9343; https://doi.org/10.1016/j.amjmed.2022.03.022.; (https://www.sciencedirect.com/science/article/pii/S0002934322002583) CC BY 4.0-https://creativecommons.org/licenses/by/4.0/. **38 (b)** © 2025 Pressbooks: Allison Calabrese / CC BY 4.0 / Illustration based on image by Allison Calabrese / CC BY 4.0- https://creativecommons.org/licenses/by/4.0/ from "Digestion and Absorption of Lipids", Copyright © by Langara College-https://pressbooks.bccampus.ca/nutr1100/chapter/digestion-and-absorption-of-lipids/

About the author

Rhiannon Lambert is celebrated as one of the UK's leading practitioners in the complex field of nutritional science. In 2016, she founded **Rhitrition**, her private clinic on London's Harley Street. Rooted in scientific evidence, the clinic stands in sharp contrast to the sea of pseudoscience often promoted by fad diets. She has worked with both individuals and globally recognized brands – including Deliveroo, Wagamama, Samsung, Alpro, Yeo Valley, and Tesco – helping them transform how they think about and approach nutrition.

Registered with the Association for Nutrition, Rhiannon obtained a first-class degree in Nutrition and Health and a Master's degree in Obesity, Risks, and Prevention. She holds additional diplomas in sports nutrition and pre- and post-natal nutrition. She is a Master Practitioner in Eating Disorders, accredited by The British Psychological Society, and a Level 3 Personal Trainer. A prolific author, Rhiannon has penned five books, two of which – *The Science of Plant-Based Nutrition* (2024) and *The Science of Nutrition* (2021) – achieved Sunday Times Bestseller status.

In 2018, Rhiannon launched her highly acclaimed podcast, *Food for Thought*, which has had over 10 million downloads since its inception. Since 2025, Rhiannon has also co-hosted the podcast *The Wellness Scoop* with Deliciously Ella founder, Ella Mills. Expanding her mission, Rhiannon re-launched **Rhitrition+** in 2023, a web-based supplement brand designed to cut through the misinformation in the supplement industry.

Rhiannon also cherishes her life as a wife and as a mother to two young boys, Zachary and Theodore – and her cat Aurora. She remains dedicated to creating a brighter, healthier future for both people and the planet.

Acknowledgments

Without the exceptional team at DK, this book wouldn't be possible. Izzy, Cara, Judy, Georgia, Rosie, Clare, Tania, Holly, Lu, Eden, Charlie, Issy P, Silvia, and everyone working behind the scenes, thank you for your unwavering support in bringing this mission to life. We managed to create a helpful and inspiring resource for everyone and should be very proud. Your dedication to your work is truly inspiring. I am deeply grateful.

Thank you to Pam Lyddon for her incredible enthusiasm and unwavering support; to the brilliant Victoria Simmonds, the most amazing stylist, for guiding us through the shoot days for this book; and to my wonderful MUA, Melissa Oldridge, for somehow making me look awake even on no sleep. And a special thank you to Claire P and Claire L for the glow up – you helped me feel my best and navigate the huge feat of book-writing throughout highs and lows of life.

My deepest thanks go to my brilliant team: Aoibhinn Connolly and Kitty Costelloe; and, above all, Abi Robertson, who has supported me at all hours to help bring this book to life. I simply could not have completed it without her tireless hard work, dedication, and calm presence, no matter what time of day. My team is the backbone of everything Rhitrition stands for – transparency, trust, and a genuine mission to help others – and they consistently go above and beyond to make that mission a reality.

As a mother and a working professional, I can't ignore the state of nutrition, in this country or across the world, nor the direction in which things are heading. My hope is that this book, in its own small way, can be a force for change: for better health, for greater understanding, and for good that lasts. My family are my constant inspiration and the reason I keep going every single day. To Billy, to my boys Zachary and Theodore, and even to our cat, Aurora, you are all my why. And to my dad, thank you for stepping in with childcare at the drop of a hat so that I can chase these dreams and help to make a difference.

Publisher's acknowledgments

DK would like to thank Georgia Levy for the recipe development, Katie Hardwicke for proofreading, and Vanessa Bird for indexing. DK would also like to thank Judy Barratt and the team at Studio Noel for all their work on this project.

Editorial Director Cara Armstrong
Project Editor Izzy Holton
Design Manager Tania Gomes
Editorial Assistant Abi Reeves
Sales and Jackets Coordinator Serena Sclocco
Senior Production Editor Becky Fallowfield
Senior Production Controller Stephanie McConnell
Art Director Maxine Pedliham
Publisher Stephanie Jackson

Editor Judy Barratt
Designer Studio Noel
Photographer Clare Winfield
Recipe Developer Georgia Levy
Food Stylist Holly Cowgill
Prop Stylist Charlie Phillips
Food Stylist Assistants Lu Cottle, Eden Owen-Jones & Katie Smith

First published in Great Britain in 2026 by
Dorling Kindersley Limited
20 Vauxhall Bridge Road,
London SW1V 2SA

The authorised representative in the EEA is Dorling Kindersley Verlag GmbH. Arnulfstr. 124, 80636 Munich, Germany

Text copyright © Rhitrition Limited 2026
Rhiannon Lambert has asserted her right to be identified as the author of this work.

Copyright © 2026 Dorling Kindersley Limited
A Penguin Random House Company
10 9 8 7 6 5 4 3 2 1
001–350622–March/2026

All rights reserved.
No part of this publication may be reproduced, stored in or introduced into a retrieval system, or transmitted, in any form, or by any means (electronic, mechanical, photocopying, recording, or otherwise), without the prior written permission of the copyright owner.
DK values and supports copyright. Thank you for respecting intellectual property laws by not reproducing, scanning or distributing any part of this publication by any means without permission. By purchasing an authorized edition, you are supporting writers and artists and enabling DK to continue to publish books that inform and inspire readers. No part of this publication may be used or reproduced in any manner for the purpose of training artificial intelligence technologies or systems. In accordance with Article 4(3) of the DSM Directive 2019/790, DK expressly reserves this work from the text and data mining exception.

A CIP catalogue record for this book
is available from the British Library.
ISBN: 978-0-2418-0331-8

Printed and bound in Germany

www.dk.com

Disclaimer

Neither the publisher nor the author is engaged in rendering professional advice or services to the individual reader. The ideas, procedures, and suggestions contained in this book are not intended as a substitute for consulting with your doctor or a professional. All matters regarding your health require supervision. Neither the author nor the publisher shall be liable or responsible for any loss or damage allegedly arising from any information or suggestion in this book.